D1559482

LOOKING THROUGH FREUD'S PHOTOS

DATE DUE

			PRINTED IN U.S.A.

The History of Psychoanalysis Series

Professor Brett Kahr and Professor Peter L. Rudnytsky (Series Editors)
Published and distributed by Karnac Books

Other titles in the Series

LOOKING THROUGH FREUD'S PHOTOS

Michael Molnar

KARNAC

First published in 2015 by
Karnac Books Ltd
118 Finchley Road, London NW3 5HT

British Library Cataloguing in Publication Data

A C.I.P. for this book is available from the British Library

  ISBN 978 1 78220 004 8

Edited, designed and produced by The Studio Publishing Services Ltd
www.publishingservicesuk.co.uk
e-mail: studio@publishingservicesuk.co.uk

www.karnacbooks.com

CONTENTS

ACKNOWLEDGEMENTS

My thanks first of all to Michael Schröter, editor of *Luzifer-Amor*, for having requested, translated, and published the series of essays which developed into this book: to John Forrester for publishing previous versions of four chapters in *Psychoanalysis and History*; to Brett Kahr for his encouragement to publish the book in Karnac's History of Psychoanalysis Series, which he co-edits with Peter Rudnytsky.

The book has grown out of the Freud Museum photo archives, and out of my years of employment at the Museum. I am grateful to my colleagues for the support I have received from them over those years, and to the Museum for its tolerance of my work, and for granting permission to reproduce the photographs.

Among the many researchers who have contributed, directly or indirectly, I should like to single out Christfried Tögel and the late Gerhard Fichtner for their scholarly generosity and for having given me access to the electronic data they had accumulated. As a corollary, TUSTEP (the database *without which,* etc.) also merits mention here.

In Chapter Three, I benefited greatly from Professor Albrecht Hirschmüller's help and in Chapter Four from that of his colleague, Professor Gerhard Fichtner. For their contributions to Chapter Four, I must thank Mariano Ruperthuz, Dr Felicitas Seebacher, Dr Helmut

Gröger, Dr Ruth Koblizek, Brigitte Kranz, and Dr Wilhelm Füßl. I owe thanks to Alan Gall and Tom Roberts for assistance with Chapter Five, and to Lesley Marshall and Malcolm Holmes for their contribution to Chapter Six. Chapter Eight relies heavily on the research of Barbara Murken and I am grateful to her both for that and for her generous response to the essay. Chapter Nine benefited from access to documentation supplied by Michael Schröter. Chapter Ten relied heavily on the research of Pierre Segond and I am further indebted to him for generously responding to my enquiries and sending more information. My thanks also to Cécile Marcoux for supplying supplementary documentation on the final chapter.

Publication notes

Earlier versions of the first eight chapters were translated by Michael Schröter and originally published in his German translation, as follows:

Chapter One. Am historischen Eckfenster 17.6.1897. *Luzifer-Amor: Zeitschrift zur Geschichte der Psychoanalyse, 33* (2004).
Chapter Two. Trottoir roulant, 1900. *Luzifer-Amor, 38* (2006).
Chapter Three. . . . ein so schweres Werk wie unsere Heirat. *Luzifer-Amor, 41* (2008).
Chapter Four. Geheimnisse der Natur. *Luzifer-Amor, 45* (2010).
Chapter Five. Freud & Co. *Luzifer-Amor, 34* (2004).
Chapter Six. Alien enemy: porträt eines Mädchens. *Luzifer-Amor, 35* (2005).
Chapter Seven. Ich bleibe da. *Luzifer-Amor, 39* (2007).
Chapter Eight. . . . das Kind soll wissen . . . *Luzifer-Amor, 36* (2005).

Earlier versions of the following chapters were subsequently published in English:

Chapter One. At the historic corner window. 17.6.1897. *Psychoanalysis and History, 7*(2) (2005). Also in: *Visual Resources: An International Journal of Documentation, XXIII*(1–2 (March–June 2007).
Chapter Four. Mysteries of nature. *Psychoanalysis and History, 13*(1) (2011).
Chapter Five. Freud & Co. *Psychoanalysis and History, 8*(2) (2006).

Chapter Six. Portrait of an alien enemy. *Psychoanalysis and History*, *10*(2) (2008).

Photograph references

Originals of all photographs are in the Archive of the Freud Museum London and are reproduced by kind permission of the Freud Museum.

IN = Freud Museum Photo Library Inventory Number
LDFRD = Freud Museum London Collection Number.

Chapter 1.   Photograph: IN 839. Photographic prints referred to in text: LDFRD 5079, 5081, 5083, 5157, 5182.
Chapter 2.   Photographs: IN 860 & IN 3837
Chapter 3.   Photograph: IN 77.
Chapter 4.   Photograph: IN 1626
Chapter 5.   Photograph: IN 3866
Chapter 6.   Document : LDFRD 6284
Chapter 7.   Photograph: T_0012 (Interim listing: final inventory number pending).
Chapter 8.   Photograph: IN 977 & Album 2, p. 29 (IN 975, 976, 977).
Chapter 9.   Photograph: IN 258.
Chapter 10.   Photograph: IN 189.

For Rita
my first reader

ABOUT THE AUTHOR

Michael Molnar was employed as researcher at the Freud Museum in London from 1986 to 2003, and as director from 2003 to 2009. He translated and annotated Freud's 1930s diary notes, published as *The Diary of Sigmund Freud 1929–39* (Scribner's and Chatto, 1992). He has published numerous contributions to the history of psychoanalysis in *Luzifer-Amor, Psychoanalysis and History*, and elsewhere.

On Tuesday, 27th September, 1938, the eighty-two-year-old Professor Sigmund Freud, a refugee from Nazi-infested Austria, moved into his very last home at 20, Maresfield Gardens, in the Swiss Cottage region of North London. Freud did not quite manage a full calendar year at Maresfield Gardens, because he died from a physician-administered overdose of morphine in the small hours of the morning of Saturday, 23rd September, 1939, just over three hundred and sixty-one days after he began to reside in his comfortable home, which has since become the Freud Museum London.

Although Freud spent less than one year in Maresfield Gardens, Michael Molnar, a highly accomplished historian of psychoanalysis, has worked for nearly quarter of a century in Freud's house, having begun his tenure there as researcher back in 1986, and then, after many years of loyal service, having become its Director, until he retired in 2009. Consequently, Molnar has spent far more time in Freud's house than the father of psychoanalysis ever had; and as a result, he has not only studied Freud's life and work in meticulous archival detail but, also, has absorbed so much of the atmosphere of Freud's surroundings. Having researched, edited, translated, and annotated Freud's appointment diary—the *Kürzeste Chronik*—published in 1992, Molnar has the distinction of having followed Freud's life in great detail on a day-by-day basis.

With such a profound scholarly immersion into not only the minutiae but, also, the broad sweep of the lives of Freud and his family, Michael Molnar has, in recent years, turned his gaze to the study of Freud's family photographs, many examined only by staff at the Freud Museum. With vigour, imagination, and perseverance, Molnar has deployed his considerable skills as historian, archivist, and occasional photographer, to craft ten chapters, unravelling the hidden meanings of some of the seemingly unremarkable photographs from the albums of Freudiana. Writing with clarity and perceptivity and, at times, with the skill of the great essayists of the nineteenth century, Michael Molnar treats us to a series of deep and engaging immersions in the world of Freud and his relatives, dis-covering buried treasures in material that one might otherwise have overlooked too readily.

We all know that remarkably piercing photograph of Sigmund Freud taken by his son-in-law Max Halberstadt, depicting the great man with a full white beard and moustache, dressed in a three-piece suit, with a partially smoked cigar—possibly a Trabuco—poised between the second and third fingers of his right hand. According to Molnar, the Freud Museum in London had received more requests for permission to reproduce Halberstadt's photo than for any other visual representation of Freud. Molnar could, no doubt, have treated us to a detailed exegesis of the secret meanings of Halberstadt's portrait. But, with the gaze of one deeply immersed in psychoanalytical ideas, Molnar has decided to focus not on the obvious, not on the hackneyed, not on the conscious, but, rather, upon the less well known, more hidden, often obscure photographs from the archives of the Freud family unconscious.

From Molnar's writings, I have come to learn that one can snap a photograph in one-thirtieth of a second. Therefore, the ten photographs that Molnar has analysed in this book represent no more than one-third of a second in time! And yet, in spite of this, he has managed to uncover an entire book full of rich hypotheses, sometimes rendered with the confidence of a successful archivist and sometimes with the humility of a clinician who offers a well-informed but by no means proven hypothesis to his or her patient. In many respects, *Looking Through Freud's Photos* may be understood not only as an essay in historical, photographic analysis but, also, as a veritable

Traumdeutung—dream analysis—in the best tradition of Sigmund Freud and his followers.

Part psychobiography, part psychohistory, part Freud scholarship, part art history, and part Sherlockian detective work, these modest, inquisitive essays—often obsessional in detail, always riveting in construction—demonstrate quite conclusively that a photograph has an unconscious mind, just as a human being might, and that beneath the surface of the shiny, laminated exterior, one can find a highly rich, deeply communicative interior, if, of course, one understands both the day residue and the early history that have combined to create that brief moment in time captured forever on film.

Molnar's chapters reveal the way in which a photographic image serves as a point of entry into the mind of Freud and his relatives, in exactly the same way that the seemingly throwaway free association of a patient might become the centrepiece of an entire psychoanalytical session. Hence, Michael Molnar's analyses become minibiographies, providing us with great insights into the life of Freud and his intimates, including his mother, his wife, his sister-in-law, several of his siblings and half-siblings and their spouses, his children, his nieces and nephews, and even a great-niece. One will read these essays and become infinitely better informed about Freud, about his world, and about the psychoanalytical emphasis on detail as a *via regia* into the depths of the human mind.

Sometimes, Molnar reinforces our hunches and impressions of Freud, and sometimes he shatters them. For instance, through his analysis of the photograph of Freud and his neuropsychiatric colleagues, taken in 1894 at a meeting of the Gesellschaft deutscher Naturforscher und Ärzte, Molnar forces us to question the age-old shibboleth, so commonplace in Freud biographies, that the father of psychoanalysis had to endure a splendid isolation, deprived of contact with, or encouragement from, his medical peers. In fact, with the skill of an ophthalmologist utilising a high-intensity lens, Molnar has detected that on this occasion, Freud wore a special ribbon on his label—virtually invisible on first glance—which indicated not only his status as a participant in the conference but, moreover, that he served as one of the secretaries to the section on neurology, and thus, formed part of the inner core of this scientific organisation.

As I read through Molnar's impeccably prepared typescript, I often found my mind turning to Freud's famous essay on "Der Moses des

xvi   SERIES EDITOR'S FOREWORD

Michelangelo" ["The Moses of Michelangelo"], published in 1914. As even the most rudimentary of Freud students will appreciate, this short but compelling work of genius represents one of the highlights of Freud's own detective skills, endeavouring to understanding why Michelangelo Buonarroti sculpted the Biblical Moses with his fingers interlaced between the folds of his beard, and with the Ten Commandments tucked so precariously by his side. Just as Freud forces us to focus upon important, revealing details that we had overlooked many times, so, too, does Molnar invite us to revel in the seemingly innocuous, ostensibly irrelevant, details of the Freud family photographs. Although Michael Molnar has worked as an historian and not as a clinician, one senses that if he had devoted himself to clinical work with patients, he would have done the work rather well!

Like all psychoanalytical detective stories, *Looking Through Freud's Photos* contains many shadows, not only the shades of dark which intermingle with the shades of light in any snapshot but, also, the shadows of a family struggling with personal tragedy, with bereavement, with anti-Semitism, with emigration, and with murder. Within the pages of Molnar's book, we meet not only the familiar figure of Sigmund Freud, sandwiched in a group photograph among his fellow Austrian physicians but, we also begin to know Freud's elder half-brother, Emanuel Freud, who plunged to his death, having fallen out of a train, as well as his sister Marie Freud, one of the four sisters who perished in a concentration camp. We also learn of Oliver Freud, the middle son of the great psychoanalyst, and of his near-death at the hands of the Nazis, saved only by having missed a certain train from Nice in the South of France. And only those with a more detailed knowledge of Freud's biography will have previously encountered his niece, Martha Gertrud Freud (later known as the children's writer and illustrator Tom Seidmann-Freud), who committed suicide. Thus, as Molnar has demonstrated, the photographic shadows often prefigure the tragic shadows that would befall Freud's loved ones, a set of stories all too familiar to Jewish families or, indeed, to those of any nationality embroiled in the insanity of war.

I have had the privilege of knowing Michael Molnar for nearly thirty years, and in that long period, I have come to admire deeply his fine mind, his warm heart, and his quiet, but passionate, commitment to the highest level of scholarship. A great exemplar to all Freud scholars and to all historians of psychoanalysis, he has offered us a poignant, insightful, and generous book which will not only educate us but which will also inspire us to pay much closer attention to our world. We take great pleasure in publishing this truly excellent book in "The History of Psychoanalysis Series", and we earnestly hope that Michael's retirement from his formal post at the Freud Museum London will in no way represent his retirement from researching, from writing, and from communicating with us all.

Professor Brett Kahr
Series Co-Editor
"The History of Psychoanalysis Series", Karnac

Introduction

Each of the ten chapters of this book explores a photograph from the Freud Museum photo archive. The first four focus on Freud himself, although only one of these photos shows him alone and, as it turns out, that solitude is illusory. In the other three he is part of a group, either relatives or colleagues. The remaining six photos and chapters feature members of the family—his half-brother Emanuel, three of his children (Anna, Ernst, and Oliver), his niece Angela, and his grand-daughter Eva. This is a family album.

The earliest photo is dated 1894, the latest 1943. The narrative ranges over ninety years of family history: the photography time (at, say, 1/30th of a second per shot) totals around a third of a second. The fragments of biography that make up this book have grown out of this disparity between the flow of events and the split seconds of the shutter.

The book began as a series of essays written between 2003 and 2013, but the impulse to write them goes further back, probably to my first contact with the Freud Museum photo archive in 1986, months before the Museum opened to the public. Some time in April or May of that year, I entered the long room at the top of the house, previously Anna Freud's consulting room, and found a person sitting in the middle of the floor—the first photo cataloguer, Brendan King—surrounded by photographs, which he was moving around and arranging as if working out a giant jigsaw puzzle. He had been allotted the (still unfinished) task of identifying and dating the collection. In due course, the same task would come my way, and I, too, would find myself working at this jigsaw puzzle, and gripped by the same archival urge to catalogue and classify. This is essential historical business. However, it can be taken too far—or take us too far. Something of that may be gathered from the topic and tone of my opening chapter.

In the penultimate chapter, "Portrait of a refugee", written ten years later, I return from another angle to the themes of accuracy and factuality, seen through the person of Oliver Freud and his numerical mode of classifying experience. If I revise my earlier and more ironic stance, this is a stylistic shift rather than a thematic development. Because the book is based on still images, each chapter is centred on a single moment with all its correlates and consequences. Whatever development might take shape, via themes revisited or otherwise, is at odds with the static images. A photograph is anti-historical, a mute moment extracted from the narrative of time. How to integrate the counterpoint of stillness and motion into a historical narrative becomes a topic of the second chapter, "*Trottoir roulant, 1900*". In general, it is the timeless nature of the photograph that has dictated the book's preoccupation with lost moments of lived experience, in contrast to the historical development of events.

Or was it not, first of all, my own preoccupation with lost moments that dictated this approach to the subject? In one of his dream interpretations Freud off-handedly dismissed another such cause-or-effect quandary: "But in any case it will do no harm to leave the point unresolved" (Freud, 1900a, p. 218).

These are historical photographs and the book is being published in a series devoted to the history of psychoanalysis. Whatever my motive for writing it, its main interest for the reader will be the light shed on the lives of Freud and his family by these "light pictures" (*Lichtbilder*) and their commentaries. When, in 2003, Michael Schröter took over as editor of *Luzifer-Amor*, a journal specialising in the history of psychoanalysis, and requested a series of articles from me, I was aware that their claim to interest this readership would have to be evidence of original research, whether new interpretations or unknown documentation. At the same time, I also felt the pressure of another demand, and this has affected my revisions and resulted in the addition of the last two chapters, which comprise two overlapping stories, the lives of Oliver Freud and his daughter Eva and their experiences during the Second World War. Although motion is tethered in photographs, the viewer's emotions run riot. Portraits are an electrical earth, a channel for discharging and grounding the emotional charge of the narrated life. What we see in front of our eyes no longer exists. Historic photos plead with us, and the historian or viewer has to come to terms with that pleading, that inordinate demand for mourning, that urge to submit to melancholia.

Clearly, a photograph is interpreted differently from written documentation. Emotional or transferential readings take precedence over other forms of information. It occurs to me now that reading photos may, for that very reason, be a peculiarly apt instrument of Freud historiography.

The Freud Museum opened at an inauspicious moment. The first designated director of the new museum had been dismissed even before it opened, for questioning the value of psychoanalysis. The core of his argument was an attack on Freud's personal and scientific integrity. This inherited public scandal, like the "hereditary taint" of Victorian psychiatry, cast a threatening shadow. It was only one raid in a widespread revisionist backlash, the "Freud Wars" which were raging at the time. In theory, they should have just been about theory, but Freud's theories are everywhere and nowhere. In practice, the war was being fought over the body and life of the man himself—and over his image.

The famous portrait by his son-in-law, Max Halberstadt, known from countless book jackets, looks like a recruitment poster for the conflict: Freud glaring at the viewer, pointed finger and levelled cigar at the ready. As administrator of the photo archive, I was taken aback by the popularity of that notorious portrait, and by the number of requests for it from media and public. It epitomised controversy. In addition, it confronted me, as an employee of the Freud Museum, with the question of our remit: how do you represent Freud to the public?

What muddies the water is that two senses of "represent" are conflated, in both public perception and in the portrait. Personal involvement is a factor of historical proximity. This is written into the subtitle of a well-known Freud biography published at that period:

A Life for Our Time. Although my book touches on questions of identification and commitment at various points, these photographs are archival objects, and consequently distanced, objectified, and contextualised. I have tried to follow the grain of their nature in that respect. Above all, this book is not a biography of Sigmund Freud.

The Freud Museum in London often receives post addressed to the Sigmund Freud Museum, London. The mistake is symptomatic, and understandable. But 20 Marefield Gardens was also the home of Martha and Anna Freud, Minna Bernays, Dorothy Burlingham, Paula Fichtl, and various chows. Freud's workshop was not just the portrait head that Halberstadt recorded for posterity, it was the family and household he inhabited. Decontextualisation is inevitable and any biography has to make a compromise with the surrounding world, fitting in only what appears relevant to the subject. Photographs, unlike biography, are indiscriminate. They are "objective reality", that is, the world seen by an object. It might have been something haphazard about these images of reality that first drew me to study them more closely. Chance is their household and context. Although it can be modified by photographer and occasion, it can never be excluded: it is the photo's unconscious, its chattering pores and fingertips.

The first picture that spoke to me in this manner was the large group portrait discussed in Chapter Four, "Mysteries of nature", and my first reaction to it was to try to compile some sort of encyclopaedic list of the congress participants, a mass portrait which would, in effect, sketch the scientific background of neurology in the 1890s. That turned out to be far beyond my scope, and soon reduced itself to the very incomplete listing that precedes the essay. Instead, curiosity about the organisation itself that brought all these scientists and doctors together sidetracked me into thoughts around the nature of Nature. In general, if there is any system to these essays, it was to follow such incidental associations and relationships.

Taking relationships literally, and trailing the contents of these family albums, the last five chapters follow the fates of children and grandchildren, and trace the conflicts and confluences of the generations, their cultural inheritance, their "hereditary taints". Like Martha and Henny Freud in the final chapter, struggling to get a clear picture of Eva Freud's life, I have in all these essays attempted to read some historical sense into these images. For that reason, the final photo has been chosen for the front cover, as an emblem of the enterprise.

At the click of a shutter a camera is flooded with information. Viewing the image, we select or ignore whatever elements suit our purpose. It is not what is visible but how we look that matters. We, the viewers, are the final subject in question.

The technology of photography—already lost to the digital age—offered Freud a curious model of the mind:

> A rough but not inadequate analogy to this supposed relation of conscious to unconscious activity might be drawn from the field of ordinary photography. The first stage of the photograph is the "negative"; every photographic picture has to pass through the "negative process", and some of these negatives which have held good in examination are admitted to the "positive process" ending in the picture. (Freud, 1912g, p. 264)

It was the process itself and not the end product that offered Freud this analogy. In all these essays I am as much looking into the processes that resulted in the image, or those that stemmed from it, as at the picture itself. That the journal which originally commissioned them was entitled *Luzifer-Amor* pleases me, because they were ultimately written for no other motive than my own pleasure. That being so, and pleasure being the deepest and most historical of motives, I sense an unconscious urge at play beneath the various reasons or justifications I have so far presented in this introduction.

Like Oliver Freud, I, too, was once an amateur photographer. When my parents converted the house to oil heating, the little coal cellar became my darkroom, where I spent hours of a lost childhood on what now looks to me like a form of alchemy, trying to convert fleeting instants into lasting images. Like the alchemists, I accepted that the tortures of science and patience were necessary; I accepted the noxious chemicals and stale air of the laboratory/dungeon, its dim red light and constant eyestrain; I accepted the tedium and isolation. All of that was redeemed by a single moment—when the first signs of an image begin arranging themselves on the white paper submerged in developer.

Adolescence brought other preoccupations and I abandoned this hobby. Vestiges must have survived, and perhaps they were obscurely revived by my contact with the Freud photo archive. Perhaps, in the end, I was just looking for revival and repetition of that experience, the anticipation of surprise, spontaneous generation, a picture welling up out of the blank paper and taking form, something once seen and only now about to be understood.

CHAPTER ONE

At the historic corner window: 17.6.1897

Um historischen Eckfenster.

Wien 17.6.1897.

> "Incidentally I have been through some kind of neurotic experience . . ."
>
> (Freud to Fliess, 22.6.1897, Masson, 1985)

E arlier photographs of Freud were all carefully posed. This may be the earliest snapshot of him. In *Sigmund Freud: His Life in Pictures and Words*, a cropped and enlarged version of this picture is spread across two pages (E. Freud, L. Freud, & Grubrich-Simitis, 1978, Plate 143). But the original print I came across was very small (77 × 50 mm). Its dimensions contributed to an effect of great distance separating the viewer from the scene. Also, a wide white border isolates this image. I could imagine looking down into a deep well.

At the same time, while looking at myself looking at the photo, I also sensed its objective challenge. It bears an inscription and date, and the figure of Freud is seen standing against an intriguing background, a wall of pictures within the picture. All this data promises real historical information.

That first sense of an isolated man in a lost world has to be immediately modified, as soon as you take its context into consideration. Even though it shows Freud alone, it has to be categorised as a family photo. The original print I was looking at forms part of a collection of family pictures that had been mounted together in a single frame like a collage, and hung for many years on the wall in the living room at Berggasse (Engelman, 1976, Plate 50).

This framed picture was in itself a mini-album, a point of reference for the family and a memento of its own composite history. Curiously enough, the theme of the collage is repeated inside this photo. When the print is examined closely, it turns out that the pictures on the wall behind Freud are recognisable as photographic prints that he brought back from his holidays in Italy during the 1890s. The children, who feature in other photos in the same frame, did not accompany him on any of these journeys, and for most of them neither did his wife. These prints were a way of bringing home traces of his life lived outside the family.

The date on the inscription, which serves as the title of this chapter, is even more relevant to the family. 17th June 1897 was the fifteenth anniversary of Freud's engagement to Martha Bernays. That raises the question whether the picture was intended as a memento or a gift to mark that occasion. If so, it seems a slightly curious one, since it shows him alone, but that could have been dictated by circumstances. On that particular date, the couple were apart.

As usual, the family, Martha, her sister Minna, and the children, were spending the summer away from Vienna. This year they were at Bad Aussee, but Freud remained behind, working until near the end of June. That particular day, Thursday 17th, was a general holiday, the Catholic festival of Corpus Christi. Freud took advantage of it by going on an outing to Schneeberg, the nearest alpine mountain to Vienna, together with his younger brother, Alexander, and his first and, as it turned out, unsatisfactory pupil, Dr Felix Gattel (Schröter & Hermanns, 1994).

There was a boyish pretext for the trip: they wanted to try out the new rack and pinion railway up the mountain. It had only been open since 1st June that year. Rail excursions were being advertised from Vienna to Puchberg, where the rack and pinion began. They had left Vienna early and arrived at the top of the mountain by 11 a.m.

The following day, Freud wrote to Martha that he had attempted to send her a congratulatory telegram from the Baumgartnerhaus, which was a hotel on the mountain and the terminus of the new railway. But the landlord, whom he referred to as "the repulsive Kronich", refused to deal with his message because of the pressure of holidaymakers that day, and because of the holiday it was already too late to send anything on the return journey (Sigmund Freud to Martha Freud, 18.6.1897, SFC).

Apart from this snub, Freud had good reason for describing Kronich as "repulsive", though it is uncertain whether Martha would have known that reason. As Peter Swales' research has shown (Swales, 1988), he was the incestuous father of the sexually abused "Katharina" in *Studies on Hysteria*.

For want of that failed telegram, Freud added that she would have nothing to mark their fifteenth engagement anniversary except some strawberries that he had sent and that he feared would not survive the journey to Aussee. If we assume the picture was a gift or commemoration of the anniversary, then it might have been an afterthought, a compensation for the failed telegram and the spoiled strawberries.

Details of the outing to Schneeberg cast doubts on whether the photo was really taken that day. The group left Vienna very early and came back late. For most of the day it had rained heavily and by the time they returned they were tired and soaked through. Given the rain and fading light, and the fact that the heavy shadow across Freud's face shows flashlight was not used for this photo, could it have been taken that day indoors and by daylight?

This question, and this entire line of enquiry, could be classed as neurotic. If the photo were indeed a compensatory offering, it could just as easily have been taken at any time around the anniversary and that date added. To know the exact date or time is entirely unnecessary.

Nevertheless, the archivist in me is disturbed by the possibility of a false (retrospective or prospective) dating in the inscription. Meanwhile, the historian in me mocks the archivist, telling him that suspicion is always obligatory, and adding that there are, anyway, further problems about that inscription.

Whatever day it was taken, it is likely that Alexander took it. A week or so previously, Freud wrote that he had become their "official" photographer. (The expression Freud uses in the letter to Martha around 11th June 1897 is "Hofphotograph", or "Court Photographer".) That year, he also took a photo of Freud and his sisters around their father's newly installed gravestone. Since Alexander was still learning to handle the camera—maybe it was a new one—and his first attempts at taking that picture failed, they had to return another day to the cemetery (Molnar, 1992, p. 208).

That is a reminder: the 1890s were still the early years of handheld cameras and snapshots. In still earlier days, photographic portraits had had to be posed, painstakingly and sometimes even painfully, almost like a visit to the dentist. By now, the days of head-clamps were over, but we can still see that this photo is not completely impromptu. Care has clearly been taken with the composition and the subject placed to good advantage in the light coming through the window. Yet the focus is not quite right. Freud's face is slightly blurred, whereas the prints pinned to the wall behind him are in sharp focus. Because of that, his expression is hard to read. The mouth is hidden by the full beard; the eyes are vague and seem to be squinting towards the space to the left of the photographer. The hunched posture and oblique glance might be seen as signifying impatience or ill-temper, or anticipation of something unknown.

Again, I sense something suspect about this desire to read such an indeterminable expression. When traces disappear into impenetrable undergrowth, trackers just have to pick up the trail elsewhere.

For instance, in a letter to Fliess the following day. (I am continuing to follow the assumption that the photo was taken on or around the date inscribed.) Setting aside questionable interpretations or dubious insights, we can refer to Freud's own assessment of his mood: "Fathomless and bottomless laziness, intellectual stagnation, summer dreariness, vegetative well-being . . ." (Masson, 1985, p. 252).

The general context of that statement in terms of Freud's intellectual biography is well known. He was, at this very time, beginning his self-analysis and on the verge of abandoning the so-called "seduction theory", according to which hysteria and neurosis were always to be traced back to actual sexual abuse, such as Kronich's daughter had suffered. This change would be announced to Fliess in the momentous letter of 21st September 1897.

The photo cannot document that intellectual drama. Even if his features could, in theory, reveal his thoughts, the expression here is, in the end, unreadable: his face is simply too fuzzy.

What a photograph can legitimately offer is specificity, an actual moment revealed with all its paraphernalia. That excludes the sitter's intellect, though some emotions may find their way through, together with a disparate collection of objects in the material world.

Meanwhile the question of the inscription—"At the historic corner window"—remains unanswered. Why was this corner "historic"? Perhaps this refers to the prints that hung there, or to some family tradition, and Martha would have recognised the reference. However, it has to be noted that this inscription is in neither Freud's nor Martha's handwriting, and I have this on the best authority, that of the late Professor Fichtner. Evidently, this is strange if the picture did commemorate the anniversary.

As evidence against the working hypothesis accumulates, a sense of frustration grows and the researcher starts (yet again!) to wonder about the whole point of the investigation. Freud's life and thought is, without doubt, of the greatest possible interest. Yet surely such close attention to purely incidental details of his daily life is suspect?

To continue, nevertheless: it is clear the inscription was written with great care and with an italic nib. Did Freud perhaps, distrusting his own untidier handwriting, ask someone known for their neat penmanship? Or did another family member (perhaps the person who compiled the composite framed photo collection) add the inscription some time later (in which case the hypothesis of an anniversary gift might no longer be valid)? As if all these uncertainties were not enough, there remains the question of that "historic corner window". Where was it? Both Lydia Marinelli, who was employed at the Vienna Freud Museum, and Christfried Tögel, who has worked there extensively, assure me that it does not appear to correspond to any possible location at Berggasse 19.

Questions accumulate and with them the pressure of the anxious meta-question: is this compulsion to nail such details no more than history as a compulsive–obsessive symptom? Medieval theology is mocked for supposedly enquiring how many angels could dance on the head of a pin. My research has apparently brought me finally to such pinpoints.

Behind the figure of Freud, in the historic window corner, the prints are fixed to the wall by tacks or small nails. All those photographic prints correspond exactly to those that belonged to Freud, and are now to be found in the archive of the Freud Museum London. Why, then, does none of these archive prints bear any pinholes?

*   *   *

". . . curious states incomprehensible to consciousness . . ."

(Sigmund Freud to Wilhelm Fliess, 22.6.1897)

It was only around 1900 that picture postcards first appeared. If Alexander Freud took his camera on any of the holidays in Italy with his brother, no evidence for it has yet been found. For their mementoes of holiday sights, the brothers had recourse to published albums of photos, some of which can be found in Freud's library, and to photographic prints, such as the ones on the wall behind Freud. These were mass-produced by Alinari, an Italian firm which still exists and claims to be the first photographic publishers. These prints (n.b. *without* the pinholes) and many other Italian scenes constitute a sizeable print archive at the Freud Museum.

A new line of speculation around this photograph is the question of what might have led to those particular ones being selected for display on this wall.

By Freud's right hand, we can make out a Venetian canal, the Riva dei Greci, just round the corner from the Casa Kirsch on the Riva Degli Schiavoni, where he stayed on his first visit in the summer of 1895, and where he was to stay again later in 1897, with his wife. A memory of that stay underlies the poignant "Breakfast Ship" dream in the *Interpretation of Dreams*. The dream associations recall his wife on the balcony of their hotel room, looking out over the lagoon and exclaiming with girlish delight, "Here comes the English warship!" In fact, this trip to Venice with her, just over two months after the date on this photo, would be a long-delayed honeymoon. He had been promising to bring her to Venice ever since his own first trip there in 1895. That her joyful behaviour, in fact and in the dream, would lead Freud to darker associations, that is, premonitions of his early death, lies far out of this picture.

The three framed pictures behind Freud's head also show Venice: scenes on St Mark's Square and the Grand Canal. Given the creative role Venice, and Italy in general, were playing in Freud's thought at the time, it almost seems as if the images had been deliberately chosen to illustrate his dreams and desires. However, this could hardly be the case for the picture next to his right elbow, an uninteresting high wall. It turns out to be a view of the front wall of the Palace of Theodoric in Ravenna. Freud had first visited the town in September 1896 and disliked it, calling Ravenna in general "a miserable den" and referring just as disdainfully to that palace in particular: "a part of the palace of Dietrich von Bern [Theodore the Great] serves as the wall for a miserable rabble-house" (Tögel, 2002, pp. 59–60).

The absence of any comprehensible motive for pinning up such a picture as this, combined with the absence of pinholes in Freud's archive prints, which include one of this wall, demands some provisional hypothesis, if only because the compulsion to date and locate needs to be satisfied. It becomes increasingly evident that this dubious compulsion is, in the end, motivated by the desire to know what is or was going on in Freud's mind. Hence, it qualifies as a form of identification.

Behind Freud's left elbow, one can make out another north Italian memento, a print of the leaning Asinelli and Garisenda towers in

Bologna. This was a city he had also visited in 1896 and which he had at least liked, for its food and cleanliness as well as for its glorious monuments. There are two more pictures from Bologna by his head, both sarcophagus details from a graveyard, the Campo Santo, Bologna: on the left two children at the bed of a third (dead?) child, from the Monumento Minghetti, and next to it a mother holding a standing infant from the Monumento Bersani. Since Freud mentions buying two prints at the Campo Santo, he is probably referring to these, or rather *his* copy of these prints (Tögel, 2002, p. 57).

A photograph shows us the material world. The mind of this man with his back to the wall of pictures is not revealed, but the Venice dream offers a template for reading a paradoxical significance into these dead babies from Bologna.

In the Venice dream of the warship, the residue of his wife's joy would lead to contradictory omens of his own death. In this photograph, the prints of dead infants behind Freud's head could be interpreted as a source of satisfaction, even an augury of success. On the face of it, they are lugubrious images, especially for the father of a large family, always anxious about his children's health. However, he was also an ambitious research scientist. Around the time of the photo, he still had high hopes of imminently receiving his Extraordinary Professorship. A key work in his academic dossier was his highly praised *magnum opus* of the 1890s on infantile hemiplegia, based on studies of the brains of dead children. From this viewpoint, the deaths of infants in Bologna might well be associated with hopes of academic success.

An iconographic fantasy? Dreams of interpretation hang in and around the photo and the photos in the photo. The researcher wants to know what Freud really thought, and knows it can only be imagined. The Italian prints behind his back are a nexus of endless associations.

Between the prints from the Bologna Campo Santo and the window there is a photo representing more infants, but these ones are rejoicing. They are, in fact, cherubs. The image shows a panel from a Donatello frieze in the Museo di S. Maria del Fiore in Florence. More exactly, it is a detail of the *Cantoria* carved between 1433 and 1438 in the Cathedral. This frieze was dismantled in 1668 and only reconstructed after 1883. The Alinari photo must have been taken before the reconstruction, since it shows the section without the two columns that would afterwards block out part of it.

When Freud visited the cathedral in September 1896, the frieze he would have seen there was half-hidden by those subsequently added columns. Like so many holiday postcards and mementos, the image in the print was (for him) imaginary, something he never saw.

These Donatello cherubs serve as a reminder of the discrepancies between image and event. Angels dancing on a pinhead are fantasy, but the stone cherubs continue dancing in the real world, although their dance was hidden behind columns. Whatever Freud might actually have seen in Florence, it differed from the images in the prints he bought.

Cherubs dancing behind columns brings us back to angels and pinheads and the fact that there are no pinholes, either in his archive print of this picture or on those from Bologna or Ravenna. The questions remain: whose prints were these on the wall and where is that historic corner window?

*   *   *

"... twilight thoughts, veiled doubts, with barely a ray of light here and there"

(Sigmund Freud to Wilhelm Fliess, 22.6.1897)

Nothing about old photos is self-evident. Or whatever seems obvious is only half the story. It has previously been accepted that this photo shows Freud at Berggasse among his possessions. He looks at home and the pictures on the wall behind relate him to his holidays. Yet contextual and architectural details tell another story. For the time being, the best hypothesis, and one which would have the great merit of also explaining the absence of pinholes, is that this photo might have been taken at Alexander's place. At the time, he was still living with their mother on Grünentorgasse, just round the corner from Berggasse (Czeike, 1993, p. 398). The prints would, therefore, be his. Since he visited the scenes depicted with his brother, it is likely he would have bought a copy of the same prints for himself. Whether the choice of which image to buy was dictated by him or his brother, or simply by the lack of any alternative pictures, remains unknown.

The actual date of the photo, too, remains undecidable. The inscription might refer to the date of the dedication rather than that of the image itself. What is evident is that definitive answers would only lead to new questions. Once we have established where and when it was taken, what can we usefully do with such facts? What can we make of a portrait of Freud at this critical period of his intellectual life?

There is only one other photo that can be assigned with any confidence to the summer of 1897 and that is the picture of Freud and his sisters around their father's grave. This could be one of the photos referred to in his letter to Martha of 22nd June. It shows a huddled group: Freud's own features can hardly be made out at all. In fact, Alexander's first attempt, on 19th June, to photograph the newly dedicated gravestone had failed (spoiled by fogging of the plate, according to Alexander, or what Freud refers to in a letter to Martha on 30th June 1897 as a "Lichtschleier"—"light-veil"), and he had to try again. Freud had been hoping not to return to the grave-yard, but obviously consented for the sake of the photograph, for Alexander's and the family's sake, for his dead father's sake.

All these family connotations lend that little scene around the grave certain hysterical undertones. A letter to Fliess earlier that year, on the 8th February, follows a sinister line of associations between family, photography, and hysteria:

> Hysterical headache with sensations of pressure on top of the head, temples, and so forth, is characteristic of the scenes where the head is held still for the purpose of actions in the mouth. (Later reluctance at photographer's, who holds head in a clamp.)

> Unfortunately, my own father was one of these perverts and is respon-sible for the hysteria of my brother (all of whose symptoms are iden-tifications) and those of several younger sisters. The frequency of this circumstance often makes me wonder. (Masson, 1985, pp. 230–231)

Although Freud's head was not clamped for the photograph in the window corner, he had suffered a bout of migraine the day before the engagement anniversary. It was this which prevented him writing to Martha that day and which consequently resulted in her receiving no adequate acknowledgement of the occasion from him. If he looks thoughtful in the photo, the question whether it is because of the effect of fathers' behaviour on their children, or of husbands on their wives, remains beyond any possible corroboration.

Certainly, Freud was concerned about his own hysterical state of mind and thwarted creativity during these days. On the 22nd June, he wrote to Fliess: "I have never before even imagined anything like this period of intellectual paralysis. Every line is torture. . . . I believe I am in a cocoon, and God knows what sort of beast will crawl out" (Masson 1985, pp. 253–254).

This brings to mind Dürer's engraving, *Melencolia I*, the image of an earthbound angel idle among strange instruments of labour. That print, which Erwin Panofsky interpreted as symbolising creative impotence, was persuasively reinterpreted by Frances Yates as a representation of inner vision, the prelude to creation (Yates, 1979, pp. 54–57). In that latter sense, the Freud seen here is a melancholic figure, hunched, his hands in his pockets, his back to mementoes of Italy, the land of inspiration and creativity. Although he may be brooding, he is by no means dejected. His letters of June 1897 re-iterate his sense of physical well-being. Alertness is implied in the structure of the image, too—the angle of the head, the wary expression, the engagement with the photographer.

Whatever is happening, or about to happen here, takes place outside the photo. Because they present the world of appearances, photographs seem to promise unmediated reality. The visual world is self-evident, we assume. Yet, even in terms of its own level of signification, the photographic image is full of allusions and ambiguities. For instance, that carved board in the lower right-hand corner—is it the back of a desk, or a bench, or the headboard of a bed? Following that last speculation, is the little white object in the lower left-hand corner perhaps the edge of an eiderdown? In that case, Freud would be standing next to a bed—a suitable position for such an active dreamer, but the viewer here has no infallible key to the signs.

Even the primary questions must finally remain unresolved: when and where the photo was taken, by whom, for what purpose. Here, as elsewhere, the visible world and its signs are perpetually being read and misread. What happens at the edge or beyond the edges of the photo remains open to interpretation. It is as if certainty were the most elusive property of the image. Perhaps this acknowledgement is where any investigation of images ends. The truth we are looking for is always outside the frame.

Meanwhile, the photo itself remains and demands an emotional response. What we are looking for are signs of life in this fragment of a dead world. This is the paradox: the photo can only be brought to life by becoming an object of the viewer's fantasies. Between the reality of the image and its image among our own unrealities, the historian has to find a counterpoise. The exact questions require exact answers—a factual time, place, function. But beyond the edges of these facts everything else emerges from the twilight of interpretation. This is where we stand (with Freud?), waiting for illumination from outside, hoping for a ray of insight.

CHAPTER TWO

Trottoir roulant, 1900

On 14 April 1900, the Exposition Universelle, the Paris World Fair, opened. The *Neue Freie Presse*, in the evening edition of 17 April, published a report on the *trottoir roulant*, the elevated moving walkway. Also called *rue de l'Avenir* (street of the future), it was the great sensation of the Fair. It transported visitors at first floor level from one pavilion to another. According to the report, more than one hundred thousand visitors had travelled on it the previous day.

Freud himself never saw it, but the idea of it must have captured his imagination, for later that year, in "On dreams" (1901a), his brief popularisation of *Interpretation of Dreams* (1900a), it appears in one of his dream associations. We are fairly used to such moving walkways nowadays, yet it is still possible for us to experience at least something of the strangeness of this *fin de siècle* innovation. The pioneer cinematographer, Georges Méliès, captured it on film at the time. We get a sense of its absurdity, as seen from outside—rows of standing people dehumanised, gliding past like machine parts on an assembly line. Then there is the subjective incongruity, which Freud must have experienced in his imagination because it penetrated his dream: the curious sense of moving and not moving at the same time.

The click of a camera shutter lets in a flood of instantaneous data and fixes a moment for good. In a photograph, nothing moves. We are so used to fixed images, in newspapers, magazines, and books, or in the photo albums of our own lives, that we easily lose sight of their essential strangeness. Each one is a dislocation in time and every photo questions the experience of time.

*   *   *

In the first photo here, the little boy in the white hat is looking at the camera open-mouthed and with surprise. Perhaps he heard that click and shouted out. The little girl to his left and the woman holding him have both turned to look at him. So has the sitting man to his right and the blurred standing figure on the right. For this one moment, the boy is the centre of their attention. Yet, at the same time, the others are ignoring him, fixing their attention on the camera, probably in obedience to the photographer's instructions.

This photo comes from one of the Freud family albums. Names, a place, and a date have been helpfully written into the frame. We already knew the blurred man on the right was Freud, but would not have identified the white-hatted boy as Hermann Graf, his nephew, and the son of his sister Rosa. Neither would we have otherwise known that the little girl to the right is the boy's little sister, "Mausi" Graf, and the man to his right his father, Heinrich Graf.

So far, so good. However, when we look more closely at the frame inscriptions, we see that there are two different and contradictory attributions. Clearly, this help has to be treated with caution. For example, the names and date in the top and bottom margins are in a different hand from those in the left margin. Below, it states "Ossiachersee 1900" and to the left, "Annenheim, Kärnten, summer 1898".

In the 1909 edition of the *Interpretation of Dreams*, Freud would accept Stekel's schema "that in dreams 'left' stands for what is wrong, forbidden and sinful . . ." (Freud, 1900a, p. 380). It fits these inscriptions at least, for it can easily be proved that the one on the left is wrong, and that the other attribution, "Ossiachersee 1900" in the bottom margin, is correct.

On the other hand, right and wrong are mixed. Despite the wrong date, Annenheim is indeed on the Ossiacher See in Kärnten (Carinthia in southern Austria). As for left and right, it has to be asked: from whose viewpoint, ours or theirs? Interpreting photographs means going in and out of the frame all the time, continually switching viewpoints and spatial co-ordinates.

The album containing the first photo includes photos up to 1956. Whoever wrote these inscriptions might have been digging deep in their memory or, more likely, working second-hand. Yet there is enough extraneous information available to us to build up a fairly detailed historical picture around this photographic one.

That group in the picture can be divided into representatives of old and new worlds. In August 1900, the Grafs, Freud's sister Rosa and her family, had rented the villa Berghof in Annenheim on the Ossiacher See. That summer, the oldest of Freud's sisters, Anna Freud-Bernays, and her five children were visiting Europe for the first time since their emigration to New York in 1892, and they spent the August with Rosa and her family.

From our perspective, the fate of these relations gathered at an Austrian villa in the summer of 1900 reads like a paradigm of the century to come. The two families around the table, the Grafs and Bernays, can be seen as representatives of Europe and America, respectively. Converting these figures in space into figures in time, the following life spans emerge. Heinrich Graf (the man with the hat) was Freud's contemporary, and died of a heart attack only eight years later. His son Hermann (the boy in the white hat) was killed at the age of twenty in the First World War. His daughter Caecilie, or Mausi (the little girl next to Hermann), committed suicide five years later at the age of twenty-three, in despair over an extra-marital pregnancy. Although their mother, Rosa, lived into her eighties, multiple bereavements made hers, by most accounts, a rather unhappy life. In addition, inevitably, her murder in a concentration camp casts a retrospective shadow across her biography.

The American family, by contrast, lived remarkably long lives, almost all the women surviving well into their nineties. Edward Bernays (the boy with the puppy on his lap) died only in 1995 at the age of 103. The concept of a natural span of life is flexible, and how far quality of life can be quantified or compared is arguable, but, by any possible standards of comparison, the European contingent here suffered a worse fate.

In 1900, the advantages of emigration had not yet become so evident. Freud had a low opinion of his oldest sister, Anna, and her husband, Eli. When he first heard that she would be coming to Europe that year, he expected the worst, some calamity that had struck the family, or perhaps the break-up of her marriage with Eli, whom he heartily detested, or perhaps a financial disaster. His premonitions turned out to be totally unfounded. If anything, the visit was proof that Eli's business was doing well. Their children, too, were fine and Freud was impressed by them, and especially by the precocity of the older daughters.

The second daughter, Lea (Lucy), stands next to him smiling, and she was also the one who was closest to him. While her parents were first getting a foothold in the USA, she had been left for almost a year in 1892–1893 in the care of Sigmund and Martha Freud and they had grown fond of her. That was reflected in a letter thirty years later, when he spoke of her as "affectionate and reasonable as ever, the only real person (*Mensch*) in the whole line" (Molnar, 1992, p. 74).

These words reveal the durability of the rift between him and his sister's family. It had deep and tangled roots and even predated Eli's marriage to Anna. In 1882, Eli had broken off his engagement to her at the insistence of his mother, Emmeline Bernays, later to be Freud's mother-in-law. As a result, Eli's name became anathema to the entire Freud family, parents and children, until he and his mother changed their minds, begged Anna's pardon, and re-established the engagement (Freud-Bernays, 2004, p. 34).

Freud himself was not much inclined to forgive and forget betrayal, or, at the very least, wavering behaviour, let alone Eli's submission to the will of his mother, a woman Freud came to see as his chief antagonist during his own long engagement. This was the background to his fury in 1886 when he learnt that Eli was speculating rashly with funds intended for Martha's dowry. It reached the point where he even risked breaking his own engagement when Martha failed to support his attack on her brother. (This episode will be dealt with more fully in the next chapter.)

These past antagonisms or premonitions are the business of the older generation in the picture. This is 1900, a date that looks to the future. It is the horde of children that steals the show. The adults are simply props, holding them up, gesturing towards them, or, like that blurred bystander at the far right, simply looking on.

The blurring might be the fault of the camera's depth of field or the quality of the lens. Freud, though, is out of focus both photographically and socially. His presence here was incidental and in passing, the culmination of several weeks of travelling through southern Austria, and the product of two coincidences.

He had spent a restless August. At the beginning of the month, he had met Wilhelm Fliess on the Achensee in Tirol. This turned out to be their last "congress", the one at which they finally clashed, according to Fliess over the question of precedence: Freud could not concede that Fliess's biological numerology might have a determining influence on his own drive-based psychology.

After that, Freud embarked on a tour of south Tirol with his wife Martha. They travelled to Trafoi, Sulden, Stilfserjoch, Meran, and on to the Mendelpass. There, by chance, they encountered an American "revenant", Freud's former student friend, Sigmund Lustgarten, who had subsequently emigrated to the USA. A letter to Fliess on 14 September 1900 takes up the itinerary:

> Martha then left for home via Bolzano and absolutely insisted that I follow Lustgarten to Venice to act as his guide. I did so, but there to my surprise I met my brother-in-law Heinrich and Rosa, who after a day and a half in Venice took me along with them to Berghof on Lake Ossiach. I was right in the swing of tramping around and was amenable to everything. In Berghof I found my sister Anna with the American children, who look just like my own, and a day later Uncle Alexander arrived unexpectedly. Finally—we have now reached August 26—came the relief. I mean Minna, with whom I drove through the Puster Valley to Trentino, making several short stops along the way. (Masson, 1985, p. 423)

The other side of all that to-ing and fro-ing was unusual passivity. Freud was allowing himself to be carried along by events, going along with each chance encounter, "right in the swing of tramping around". (The German is *"recht im Bummel"* and instead of "tramping", with its undertones of effort, "bumming around" might be a closer translation, both in sound and sense.)

Something of this comes through in the photos, in his stance and clothes. Both Freud and Heinrich Graf are holding walking sticks and perhaps the two of them had either just returned from a stroll, or were planning a walk. Another lakeside walk, perhaps. This month began with that highly charged lakeside walk with Fliess, and the themes that it had set in motion are still far from exhausted.

The house, Berghof, stands on a hill above the Ossiachersee, not far from the Hotel Annenheim, where Freud stayed seven years later. From that hotel, he wrote to Jung,

> I wish I were with you, taking pleasure in no longer being alone, and, if you are in need of encouragement, telling you about my long years of honourable but painful solitude, which began after I cast my first glance into the new world, about the indifference and incomprehension of my closest friends . . . (McGuire, 1974, p. 82)

The image has been fixed, but imagination unfreezes the instant. There is evidently a lot going on here. If this is a microscopic cross-section of the past, the slide is a droplet swarming with infusoria.

On the one hand, there is the local commotion among the children and the little boy's outcry, which may have been caused by the photographer himself (perhaps Freud's brother, Alexander). On the other hand, the interpretation of this activity stirs up more and more associations.

A week after the opening of the Paris World Fair, Freud gave a talk to the B'nai B'rith, the Jewish brotherhood, which was his only non-medical audience at the time. The lecture was on Zola's *Fecundity*, a novel that struck him sufficiently for it to be included on his list of ten memorable works a few years later. The following day, 25 April 1900, he wrote to Fliess that he only prepared these B'nai B'rith lectures an hour before. He must have worried about this, because the night before the event he had a series of dreams of deferring his badly prepared lecture (Masson, 1985, p. 410).

The horde of children in this scene a few months after the lecture might have reminded Freud of the theme of fecundity. From a viewer's perspective, they look like an expectant audience, waiting for a lecture to begin. With that analogy, anxiety enters the picture. Not among the subjects, who seem to be relaxed and in a holiday mood; it is the viewer who, under their unblinking gaze, begins to feel that they are waiting for something to be said or done.

The *trottoir roulant* dream is undated. It might even have happened earlier than that year, for the reference to the World Fair is in his associations, not manifested in the dream itself. From university on, Freud frequented, and gave, lectures: for most of his life he was a spectator or actor in these theatres. The dream's manifest content pastes a curious sense of movement on to this stable and generic background:

> Thus, I dreamt on one occasion that I was sitting on a bench with one of my former University teachers, and that the bench, which was surrounded by other benches, was moving forward at a rapid pace. This was a combination of lecture theatre and a *trottoir roulant*. (Freud, 1901a, pp. 651–652)

An unnamed university lecture and the dreamer, propelled rapidly forward on their benches, experience the flow of ideas as time and motion. Reduced to this single sentence description and with no further associations, the dream serves in Freud's text only as a basic example of composite dream imagery—in this case the condensation of lecture theatre benches with a *trottoir roulant*.

Incidentally, if Freud had read the *Neue Freie Presse* report, he would have known that the real Paris *trottoir roulant* had two parallel components, a walkway moving at 8 km/hr and by its side a faster one, moving at 15 km/hr. Did the dream benches move at different speeds?

By the same process of condensation, the audience of holiday-makers on the Ossiacher See takes on dual or multiple identities for the viewer. A photographer shot them in 1900: the viewer, the photographer in reverse, now faces a menacing combination of lecture audience and firing squad.

The image has been refracted through the lens of a camera and distorted in the viewer's imagination: its relation to any conscious moment is fuzzy. Yet photos present themselves to us as absolute visibility, an instant of total consciousness. As if in that mechanical image everything possible has been revealed.

This particular absolute moment is anchored in a specific time and here a reasonable guess is possible, if not down to the second, at least to a day or so. Freud was visiting Annenheim for only a few days and this must be shortly before 27 August, when he left with his sister-in-law, Minna Bernays, for a tour of South Tyrol. Heinrich Graf could come down from Vienna to be with his family only at weekends. Consequently, the photo was probably taken on Saturday 25th or Sunday 26th August. If we choose to interpret the spray of flowers on the table as festive, as well as decorative, then we could fix on the 25th, since that was Lucie Bernays' fourteenth birthday. It was also the date of Nietzsche's death.

*   *   *

The second of these two photos turned up among material left by Tini Maresch, Mathilde Freud's companion. It is common enough to find duplicate photos in the archives and albums, and it was only when I saw the two side by side that I realised one was not, as I had assumed, simply a cropped version of the other. A quick comparison shows that a second or so must have passed between the two snaps; the angle is lower on the second and everybody has turned to the camera. In effect, the two photos form a minimal film, a micro-action of two frames. Only it is uncertain which way the film should be played.

The second photo, in which everyone is dutifully facing the camera, is clearly the more deliberately posed shot. It is also badly composed, two of the front row children blocking our view of those behind. There is, therefore, an argument both ways for order of precedence: that the first photo was snapped, and then everybody persuaded to "watch the birdy", or that the unsatisfactory posed shot was followed by an attempt to close in on the subject.

At this rudimentary level, the order of action is of no practical consequence. What does make a difference is the evidence of activities that a single photo never records, the fact that between frames some microscopic agitation has determined the position and expression of the figures. Between one click and the other heads turn, expressions alter, the little girl takes her thumb out of her mouth: time happens.

"Photography is truth. And cinema is truth 24 frames a second." Godard's famous dictum equates truth and visibility. It ignores the unseen, unconscious gaps between frames, but that is where everything is going on.

The two photographs from the summer of 1900 evoke the moving pavement through paradoxes—immobile motion, silent speech. Visitors glide along the walkway like dreamers and step off to visit the various pavilions of the fair as if waking up.

In his abandoned "Project for a scientific psychology" (1895), Freud wrote,

> Consciousness of dream ideas is above all discontinuous. What
> becomes conscious is not a whole succession of associations, but

separate stopping points in it. Between these there lie unconscious intermediate links which we can easily discover when we are awake. (Freud, 1950a, p. 341)

Both continuity and language are barred from photographs. Perhaps the stillness and silence heighten the sense of a space between two moments of perception. We cannot hear these people; they cannot hear us. They smile meaningfully or shout; their messages come up against a glass wall. They need someone to speak for them: their efforts were being thwarted by some internal resistance that must be overcome.

In January that year Freud had acquired something by Nietzsche ". . . in whom I hope to find words for much that remains mute in me . . ." (Masson, 1985, p. 398). He does not say what it was, but does say he had not yet opened it. Open or closed, Nietzsche was in the air.

In the *Interpretation of Dreams*, Freud describes the process of displacement, in what seems deliberately Nietzschean terms, as the "transvaluation of all psychical values" (Freud, 1900a, pp. 654–655) and in "On dreams", written in the autumn of 1900, he repeated the phrase. Nietzsche undermined moral values by giving them a genealogy, and setting them in a historical context. Freud's phrase implicitly made an equivalent claim for his own evolutionary natural history of mental phenomena.

Although he later denied having read him, Freud probably heard of Nietzsche as early as 1874, through his contacts with the student *Leseverein*, a reading group where he was discussed. During the winter of 1883–1834, his friend Joseph Paneth was in Nice, reporting his conversations there with Nietzsche to his fiancée, and perhaps to Freud, too (their correspondence has not survived). Even if the Freud of 1900 had only known as much as was culturally current, he would have been well aware of Nietzsche's reversal of Christian morality and, above all, of his dominating concept, the anti-teleology—time conceived as eternal recurrence, endless becoming.

The dream of the lecture benches as *trottoir roulant*, gliding endlessly forward, round and round the World Fair.

Standing on the fringe of this extended family group, Freud is only an incidental figure. His presence at Annenheim was in itself accidental. He was peripheral and in transition, dissatisfied with the present, preoccupied with the unknown work ahead. The dream interpretation, his great work, had now been published, yet apparently nothing had been achieved. Was life moving or not moving? Such moods may be reflected in familiar dreams of impeded activity.

The problem of being a scientific dream interpreter is existential. As there is no established academic place or identity for him, was he casting his first glances at this new world as a pseudo-artist or, as he declared to Fliess on 1 February 1900, in the same letter in which he mentions Nietzsche, was he "nothing but a conquistador"? The obituary for Nietzsche on the front page of the *Neue Freie Presse* for 26 August praised him above all for his "extreme intransigent individualism", but even Zarathustra has to come down the mountain to find, or create, his audience.

On 12 May 1900, six days after his forty-fourth birthday, Freud began lecturing on dreams. For this first lecture, he had an audience of three people. Five days earlier, he had written to Fliess, "I would have no objection to the fact of *splendid isolation* if it were not carried too far and did not come between you and me as well". His fear was premonitory, or an admission of an unspoken distance. What he mentioned in his 1907 letter to Jung was here becoming evident: Fliess, his first audience, was imperceptibly drifting away.

At their meeting in early August 1900 on the shores of the Achensee, a discussion had occurred that finally laid bare the radical difference between their world views. Fliess later reported, "At that time Freud's violence towards me was inexplicable to me, because in a discussion of his observation of his patients I claimed that periodic events also absolutely determined the mind . . ." (Masson, 1986, p. 464, n.1). Any illusion Freud might have had that their respective theories were compatible was now dispelled: this was the end of the affair. If psychological disturbances were absolutely determined by Fliessian periods, any other factors would have to be considered secondary. It was evident that the two of them were engaged in a duel for conceptual primacy.

Perhaps it was less a question of whether periodicity or unconscious drives ruled than one of reductionism. Years later, Freud spelled this out in a letter to Abraham on 6 April 1914. Subordinating psychoanalysis to Fliess's sexual biology would have been as much of a disaster as subordinating it to ethics, metaphysics, or any such ready-made system (Falzeder, 2002, p. 229). The violence was on both sides, and was as personal as it was ideological. Another version, from a letter to Ferenczi on 10 January 1910, was that he had unleashed Fliess's fury by offering a psychoanalytical explanation of his obsession with numbers (Brabant, Falzeder, & Giampieri-Deutsch, 1993, p. 122).

These explanations were written a decade or more after the events. At the time, the correspondence between Fliess and Freud continued until early 1902, though at an ever diminishing rate, and, for the time being, without an attempt to discuss their differences.

These two photographs are in this time and out of this time, an interval of inactivity, a rest from the major themes and preoccupations, a flurry of family trivia. All that continuity of thought and unconscious activity plays out in the gap between them.

*   *   *

In Borges' *The Secret Miracle*, the condemned hero writes an entire book in his head while the bullets of the firing squad and the smoke from his last cigarette hang in the air. The miracle, his plea for time to finish his work before dying, has been granted, and it is a Nietzschean one, an expansion of the lived moment to its utmost limits.

Despite the blurring and grain of these two images, we can just make out the cigar in Freud's left hand, distinguishable mainly by its tip of grey ash. Even on the closest possible examination, there is no perceptible difference in the length of the ash between the two photos.

Whatever has just happened, or is about to happen, has to be inferred: from the hand with the cigar, from the walking sticks, from the jacket or cape loose over Heinrich Graf's left shoulder as if he had just sat down. If there was a walk, it could have been anywhere, by the lake or into the woods. Every moment contains its predecessors, is compacted with its history, and most of it leaks out into the outside world without leaving any trace. Memory is not photographic and not every moment of life is photographed. The image swarms with inferences, implied stories hanging in the air between the snapshots, walks in the mountains or by lakesides.

Whatever happened by the other lakeside earlier that month, however unexpected it might have appeared to Fliess, had already been heralded by hints and undertones in the correspondence. In the preceding weeks, Freud's letters had contained phrases that would seem portentous in retrospect. On 23 March that year, he expressed envy of Fliess's biological discoveries. A month later, on 25 April, he was pouring cold water on Fliess's apparent hope of a meeting in Rome: "Well, do you realize now that Rome cannot be forced? I often have fatalistic convictions of this kind which serve my inertia very well. I am really not making any headway". A few paragraphs further on in the same letter, the same phrase is repeated: ". . . and got lost; the weather was miserable, I made no headway" (Masson, 1985, p. 410).

Themes of time and space go round and round; restless movement and paralysis in the dream before the B'nai B'rith; *"splendid isolation"*, a lakeside walk, a lost companion, abandonment.

Time as repetition and time as progression; the similarities and differences of the two photos present both aspects of what is a single phenomenon. Between the two images the self-assured boy in the foreground forms a counterweight to the shouting infant behind him. He is Edward Bernays, the future founder of public relations. His expression and position do not alter from one photo to the other. Perhaps it is the responsibility of holding the dog that keeps him still; perhaps he is pondering the potentialities of photography. Behind them and at the edge of the group expressions change or heads turn, a smile slips or broadens, Anna Bernays' disapproval turns to, or from, resignation, Lucy's smile broadens, or fades: all the adjustments and mechanics of change that carry us from one state to another.

*   *   *

At the end of Fellini's *Satyricon,* the characters sail away or disperse into the scenery, and in the final scene are transformed into fragments of a fresco painted on a shattered wall. This device switches between two relations to the image and two versions of time: the intimate flow of transient living figures transformed into the remote immobile images of a distant age.

When the camera draws back from a scene, as in the bottom photo, it alters our relation with the object. In the album photo, the figures fill the frame. There is little internal perspective: the image is a sort of frieze. The wider angle of the other shot imposes a different scale. The white wall of the house, the bush outside the door, and the over-hanging branch enter the picture, together with the window shutters, the tiled floor of the yard, even some unidentifiable pan or bowl in the plant tub behind Freud.

The figures have to work harder to stop our attention wandering. If it were not for the hat, nose, and forehead of Hermann poking over

Edward's hat, the spiral composition that holds the human scene together in both photos would be interrupted in this one. As it is, the line is broken, but held together by the vase of unidentified plants and the flag in front of the window. In this wider composition, though the characters do not actually fade into the natural scene, they are visibly part of a wider world and context.

"Rome cannot be forced." Inertia holds everything in place. But everything is moving, even though we cannot see it. (A year later, Freud would finally reach Rome for the first time.) Only the running commentary, as a spatial consciousness extended in time, speaks for that world in motion between the fixed scenes.

". . . such a difficult task as our marriage . . ."

The earliest preserved photographic image of the world, Nicéphore Niepce's view from his window at Le Gras around 1827, shows a side of a building and opposite it a sloping roof. The view is faded to the verge of being indecipherable: the original plate is almost as shiny as a mirror (Newhall, 1982, p. 15). Presumably, the forms of the roof and building are true to life, but the unearthly lighting is impossible, because a facing wall and roof are both, simultaneously, sunlit. During the eight hours or so of exposure that the image had required, the sun had crossed the sky and illuminated the scene from both sides. Niepce termed his images "heliographs": the unreal view from his window shows us a scene "written by the sun" as the photo-history of a single day

Later and more technically advanced "light drawings" show another effect of long exposure. In Daguerre's views of the Boulevard du Temple in 1838, the beautifully detailed boulevard is eerily empty, except for a stationary bootblack and client—the first people ever to be photographed. All movement and other human activity has been eliminated from the image.

Technical development changed the nature of the image. Fast shutter speeds excluded the passing of time, but introduced chance and surprise. The accidental components of a snapshot have a way of capturing our attention. In this photo, for example, the curious white conduit slanting up from the right margin, resting on a tripod arrangement and pointed like a gun at Minna Bernays' head. Or the expression of disapproval on the face of Freud's mother, Amalia, who stands half out of frame to the left of the central trio. In fact, her presence itself looks unintentional. In some published versions of this photo she has even been trimmed out. Just before or after this photo was taken, she had her intended moment in front of the camera. There is another shot taken against the same rock and in the same clothes, in which she stands at the centre, in the place of honour between her son and her daughter-in-law, clutching a bunch of wild flowers, but with the same desolate expression on her face (E. Freud, L. Freud, & Grubrich-Simitis, 1978, Plate 186). In the shot here, however, she is an intruder, as if she had just stumbled on to this scene and did not like what she saw.

The three central figures appear oblivious of her presence, contentedly posing for the camera in a symmetrical arrangement, Freud in serviceable country clothes flanked by his wife, Martha, and Minna, his sister-in-law, both splendid in their holiday finery, their grand hats and parasols and white muslin dresses. In a letter from his voyage to Greece the previous year, Freud described the white-clad ladies on board their ship as "vanilla-ice lionesses" ("*Löwinnen aus Vanilleeis*") (Tögel, 2002, p. 185). That description could be applied to his companions on this country outing, and, evoking the Lion Gate at Mycenae, Freud himself seen as the pillar between the two rampant lionesses. All three figures here have their hands joined on the crook of their parasols or walking stick. The two women both stand with heads and bodies at the same slight angle to the central figure, and both are almost identically dressed. However, the symmetry is not perfect: Minna stands at a slightly greater distance from Freud than her sister.

There are many reasons for taking a photograph at a particular time and place. Family photos would often be taken to mark some special occasion and, as such, they performed another and more important function, which was to signify relationships. So, what sort of relationships are signified by this photograph of a man, his wife, his sister-in-law, and his mother in an alpine landscape?

In its album, this photo is labelled "Alt-Aussee 1905" and, to judge by the age of the figures, the fashion of their dress, and the surroundings there is no reason to question the date or place.[1] The date may even have a bearing on the mother's presence and on her mood. Her seventieth birthday was on 18 August 1905, when the Freud family was on holiday in Altaussee. She might not have been staying with them; she could have been with Dolfi, her youngest daughter, at her favourite resort of Bad Ischl. However, since that is within easy reach of Altaussee, a reunion could easily have been arranged on that occasion, and it would certainly have justified a commemorative photo or two. If that is so, Dolfi's absence from the photos would then need explaining. Perhaps, since her brother was looking after her that day, she was allowed a brief holiday from her lifelong task of looking after her mother.

If we choose to read the mother's expression as bitter, it would be understandable that a birthday for such a woman as Amalia Freud would have been no occasion for rejoicing. The sight of the younger women would only have rubbed salt in the wound. Whatever the reasons for her pained or puzzled expression, the mood of the other three appears light-hearted. Their smiles may be restrained, that of

Sigmund Freud in fact concealed in his beard, but they signal pleasure with the occasion. Whether that refers to a birthday celebration, or a walk in the country, or just lining up to be photographed is of no relevance to a wider question the photo raises, which is the patterns of relationship between these women and this man.

Because this is the only photo that presents Freud together with these three women, two of whom shared his life, it has acquired iconic quality. When Franz Maciejewski's recent (2006) discovery of Freud's entry in a Maloja hotel register revived a long-standing discussion around Freud's relationship with his sister-in-law, Minna Bernays, some newspapers used this picture to illustrate their stories. In fact, the subliminal message of the photo does work in favour of a Martha–Minna equivalence. The women in white seem to reflect each other. One might even read the mother's baffled expression as a reaction to that duplication. A mother can find ways of dealing with a daughter-in-law, but getting to her son past *two* "daughters-in-law" is a much harder proposition.

Apart from dating the photograph to the first decade of the twentieth century, the clothes tell us something else about the occasion. Dressed as they are, it is obvious that the women cannot leave the more sedate footpaths around the resort, but the man, with his boots and gaiters and walking stick, is well equipped to hack his way through the woods. As far back as 1898, Freud had written to Fliess, on 26 August, that the local footpaths were already long familiar—and boring—to him.

It might have been his intention, after a short stroll with the women, to let them return together and to leave on his own, or accompanied by the photographer, to climb the hills or hunt for mushrooms. The clothes establish a well-defined boundary between the respective worlds of women and men.

Freud's publications for 1905 illuminate this photograph from another angle. After a comparatively fallow period, three major works appeared that year: *Jokes and their Relation to the Unconscious* (1905c), *Fragment of an Analysis of a Case of Hysteria* (1905e), and *Three Essays on the Theory of Sexuality* (1905d). If the figure in the photo seems to exude a certain self-satisfaction, these achievements gave him good grounds. Above all, he had now set sexuality and its vicissitudes as firmly at the centre of his work as that background rock, which the photographer used to unify the elements of this composition.

However, each of the protagonists stands separately, hands crossed below the midriff as if barring access to their private lives. If this photograph illustrates a story, it is indicated chiefly by the central triangle, the symmetry and proximity of the man and the two sisters.

Before this triangle ever developed, there had been a rectangle. In the early 1880s, it had consisted of two sets of betrothed, Freud engaged to Martha Bernays, and Minna Bernays to the Sanskrit scholar, Ignaz Schönberg. Since both sisters had found themselves impoverished academic researchers as fiancés, it was small wonder that their mother, Emmeline Bernays, remained sceptical of their prospects and did little to encourage her daughters' suitors. Thus, another mother haunts the frame of this photograph, as if her disapproving gaze also falls across the scene. For the quartet of young lovers were all under the influence of "Mama", as Freud always referred to Emmeline Bernays in his correspondence with Martha when they were engaged. Her influence dominated all their relationships after she decided to take her daughters back with her from Vienna to Wandsbek near Hamburg in early 1883.

Schönberg's reaction to Mama's abduction of his beloved was dramatic. He accused Emmeline Bernays of selfishness and failing to be the benevolent mother he had thought her to be. Freud took a cooler view of their situation and criticised Schönberg's emotional response. A letter to Minna on 21 February 1883 shows that his criticism was also aimed at Schönberg's (and Minna's) failure to preserve the exclusivity of their own relationship:

> But he [Schönberg] places demands on her [Emmeline Bernays], as if she were the malleable young wife who had not yet exhausted herself in sacrifices and suffering, who could still expect happiness from life, who still had the zest, the fine vivacity, the self-criticism of youth. To some extent I believe it was your fault; you allowed the two of them to get too close to one another. Such harmony as Schönberg demanded, with all its self-sacrifice, can be established between two but never between three people, and is totally superfluous with that number. I believe you should be a bit more jealous of him, how was he allowed to disturb his relationship to you through his links with any third person. (Hirschmüller, 2005, p. 50)

That final sentence above seems to me to require a question mark at the end and there is none. These letters were often written in haste and high feelings. Clearly, however, Freud was not asking a question; he was making an affirmation, of the necessity of jealousy.

This advocacy of jealous possessiveness might be taken for Freud's art of loving, even allowing for the fact that Schönberg's "promiscuity" was intergenerational and that his affective triangle included a prospective mother-in-law. Parents and in-laws must be kept at a distance. Lovers must, above all, protect their own interests.

Freud's (real) mother is half out of the frame in 1905. Already at the time of his engagement, she was seldom referred to in the correspondences. The figure of Mama, Emmeline Bernays, the obstacle to lovers' plans, had edged her out of the picture. Schönberg's error in relation to her can be seen as an instance of a general rule that Freud would later state. Love overvalues and insists on the uniqueness of its object. Consequently, the mother-in-law's distorted similarity to the beloved confuses the suitor.

That rule is spelled out in *Totem and Taboo*:

> On the side of the mother-in-law there is reluctance to give up the possession of her daughter, distrust of the stranger to whom she is to be handed over, an impulse to retain the dominating position which she has occupied in her own house. On the man's side there is a determination not to submit any longer to someone else's will, jealousy of anyone who possessed his wife's affection before he did, and, last but not least, an unwillingness to allow anything to interfere with the illusory overvaluation bred of his sexual feelings. The figure of his mother-in-law usually causes such an interference, for she has many features which remind him of her daughter and yet lacks all the charms of youth, beauty and spiritual freshness which endear his wife to him. (Freud, 1912–1913, pp. 14–15)

The disturbance caused by similarity may remain unconscious. What dominates conscious attention, and inspires lovers' antipathy, is the mother's power over her sons and daughters.

To read Freud's engagement correspondence is to follow a long struggle for control over the daughter. The antagonist was not only the mother-in-law. Only five days after the engagement had been sealed by a secret pact, Martha had (temporarily on this occasion) left Vienna for Hamburg with her mother. On 22–23 June 1882, Freud wrote to her,

Eli and Schönberg have been with us every evening since your departure. We who love Martha and Minna always have something to tell each other; we forge plans for and against to make us masters of the situation in your house. To me it is certain that one must keep Eli under control instead of flattering him as the one in power. (Fichtner, Grubrich-Simitis, & Hirschmüller, 2011, p. 103)

Here, the two lovers are up against Eli Bernays, the guardian-brother of their fiancées.[2] Whereas Freud could accept Emmeline's power over her daughter, and was consequently able to attain some sort of an understanding of the mother, he could by no means accept that the upstart son, Eli, had any natural right to be in control of the fate and finances of the Bernays family.

Since his bankrupt father's death in 1879, Eli Bernays had been responsible for the family finances and for earning their living. If Freud ever took this into account, he never mentioned it as mitigation. His hostility to Eli was broad-based, and (as I mentioned in the previous chapter) initially stemmed from his jilting of Freud's sister, Anna. Its eventual consequences were serious enough to bring him in 1886 to the very verge of breaking his engagement to Martha.

Perhaps Freud's air of confidence in this photograph is multivalent, and not just a result of recent intellectual conquests. On 25 August that year, he wrote to Emma Eckstein that he was spending his time hunting berries and mushrooms, and was indifferent towards science. Perhaps (and the reader should be aware that this is sheer historical extrapolation) his jovial stance reflects some afterglow of his old victory over the Bernays family two decades earlier. To gain the woman at his side he had overcome adversity and adversaries, risked his future happiness, and won. That past period of combat might be imagined as the negative or reverse of this photograph.

In the photo, the parent in the background appears to have been barred from the life and loves of the children. The younger generation forms a closed group. Yet their self-satisfaction might only be apparent, the symmetry unstable. The rectangle of the engagement period, as described by Freud, was held in balance by a counterweight of opposites. The secret of its stability, as Freud told Martha on 27 December 1883, was that the two good-natured and submissive ones, she and Schönberg, were each paired to a wilful and passionate partner. The loss of one angle (Schönberg's disappearance) created a triangle and a new equilibrium of their *balances sentimentales*. That, in turn, could easily collapse with any shift in the subsequent delicate balance of their respective affections.

A photographic image is reducible to static figures in a landscape or even to a geometrical design, if history is excluded from it. Since human relationships are dynamic and historical, whatever is not visible here has to be extrapolated from gestures or deduced from the expressions. For example, there is something hesitant and uncertain about Minna's smile. The shadow over her face accentuates the whites of her eyes and brings out a sense of timidity. An effect of her marginality, perhaps?

In 1885, Schönberg's tuberculosis worsened, partly as a result of his choosing to spend the year working in damp, cold Oxford rather than tending his health. In November 1884, he had been appointed first librarian of the newly founded Indian Institute at the University of Oxford. Whether his affections also cooled down with the deterioration in his health, or whether it was from self-abnegation (not wanting to bind Minna to a dying man), he broke off their engagement, and, in January 1886, death subtracted him definitively from the equation. Minna's relationship to the other two shifted. Solitude rendered her vulnerable. They immediately offered to look after her, even though this was before their wedding and they still had no place of their own.

It was to be another nine years before she actually moved in with them. Their first holiday after she had joined the household was to Altaussee in the summer of 1896, to the family's "holiday paradise" in Obertressen, the presumed landscape of this photo. It was here they also spent the summers of 1897 and 1898. Martin Freud would affectionately commemorate these summer holidays in his memoir, *Glory Reflected* (1957). It was from Obertressen that Freud and Minna set out in 1898 on the walking tour that would take them to the pension in Maloja, where their names remain notoriously recorded in the register as "Dr Sigm. Freud & wife" ("Dr Sigm. Freud u Frau").

In *Jokes and Their Relation to the Unconscious,* there is an anecdote of a young girl left by her father in the care of a friend. He assigns her a bed in his son's bedroom. The girl duly becomes pregnant. Outraged, the girl's father asks his friend how he could have allowed such a thing to happen. The other protests: but there was a screen in the bedroom between the two. The girl's father objects: but the boy might easily have walked round the screen . . . "'Yes, there is that,' replied the other thoughtfully; 'it might have happened like that'" (Freud, 1905c, p. 58). The story illustrates the "nonsense joke": one absurdity is used to illuminate another, greater absurdity.

The screen itself is the minor absurdity: it is the stupidity of the couple's fathers that is the butt of the joke. In Freud historiography, an overriding sense of absurdity hangs over all attempts to prove— or disprove—Freud's alleged affair with Minna Bernays. Couples can share rooms for whatever reason (parsimony, lack of alternative accommodation, etc.), and, whether or not there was a screen in the room, without physical intimacy. The ultimate screen, the one no one easily walks round, is the superego or conscience, or the moral code that rules our conduct, and that leaves its traces everywhere and nowhere.

As for the traces of sexual intercourse, the act only becomes fact through narrative (witnessed intimacy, letters, confessions) or through its physical consequences (pregnancy). Neither shared holidays nor the curious situation of Minna's bedroom in Berggasse constitute evidence of a sexual relationship. Inconvenient as it was that she could only get to her bedroom through the Freuds' bedroom, she was one of the family, and inside its boundaries of privacy. Concerning the impracticality of the arrangement, chamber-pots deal with one possible type of awkwardness, knocking before entry another.

One curious explanation as to why they should have chosen this awkward set-up in the first place further illustrates some of the absurdity surrounding this discussion. It comes from a document written by Freud's grandson, W. Ernest Freud, and intended to refute the allegations contained in a biography of the Freuds' maid, Paula Fichtl:

> Minna Bernays had a travel-grammophone [sic] and was very fond of music. The statement that there was no grammophone in the Freud flat is wrong. Because Sigmund Freud disliked hearing music (or Minna's singing) when he wanted to concentrate Minna was allocated her bedroom in the farthest corner of the flat, and her living room was similarly situated.[3]

In the days before consensual divorce was facilitated in British courts, the practice existed of arranging for a photographer to burst into a hotel room where the "erring couple" had also arranged to be incriminatingly discovered together in bed. In Freud's instance, such photographs are lacking. All the evidence is circumstantial and requires a justifying narrative that will weave the episode into the fabric of history. One such example, with a deduced abortion as a corroborating item, connects with a polemic against Freud's habitual bad faith. Another, concerned with consequences of the imperfect separation of psychoanalysis from its founder, traces the authoritarian tendencies within the psychoanalytic movement back to Freud's need to suppress evidence of his affair. Well over a century later, what went on behind the screens remains undecided. The longer it does, the deeper it embeds itself into the folklore, persisting as a virtual image in a clouded mirror in which one can only make out a reflection of the historians' own motives for wanting an affair with Minna to be true or untrue.

*　*　*

Sometimes a real object or image intervenes into the phantasmic interactions between people. On Freud's thirtieth birthday in 1886, the two sisters, Martha and Minna, clubbed together with Mama to buy him a bust of the nymph Clytie (Hirschmüller, 2005, pp. 148–149).

In Ovid's *Metamorphoses*, the sun god Helios loves and seduces Leucothoe. But Clytie is unrequitedly in love with Helios and she informs Leucothoe's father of the affair. Thereupon, he buries his daughter alive. However, Helios continues to spurn Clytie, and she pines away in the wilderness, her face perpetually following Helios the sun in his passage across the sky. Finally, she is transformed into a flower that forever follows the sun, the heliotrope.

Freud's terracotta copy was presumably based on a Roman bust in the British Museum, depicting a woman's head emerging from flower petals. (There is no trace of it in his collection at the Freud Museum London.) Such copies were extremely popular during the nineteenth century, the bust expressing a blend of melancholy and submission that evidently suited the taste of that time, and perhaps ours, too, since the British Museum still sells them.

When the gift arrived, Freud wrote to Martha, on 8 May 1886, that it reminded him slightly of her. Such effigies channel affection and anxiety. The Clytie bust gave Martha a vicarious focus for some concerns about their relationship:

> You must allow me some "corrections": it is very flattering to me
> that you attribute to me a slight similarity to the Lady Clytie, but I

would prefer it if you did not fall too much in love with the classical terracotta beauty, so as not to be too disappointed when we meet again with your measly other one made of flesh and bone. That is one thing: secondly the tablet is made for hanging on the wall and not for propping up . . . (Martha Bernays to Freud 11.5.1886, SFC)

Treating the surrogate figure on his desk as a rival might be playful, like her other jocular "corrections", but together they carry a serious implication—the question of trust.

The "tablet" she mentions was actually a sampler. He had asked her to embroider a Charcot quote for him. It read: "Il faut avoir la foi" ("One must have faith"). Freud had approached his thirtieth birthday in a subdued, even depressed, state of mind. Continual uncertainty about their prospects had exhausted him, as had his four-year struggle against the Bernays family. In the end, it was not the battle against Eli and Emmeline that had worn him down. After all, he was always a good fighter. What had got under his skin was the effort to eradicate the Bernays spirit in Martha herself. What seemed a simple either/or question of loyalty had turned into a double-bind. His efforts to mould her character were at odds with his love of her as an independent personality.

In 1882, within a week of their engagement, Freud had already revealed both his jealousy (for Max Mayer) and his educative urge. He declared that his ideal wife should have her own voice and be "no little children's doll"—"*kein Spielpüppchen*" (Fichtner, Grubrich-Simitis, & Hirschmüller, 2011, p. 108). But the problem he was to encounter over the coming year was that he began hearing echoes of her brother's and mother's voices through her mouth. This was summed up in a bitter letter of 30 June 1883: "Can you demand that I should love you when you show those characteristics I detest so much and which I resent so much in your family?" (Fichtner, Grubrich-Simitis, & Hirschmüller, 2011, p. 476).

In this challenge to her self-respect, he hurls the same derogatory term at her:

If you feel like a little doll and want to be treated as one, then tell me, after a time I might even be able to write affectionate letters. But up to now I wanted to make something else out of you. (Fichtner, Grubrich-Simitis, & Hirschmüller, 2011, p. 477)

Here, the tension between the real and the imagined Martha leaves Freud suspended somewhere between *Pygmalion* and Ibsen's *Doll's House* (*Puppenheim*). Love—and reality—exacted a compromise. The following day, he withdrew his plea for a "comrade in arms" ("*Kampfgenosse*") and vowed his readiness to accept only what he needed most of all, her affection (Fichtner, Grubrich-Simitis, & Hirschmüller, 2011, p. 482).

Over the four years of their engagement, Martha had had to withstand an assault of images and expectations, and had learnt to defend herself as best she could. By 1886, she had endured a long enough initiation into Freud's character to be able to reverse the roles. When he admitted withholding from her the extent of his temporary depression, she was able to reproach him that she was mature enough to deal with it: ". . . I am not such a little doll" ("*so ein Püppchen*", Martha Bernays to Freud, 9.5.1886).

The bust was not the only image to focus their conflicts. Only a week after the arrival of the Clytie, on the 13th May, Freud wrote to Martha of an American patient with a beautiful and interesting wife. This was also, incidentally, a mere three weeks after he had opened his private practice. On both occasions when the wife had visited, he wrote, Martha's portrait had fallen from his desk. This mixed message put Martha to a curious test. She rose to the challenge:

> You know, my darling, that I am not at all superstitious and even less am I jealous and would not be capable of tormenting you if I noticed that your love for me had diminished. I always have the feeling that you would tell me if it came to that, we spoke about it the last time you were here, if you remember, on that occasion you laughed me out, yet I am serious about it. And today you might laugh me out again that I have gone from the falling picture to such serious matters. . . .
>
> You are no monk and I would not want one, as little as I feel that there is anything of the nun about me. (Martha Bernays to Freud 15.5.1886, SFC)

This promise, then, emerged from the episode of the fallen picture: she could trust him to be honest with her and in return he could trust her not to torment him with jealousy. Yet he had still not received the one proof of trust he required—that she should root out all affective links with her brother.

The decision to marry in autumn 1886 precipitated a frantic search for the funds to establish their new home, and Martha's dowry, held in trust by her brother, Eli, would be their prime source. Unfortunately, Eli seemed to have invested it and was unable to pay up immediately on request. The first sign of an impending crisis, the worst in the couple's long engagement, was a confidential letter from Freud to Minna detailing Eli's underhand dealings (Hirschmüller, 2005, pp. 151–156). In asking Minna to keep the letter secret, Freud was confessing his distrust of Martha's judgement and ability to face the situation dispassionately. But he, in turn, misjudged the intimacy between the sisters—Minna could not keep the letter secret: "We two are always alone and always together now, no suppression is possible and sooner or later she would have to find out what will certainly not stay a family secret for long" (Hirschmüller, 2005, p. 156).

In that response, Minna was anticipating a repeat of the public disgrace that the family had experienced in 1868, when their father, Berman, had been condemned to a year in gaol for bankruptcy with intent to defraud. But the scandal that broke was of a more private nature. Against Martha's advice and wishes, Freud threatened to expose not only Eli's financial dealings, but also his personal affairs. He had an ex-mistress and an illegitimate child he was supporting. Freud was hoping, thus, to compel him to pay the money he owed. Martha was appalled by this blackmail against the brother who had supported her and her family since her father's death in 1879, but it worked. Eli raised the money and sent it, with bad grace, to Martha. She, in turn, sent the money on to Freud, telling him she wanted nothing to do with it (Martha Bernays to Freud, 23.6.1886, SFC).

An increasingly embittered exchange of letters culminated in a sort of ultimatum from Freud. She would have to decide between him and Eli, between loyalty to family or to him:

> Just a few days ago I would have laughed if someone had presented me with the possibility that we two might not marry at all because we were not together and did not have faith in our respective love. And yet we have now reached that point. And I see no way out because I cannot give in and I also do not have the courage to propose to us both that we should undertake such a difficult task as our marriage [*ein so schweres Werk wie unsere Heirat*] in any other way than with full mutual desire. (Freud to Martha Bernays, 25.6.1886, SFC)

In this title line, I have chosen to translate *"Werk"* as *"task"*, and that means I have biased the sense in the direction of hard labour and duty. Translated as "a work", it would be more open to meaning a creative act. Perhaps that would be preferable, but the sense in this letter has already been biased towards bitterness by the context.

Two days later, on 27 June 1886, an exchange of letters brought the affair to a cathartic climax. Freud wrote,

> I will comply with your request to write calmly . . . because I sense how easily one can convert the most heartfelt love into bitterness.
>
> You seem not to have noticed at all how your behaviour recently must result in my hardly being able to view you as my wife . . .

He went on to accuse her of showing more respect for Eli's feelings than for his own. Yet, once again, as it had three years previously, his tirade ended in submission: "Actually, my darling, I have now talked everything out and I ask you earnestly to think that I can have you in September never to lose you again, for I love you too much" (Freud to Martha Bernays, 27.6.1886, SFC).

On the same day, Martha wrote a letter revealing her own ordeal. She could not respect Eli, yet nothing could persuade her that Freud had acted rightly or fairly towards her brother. After standing firmly on the grounds of their disagreement, she, too, refused to take the quarrel to its extreme conclusion: "From all of this you can see, my beloved man, that I am firmly counting on us getting married, although I have ventured for once to have a somewhat different opinion from you" (Martha Bernays to Freud, 27.6.1886, SFC).

How much of this bitterly intimate correspondence did Minna see? The opening words of her letter of 11 July 1886 hint that she has at least followed the progress of the lovers' quarrel. Given her sister's inevitable agitation over the previous fortnight, it would have been difficult to have ignored it. Yet she did not try to intervene: ". . . even without me enough, already more than too much has been written" (Hirschmüller. 2005, p. 165).

At that time, it seems, there were no secrets between the sisters, and although they were to be separated by Martha's marriage a few months later and to live apart until late 1895, when Minna finally joined the Freud household as a permanent resident, no radical alteration of that close relationship has been attested. Hence, any

Freud–Minna romance would need to be imagined as a highly secretive and mutually acknowledged *ménage à trois*. Indeed, if a voyage to Italy is punningly translated into French as a "voyage de lit à lit" ("journey from bed to bed"), and if a supposed foreign affair is farcically transposed to Vienna as bed-hopping between connected rooms, then this would all certainly require the consent of both sisters.

Another of Freud's grandsons, Anton Walter Freud, offered his own take on that scenario:

> I find it hard to believe that Grandfather had a tachtel machtel with his sister in law. Grandmother was no Washlappen [*sic*], I can assure you, and she would have given her sister her marching orders very quickly if she had known about it. The 2 sisters were in fact very good friends to the end of Minna's life. The way grandmother used to talk about her husband, to me and in letters to friends, makes it highly unlikely that her husband had deceived her. My father [Martin Freud], who adored his mother, would have taken it very amiss if his father had "carried on" with Tanta Minna. There was never the least indication by him that anything of that sort had happened.[4]

* * *

Relatives' evidence may only be of relative value. Also, a photo of Freud with his women, even in conjunction with his engagement letters, is no evidence at all, whether or not Freud was (once or serially, with or without his wife's knowledge or permission) "unfaithful". The photo serves me here mainly as an entry into something of more moment for his biography, the unceasing work behind the marriage and the negotiated adjustments and agreements on which a long marital life was founded.

In this picture, the pleasure expressed by the central three figures is offset by the unease of the observer standing in the frame. Some impression of the trio's mood emerges—their pride or content—but it is the mother's unease that breaks the frame and opens out to the larger picture, the history of that instant, the historiography of the protagonists. Reading this photograph, my concern has been less with any fixed incident than with the nature of the evidence. The facts depend on how they are framed.

At the time when Ignaz Schönberg was Freud's companion-in-arms against the Bernays family, he was translating a Sanskrit collection of animal fables, the *Hitopadesha*. It was published in 1884. In his foreword, dated July 1883, Schönberg wrote: "Our Hitopadesha is a collection, in which the tales are grouped in four sections, of which each one is circumscribed by a framing story; these in turn are linked to each other quite superficially by a main story" (Schönberg, 1884, p. iv).

That main story is of a wise ruler who wishes to educate his frivolous sons and can only do so by entertaining them. What holds the collection together is a counterbalance of frame and framed story, of moral education and sheer entertainment. The levels of narrative are kept well segregated. (Incidentally, as Freud pointed out, at that very period Schönberg was failing to segregate his attachment to Minna from a transferential attachment on to "Mama"—the mother in the frame of his love affair.)

In another, far more influential collection of tales, Ovid's *Metamorphoses* (1955), one story flows into another. In the fourth book, a framing narrative tells the story of the daughters of Minyas, who refuse to go out and worship the new, orgiastic god Dionysus. Instead, they stay at home and tell each other stories. One of them is about Pyramus and Thisbe (which Shakespeare would recycle as the "play within a play" in *Midsummer Night's Dream*); another is the tale of Leucothoe and Clytie. Both of them treat the miseries of thwarted desire. In the framing narrative, the narrators of these tales will, in due course, be punished for their refusal to obey Dionysus, the god of instinct. Their punishment is for them to be transformed into twittering bats, creatures of the dusk, neither bird nor beast. The storytellers become the story.

What is visible in the photo is no more than signs and indications, silently crying out for interpretation—the mother's expression, the relative distance between the three central figures, the "gun" pointing at Minna's head. What is going on here? Looking at it again and again, stories keep merging into one another, themes as well as characters undergoing metamorphoses. History keeps breaking out of its frame.

If the title *Metamorphoses* indicates what is going on, *In Search of Lost Time* summarises what photo-history is after. Since this investigation is, by its nature, inconclusive, in place of a conclusion I offer this passage from Proust's *Swann's Way*; a meditation on love, jealousy, and the historical method:

But in this strange phase of love the personality of another person becomes so enlarged, so deepened, that the curiosity which he could now feel aroused in himself, to know the least details of a woman's daily occupation, was the same thirst for knowledge with which he had once studied history. And all manner of actions, from which, until now, he would have recoiled in shame, such as spying, to-night, outside a window, to-morrow, for all he knew, putting adroitly provocative questions to casual witnesses, bribing servants, listening at doors, seemed to him, now, to be precisely on a level with the deciphering of manuscripts, the weighing of evidence, the interpretation of old monuments, that was to say, so many different methods of scientific investigation, each one having a definite intellectual value and being legitimately employable in the search for truth. (Proust, 1922)

CHAPTER FOUR

Mysteries of nature

Woyzeck: "You see, Doctor, sometimes a person has that sort of character, that sort of structure. – But nature's different, you see with nature (*he clicks his fingers*) that's something, how can I say, for example –"
Doctor: "Woyzeck, you are philosophizing again."

(Büchner, 1999, *Woyzeck*)

reud's copy of this photograph is mounted and bears the prin-
ted inscription: "66th Meeting of German Natural Scientists and
Doctors in Vienna 24–30 September 1894. Psychiatry and
Neurology. Taken in the Arcade Court of the University".

The Society of German Natural Scientists and Doctors—*Gesellschaft deutscher Naturforscher und Ärzte*—still exists. Its original archive was lost at the end of the Second World War and its present archive lacks any copy of this photograph or any identifications. Some of the identifications I have suggested below remain tentative.

Key to photograph.
1. Max Kassowitz (1842–1913). 3. Otto Binswanger (1852–1929). 4. Albert Moll (1862–1939). 5. Auguste Forel (1848–1931). 6. Constantin v. Monakow (1853–1930). 7. Karl Ludwig Kahlbaum (1828–1899). 8. Richard Krafft-Ebing (1840–1902). 9. Friedrich Jolly (1844–1904). 10. Gabriel Anton (1858–1933). 11. Heinrich Obersteiner (1847–1922). 12. Salomon Stricker (1834–1898). 18. Karl Mayer (1862–1936). 21. Emilio Conde Flores (1869–1928). 22. Germán Greve Schlegel (1869–1954). 25. Max Herz (1865–1956). 26. C.S. Freund (1862–1932). 27. Sigmund Freud (1856–1939). 28. Olga v. Leonowa (1867–?). 33. August Smith (Marbach a. Bodensee). 35. Alois Alzheimer (1864–1915). 36. Emanuel Mendel (1839–1907). 40. Friedrich Pineles (1868–1936). 41. Lothar Frankl-Hochwart (1862–1914). 47. Alexander Spitzer (1868–1943). 50. F. L. Stüever (Wien). 51. Josef Adolf Hirschl (1865–1914). 55. Robert Sommer (1864–1937). 59. Julius Wagner-Jauregg (1857–1940).

Further participants in the Psychiatry and Neurology section (speakers or discussants) who might appear in the photo:

Bayer (Karlsbad); E. Bregmann; Jonas Großmann; Heinrich Higier; M. Löwit; Alessandro Marina; Ludwig Heinrich Friedrich Moritz; Edmund von Neusser; Jakob Pal; Arnold Pick; A. Poehl; Heinrich Rehm; Emil Schiff; Hermann Schlesinger; Victor Stern; Maximilian Sternberg; Franz Tuczek; Weiss (Wien); Hugo v. Ziemssen. (*Sources*: Kerner & Exner (1894); Wangerin & Taschenberg (1895).)

Photographs appear unnatural because they have been stopped in time. Their hallucinatory quality is an instantaneous *"alienation between the somatic and the psychic"* (Masson, 1985, p. 93). They interrupt experience and detach themselves from it in the same way as a scientific experiment isolates elements of reality for examination. But what experiment might be taking place in this photo?

There are sixty figures facing us, all with their own life story. As if that were not already far too much to deal with, the group they belong to has its own long history. Founded in 1822, the Society of German Natural Scientists and Doctors ((henceforth referred as GDNÄ) still exists today. The best that can be done is to question the moment itself, and look at Freud's encounter with this society and its members in 1894.

If this is an experiment, a staged group photo such as this seems at first sight to demonstrate no more than the mechanics of its own staging. Accordingly, the Freud in this photograph, standing as he does nearly at the edge of the group, would have to be seen as peripheral. In fact, the meeting itself was peripheral as far as his official biography was concerned. Jones, who had evidently not seen this picture, even remained uncertain whether Freud had attended the event (Jones, 1980[1953], p. 377).

In terms of Freud's biography, the most interesting thing about this photograph is that he is seen among his scientific mentors and his peer group. This contrasts with the biography that stresses his sense of solitude in the 1890s. In 1894, his life was in question. Literally— symptoms and premonitions led him to ask himself whether he was about to die—and, in terms of his career, there was the uncertainty what place there might be in this world for his work in progress.

In the august company of these natural scientists, he was, if only momentarily, placing himself in the tradition of the GDNÄ. Over the course of the century, the Society had progressed from its origins in a mystical nature philosophy to systematic materialism. Nothing here could be taken for granted. The air of the photo is suffused with voices questioning the status and scope of science. In that respect, they echo Freud's own experiences that year.

Like it or not, the philosophical questions never go away, and, though he was no philosopher, Freud was forced to philosophise. He would continue doing so. A lifetime later, on 22 August 1938, he would jot down the suggestion that spatiality is a projection of the mind's own self-perception on to the world: "Instead of Kant's *a priori* determinants of our psychic apparatus" (Freud, 1941f, p. 152). This late idea of turning Kant upside down is a final trace of a continuous undercurrent in his thought. Long before that, and long after this photo, he marked a passage on the modality of perception in his 1911 edition of Pearson's *The Grammar of Science*: "Our notion of 'being' is essentially associated with space and time, and it may well be questioned whether it is intelligible to use the word except in association with these modes of perception" (Pearson, 1911 p. 207 fn.).

Probably it is the shadow of Ernst Mach that falls across Pearson's anti-metaphysical questionings. At this 1894 event, Mach was a keynote speaker. His shadow also falls across the photograph.

What is the status of a description, Mach asked, and what is it that measurement actually measures?

As if parodying that voice and those questions, a pathetic appeal for information appeared in the *Tagblatt*, the news-sheet of the 1894 Meeting. Perhaps some of the participants in this photo read it and grimaced, or reflected wryly on the mishaps that beset theory in the lived world: "Lost on the Kärntnerstrasse a manuscript (Mathematical Treatise 'Proposal for a New Measurement of Time and Space')" (Kerner & Exner, 1894, p. 442).

* * *

Freud's peripheral position in the photo may have been self-chosen. In fact, he should have been fairly central: he was an official at the event. Taking a magnifying glass to the photo, we see that many of the participants are wearing small, round, lapel badges. Among them only a few, including the eminent Richard Krafft-Ebing, Frankl-Hochwart, a colleague of Freud's, and Freud himself, are wearing larger badges with two ribbons. These might distinguish those involved in the organisation.

In a letter earlier that year, Freud had written to Fliess, "I do not know if I have already written to you that at the meeting of natural scientists I must function as 1st Secretary for the neurological section". He had, in fact, already mentioned it three months previously. That first reference spoke of "the natural scientists' meeting at which I am to perform the duty of 1st secretary of the neurological section" (Masson, 1986, pp. 66 & 63).

In terms of their emotional neutrality and apparent lack of enthusiasm, there is little to choose between these two casual references.

The words "*must* function" could even be understood as betraying reluctance, as if Freud were under some obligation to fulfil the function. To some extent, that might have been the case. Sigmund Exner was the overall Viennese representative at the Meeting, and Krafft-Ebing was in charge of the neurology section. The support of both these influential professors would be vital in any future academic application Freud might want to submit.

Krafft-Ebing himself features unmistakably and prominently in the photo, at the centre of the front row, leaning forward with his hand on his knee as if about to stand up and address the photographer. Since Sigmund Exner was his co-organiser, he might be expected to occupy the prominent position to his right, but protocol and visual evidence are at odds. Although later photos of Exner do indeed show him bald and with a long white beard, at this time he was only forty-eight years old and still dark-bearded. Assuming that the white-bearded elder to Krafft-Ebing's right was also of high status, perhaps he should be identified as another prominent participant, the German psychiatrist Karl Ludwig Kahlbaum.

We are dealing here with only one contingent of the enormous gathering of 1894: the Psychiatry and Neurology section. Jones had even expressed doubts whether this section was constituted at all (Jones, 1980, p. 377). The full gathering that year consisted of thirty-nine sections in all and over a thousand participants, not all of whom appeared in the attendance register. The franchise to photograph all the scientific sections of the Meeting had been granted to the Photo-atelier Nina. The photographs were taken by arrangement with each section, at the end of their morning sessions. Perhaps the GDNÄ itself paid the atelier, for participants received a free copy of the photo (*Einladung*, 1894, p. 19).

In the left-hand background of the photo a hoarding is visible. This might form part of a temporary scientific exhibition that accompanied the congress (Kerner & Exner, 1894, p. 8). There appear to be something like flasks or instruments under the board in the second arch from the left. The decorative signboard in the third arcade from the left bears an inscription that is just beyond the limits of legibility. Could it have belonged to the Photoatelier Nina, for there seem to be racks of pictures below the sign, which might be samples of photos?

The background itself is unmistakeably, as indicated on the label, the Arcade Court of the University. That already housed a far more permanent exhibition of sorts. Since 1888, busts of famous academic figures had been erected there, so that it had already become what it remains today, a sculpture gallery, or hall of fame. Freud's own bust would be unveiled there in 1955. In a way, it is fitting that this group of living men should back on to that memorial of death and posthumous fame, somewhere behind the pillars.

Freud's second reference to the Meeting quoted above from a letter of 7th February 1894 was immediately followed by a comment that betrays the presence of both fame and death in the arcades of his own mind. "Billroth's death is the news of the day. Enviable not to have outlived himself" (Masson, 1985, p. 66). Fear of a wasted life could be read into this remark, as if Freud were worrying whether fate might not doom him, in contrast to Billroth, to years of repetition, or to an unproductive old age. That is, if he survived at all. His anxiety and hypochondria during the early months of 1894 is well documented. The reference to Billroth's death could even be read as a conversion of fear into desire. There is the implication that Freud could accept the prospect of an early death, as long as his work brought him fame. This version of fame entails relentless duty to "scorn delights, and live laborious days" (Milton, *Lycidas*). His remark, then, becomes a sort of vow of devotion to personal and scientific progress.

For us, looking at this photograph, fame is one form of evidence. Many here, apart from such prominent members of this section as Krafft-Ebing or Forel, were already, or would become, famous in their own right. Among them, Monakow, Jolly, Anton, Obersteiner, Frankl-Hochwart, Alzheimer, and Wagner-Jauregg have all given their names to the anatomical areas, syndromes, sicknesses, or cures which they discovered or described. Some of the others are flash-lit by reflected fame, such as Freud's teachers or colleagues (Salomon Stricker or Max Kassowitz), or for having crossed his path on this and other occasions (Freund, Herz, or Mayer).

Yet others here—Conde Flores from Venezuela or Germán Greve Schlegel from Chile—appear as visitors from another world: the New World waiting for its conquistador. In due course, Germán Greve Schelling, who is standing directly behind Krafft-Ebing, would become a pioneer psychoanalyst in Chile. In 1911, Freud reviewed with approval a paper on anxiety states given by him in Buenos Aires in 1910 (Freud, 1911g). This paper would later be hailed as the first presentation of Freudian ideas in Argentina (Ruperthuz Honorato, 2012).

Like any other congress, the 1894 gathering was intended as an opportunity to network and its function was social as much as scientific. The very first statute of the GDNÄ states:

> The purpose of the Society of German Natural Scientists and Doctors, founded on 18. September 1822 in Leipzig by a number of German natural scientists and doctors, consists in the advancement of the natural sciences and of medicine and in fostering personal relations among German natural scientists and doctors. (*Einladung*, 1894, p. 1)

What this early statute could not take into account was the divisive potential of gatherings where each speciality forms its own ghetto. In 1894, medicine alone was divided into five groups that were, in turn, subdivided. Psychiatry and Neurology (Section 26) was in the second group, between Paediatric Medicine (No. 25) and Ophthalmic Medicine (No. 27). This proliferation of sections and groups is the expression of a philosophical conundrum that only began to confront the GDNÄ a few years after its founding. Lorenz Oken had set up the society on the basis of the unifying vision of *Naturphilosophie*, which aims to derive universal principles from all natural phenomena. Subdivision of knowledge was alien to this project, and when Alexander von Humboldt first announced the formation of sections at the Berlin meeting in 1828 there was a certain amount of resistance (Engelhardt, 2007). Universalising aspirations had to be reconciled with growths in technology and information. These developments inaugurated specialisation, and with it mutually incomprehensible scientific dialects.

The brief and brilliant career of the artist–scientist Georg Büchner, whose path crossed Oken's a few years later, illustrates the polymath aspirations characteristic of the early years of the GDNÄ. (Goethe and Carl Gustav Carus were other notable examples.) Oken would recognise his own evolutionary ideas reflected in Büchner's Probationary Lecture "On cranial nerves", delivered on 18 November 1836 at the University of Zurich. Oken, as newly appointed Rector, was in the audience, and it was on his recommendation that Büchner was awarded the title of Docent without further examination.

From the opening of his lecture, it was evident that Büchner was philosophising with a scalpel. He began by contrasting the teleological method prevalent in anatomy as practised in England and

France with the German attitude that sees Nature as a self-sufficient entity governed by its own mysterious law:

> To seek the law of this Being is the aim of the viewpoint that stands in opposition to the teleological, and which I will term the *philosophical*. Everything that for the former was a means is, for the latter, an effect. Where the teleological school has a ready answer is where the question begins for the philosophical. This question which addresses us at each point can only find its answer in a fundamental law for the whole organisation, and so for the philosophical method the entire corporeal existence of the individual is not set up for its own survival but is a manifestation of a primal law, a law of beauty that produces the highest and purest forms from the simplest plans and lines. (Büchner, 1999, p. 158)

Here, Büchner is, in his own way, as concerned with economy of form and description as Ernst Mach would be in his opening lecture to the 1894 Meeting, when he stated ". . . that natural science is always concerned only with the economic expression of the real" (Mach, 1896, p. 251). The fundamental law of nature, Büchner speculates, may be sensed in a beauty achieved by the most economical means and through the ideal archetype, made manifest in the form of each individual specimen.

In some respects, there is a certain congruence between Büchner and Freud. Freud's scientific origins in his study of Petromyzon are prefigured in Büchner's theis, *On the Cranial Nerves of the Barbel*. More generally, but perhaps more significantly, Büchner also came to experimental science only after overcoming the temptations of philosophy. Before settling on anatomical research, Büchner had considered writing his thesis on Descartes and Spinoza. This would surely have involved the need to situate mind in the natural world. That project was set aside, but his two greatest literary works, *Lenz* and *Woyzek*, are both case histories illustrating a drastic misalignment of real and imagined worlds.

Freud's own temptation came at university under the influence of Franz Brentano and threatened briefly to side-track him into working on a doctorate in philosophy. His subsequent denigration of philosophy comes to look something like a shamefaced covering of his own traces. His niece, Lilly Freud-Marlé, records an aphorism of her uncle's that typifies this attitude: "Philosophy sometimes seems to me like a person who keeps cleaning their glasses and yet they stay misted" (Freud-Marlé, 2006, p. 270). This could be read as a reaction to the philosophically problematic bases of his own science, psychology, or even to the disjunction between observation and defining one's terms in scientific practice. Theodor Reik also reports the "dirty glasses" aphorism, but, instead of "philosophy", his version blames "critics who limit their studies to methodological investigations" (Reik, 1942, p. 126).

One finds evidence of a similar unease about "philosophy" even in such a philosophically minded scientist as Ernst Mach. He would deny that he was a philosopher at all, or that what he wrote was philosophy. It was, Mach insisted, only "natural science methodology", adding, "For this reason I have already categorically stated that I am *not a philosopher but a natural scientist*" (Mach, 1905, p. VII). Mach's "methodology" might seem like a quibbling redefinition of philosophy—after all, science itself starts out under the rubric of "natural philosophy". However, it advances with the shifting of categories and paradigms, and in the background and atmosphere of this photo some such movements can be made out.

In his keynote lecture on the morning of 24 September 1894, Mach addressed the Meeting on, among other things, the resistance of practical scientists to philosophy (Mach, 1896, p. 252). Some aspect of that resistance would be practically demonstrated the very next day, in one of the scientific sessions of the Neurology and Psychiatry section.

We do not know exactly on which day of the Meeting this photograph was taken. If it had been taken at the end of the morning session on 25 September, its participants would just have emerged from a paper given by Max Herz (the fourth figure from the right in the second row). His paper was entitled "On critical psychiatry": it suggested that psychiatric disorders could be conceptualised as disturbances to the mechanisms of Kantian pure reason. But the reception of his ideas by the section appears to have been hostile. The record of discussion published in the *Tagblatt* is limited to the following curt report: "Sommer warns against transferring Kantian concepts on to psychiatry. Emil Schiff expresses similar sentiments" (Kerner & Exner, 1894, p. 241). Who knows? Possibly there was more, unreported, discussion. Or perhaps the hungry participants were by now getting impatient for their lunch, or were, at that point, summoned to be photographed.

Apparently undeterred by that initial reception, Herz continued his Kantian campaign in the morning of 27 September, with another paper, "On the material bases of consciousness", in which he rebuked psychology for concentrating on the effects of physical experience and excluding the most essential component of human thought, concepts (Kerner & Exner, 1894, p. 388). This was entirely in key with Mach, who, in his lecture on 24 September, had stated, "A concept is for the natural scientist what a note is for the pianist" (Mach, 1896, p. 267). But again, one senses resistance to such ideas, for after this second intervention no discussion at all is recorded. It seems that Herz, no less than Freud, though for different reasons, was out of key with the mood of this gathering (Andersson, 1962, pp. 195–197). That might even account for what, on closer inspection, could be seen as his somewhat wistful expression in this photograph.

Several times Freud quoted, with approval, Charcot's down-to-earth remark: "Theory is good, but it does not stop something existing" ("*La théorie, c'est bon, mais ça n'empêche pas d'exister*", Charcot, 1892–1895, p. 210; Anm. 1; Freud, 1893f, p. 24). Applied science is committed to empiricism, and it is theory that must adapt or change to assimilate contrary evidence. But, on the other hand, as Mach had told the participants at this gathering, science is conveyed through a narrative of concepts and comparisons (Mach, 1896, pp. 266–268). A functional methodology of science defines the limits of observation and description.

How much attention Freud paid to Mach's lecture, or even whether he attended it at all, remains unknown. The lecture survives in his library in its printed form as one of Mach's "Popular Scientific Lectures" (1896). However, Freud's copy of the book is entirely unmarked (Mach, 1896, pp. 251–274). Yet, years later, in his marked-up copy of *The Grammar of Science*, Freud would underline this very Machian phrase, "We conceal the fact that all knowledge is concise description" (Pearson, 1911, p. 133).

*   *   *

A photo incorporates a wealth of evidence. What rules regulate its description? As Charcot implied, theory should not prejudice observation. According to his method, one should only generalise after a meticulous examination of details.

Encountering the dozens of male faces in this photo, the observer's eye is at first overwhelmed by beards, moustaches, and whiskers. It would be premature to conclude that masculinity is a prerequisite of science at this moment and in this company. Suddenly, the eye fixes on one single hairless face. At first, one might tempted to assume that this was a shaved man. But her clothing gives her away. This lone, anomalous woman stands second from the right in the second row, and next to Freud.

Not only does she disrupt hasty generalisations about sex and science in 1894, she also seems to have disturbed Freud in some way. For he appears to be leaning conspicuously away from her, way over to his right. In doing so, he also seems to be forcing the man standing to his right (C. S. Freund) into an oblique and highly constrained posture.

What a photo fixes is a fraction of a second. Obviously, everyone was told to look at the camera, but at that moment, Friedrich Jolly, the eminent gentleman in the middle of the front row, happened to have turned his head to his left and on the back row the future Nobel laureate, Julius Wagner-Jauregg, as well as another man two places to his right, have both turned their heads to their right. In reclaiming the scene for history, we have to imagine reasons for any momentary disturbances of order. Freud's move to the right, forcing his neighbour into such an awkward attitude, requires explanation. Did he feel awkward about the risk of standing closer to the woman than convention might approve, and did he overcompensate by shifting too far to the right? Or did he think he was blocking the camera's view of Frankl-Hochwart, the colleague behind him, and shifted aside for that reason? In real time, such a momentary movement might hardly be noticed. Extracted from the flow of events, it acquires cryptic, even ominous, significance.

If this photo was taken at the end of the morning session of 25 September, it would have followed the woman's contribution. The *Tagblatt* presents her as Frau Dr von Leonowa and hers was the first morning presentation that day. It was on the comparative degree of development of nerves and sense organs in malformed embryos. In the subsequent discussion of her work, it was praised by Constantin von Monakow for the light it shed on the development of the central nervous system (Kerner & Exner, 1894, p. 239).

Freud's work on infant hemiplegia might have given him and Leonowa a common topic. She was a Russian (Olga Vasilevna Leonova): in 1890, she had published a study of anencephaly, under the auspices of the Moscow Anatomical Institute, and in 1896, she produced a five-page pamphlet on neonate brains, in German. According to his library catalogue, Freud once had a copy of it. Did she send it to him? Subsequently, it disappeared from his library, and she herself disappeared from history. The citizens of Laufenburg in Germany have still not solved the mystery of the "Russian villa" that she bought there in 1910. In 1916, she vanished. Over the years, the fully furnished house fell into disrepair. Eventually, the municipality sold off the furniture and took possession of the derelict property. Her story remains untold.

For lack of evidence, and in the face of unanswered questions, all we can now do is speculate. I have no further information that might cast light on Freud's marked shift away from his left-hand neighbour. All I can offer is a query that has nothing to do with either conscious or instinctive motives. I leave it hovering in a historical no-man's-land between attributed unconscious forces and symbolical representations of events.

What if Freud was edging away from Dr Olga von Leonowa because she represented Anatomy?

* * *

On 6 May 1894, his thirty-eighth birthday, Freud had written Fliess a brief letter in which he remarked, "In summer I should like to return a little to anatomy. It is after all the one source of satisfaction".

Like a photograph, such a quotation fixes what might have been a fleeting intention or one that was not fully carried out. At any rate, the proviso "a little" modifies it considerably. It might refer to Freud's continuing work on infantile hemiplegia, under the aegis of Max Kassowitz and his clinic. Certainly, Freud's initial scientific reputation had been built on respected anatomical research. However, his studies on hysteria and the aetiology of the neuroses were seducing him away from the gold circles of microscope slides with all the attractions of direct observation—and, furthermore, seducing him into the less attractive twilight of theory. Psychological speculation, albeit based on observation, may well engender the anxiety latent in Freud's nostalgic reference to anatomy as, by contrast, "the one source of satisfaction".

That phrase curiously echoes an early letter to his fiancée on 18 November 1882:

How beautiful you are, how sweet and dear, how the sight of you lifts the poor weak man above the limits set by his personality, how I feel that in you I possess the truth, the one source of satisfaction, what all men strive for. (Fichtner, 2011, p. 399)

If we construct a Galtonian complex portrait from the disparate contexts of those two instances of an identical phrase, it is as if Anatomy delivers the practitioner from his neurotic anxieties into the arms of his heart's desire.

Yet, if anatomical research is equivalent to marital love, what sort of guilty and illicit affair is psychology? Years later, Freud would make a point of insisting on the legitimacy of this difficult task and long relationship:

> I am well aware that it is one thing to give utterance to an idea once or twice in the form of a passing aperçu, and quite another to mean it seriously – to take it literally and pursue it in the face of every contradictory detail, and to win it a place among accepted truths. It is the difference between a casual flirtation and a legal marriage with all its duties and difficulties. 'Épouser les idées de . . .' is no uncommon figure of speech, at any rate in French. (Freud, 1914d, p. 15)

By the last week of September when this photo was taken, the weather was already wintry. The summer of Anatomy (if it even happened at all) was now over. In mid-August, Freud had a "congress" with Fliess in Munich to discuss the evolution of his aetiological ideas. The Freud in this photo who stares fixedly, as if hypnotically, at the camera appears once more in the guise of a "monomaniac" of the neuroses. Although his best received work of the 1890s would be his anatomically based study of infantile hemiplegia, and though he appears here in this photograph in the close company of such anatomists as Monakow and Leonowa, he had already distanced himself emotionally from their science and their endeavours, and his own first love.

*   *   *

The future is in the photograph by default, through what is missing as much as what is present. We find only one single woman among such an intolerable deal of men, and we can hardly refrain from comparing that situation with what was to come.

Ernst Mach's lecture on 24 September 1894 was entitled "On the principle of comparison in physics" and he spoke of comparison as "the most powerful vital inner element of science". As one example among others, he noted, "The zoologist . . . compares the cranial bone to the vertebra" (Mach, 1896, p. 254). His audience would have understood that the allusion referred back to Oken's (and Goethe's) famous speculation that the skull is a modification of the backbone. This idea inaugurated evolutionary anatomy and served as a fundamental doctrine of the early GDNÄ.

As well as shimmering with the intellectual and social relationships of the moment, the photograph also incorporates future modifications.

The only other known photo of the professional Freud in the 1890s shows him with Max Kassowitz and co-workers at his clinic (Berner et al., 1983, pp. 100–101). As for this 1894 group, it is the only existing pre-analytic photo that shows him at a conference among colleagues and peers. The next known group photo of Freud at a conference would not come until September 1909, at Clark University in Massachusetts. In the intervening thirteen years, the neurologist had transmuted into the psychoanalyst.

The Clark University photo, like this 1894 photo, also shows a group of disparate male specialists. The first extant photo of a specifically psychoanalytic conference comes only two years later, at Weimar in 1911. It includes about the same number of participants as the Vienna gathering in 1894. What immediately strikes the observer of the 1911 photo is the presence of the women and their prominent position. In 1894, the single and peripheral woman is ungallantly left standing behind a seated man. At Weimar, the women are literally foregrounded, all seated in the front row so that our attention is held both by their corporate presence and by the singularities of each one's appearance: Lou Andreas-Salomé, magnificent in her eye-catching fur coat, or Frau Jung, facing the camera stiffly upright and brightly attentive, seemingly unaware of her husband crouched over the back of her chair, or of the presence, two seats to her left, of his farouche mistress, Toni Wolff.

Although Russian women students had been enrolling at the University of Zurich since the 1860s, the University of Vienna began admitting women only in 1897. The idea and image of woman was slowly changing. Between Vienna 1894 and Weimar 1911, the emergence of psychoanalysis coincided with this visible shift in the psychosocial fault lines separating the sexes. Missing at that earlier moment (but for that one precursor, Olga Leonowa), women were gradually entering the scientific picture—and these photographs.

*   *   *

There are other significant absences from this photo, apart from the women. Evidently Oken, the founder-father of the GDNÄ, who died in 1851, cannot be visibly present, and even the ideas he stamped on the early society could only be detected in fossil form or as skeletal traces. But even Helmholtz, whose influence in 1894 was overwhelming, is not to be seen. He was to have given a keynote lecture, entitled "On residual motion and apparent substance" at this 1894 Meeting, but he died on 8 September, just over two weeks before the opening. The invitation, which must have gone to print earlier, had announced his talk for the 26 September 1894, but added "cancelled owing to sickness".

The reason for these absences is obvious. On the other hand, I can see no reason except pure chance why Josef Breuer does not appear in this photo. He was a registered participant. His absence, and not just from this photo, is of the greatest significance for Freud at this period.

The "Breuer–Freud" method of therapy had already gained currency among some in this group. One of them is the saturnine figure standing fourth from the left in the second row—Karl Mayer, newly appointed Professor of Psychiatry and Nervous Pathology at the University of Innsbruck. Together with Rudolf Meringer, he would publish in 1895 *Versprechen und Verlesen* ("Misspeaking and Misreading"). The book is cited with approval several times in the *Psychopathology of Everyday Life* (Freud, 1901b) and Freud borrowed from it such exemplary slips of the tongue as "Sister/Breast" and "*Vorschein/Vorschwein*". In the section "How misspeaking occurs", Mayer presented one of his own examples of a *lapsus linguae*: "The Freuer–Breud Method" instead of "Breuer–Freud". If this is interpreted in Freudian terms, we might say that it disputes Breuer's nominal priority over Freud, as far as their respective contributions to the cathartic method of treatment was concerned (Meringer & Mayer, 1895, p. 20).

In the autumn of 1893, Freud had been complaining to Fliess that Breuer was unhelpful and standing in the way of his professional advancement (Masson, 1985, p. 56). The situation would worsen in 1894 and "scientific collaboration" between them came near to breaking down, at least until the end of that year (Hirschmüller, 1978a, pp. 230–232). In the absence of Breuer's maieutic partnership, Freud was forced back on his own devices. One result was that his work towards an aetiology of the neuroses progressed more slowly. Another result was that the bond with Fliess became more intense.

Fliess, too, is absent from this gathering. Although he had intended coming, bad health had prevented his attendance.

Already, in a letter of 21 May 1894, Freud was referring to Fliess as "the only Other" and was complaining of his own intellectual isolation:

> I am quite alone here in resolving the neuroses. They view me as quite a monomaniac and I have the distinct impression of having touched upon one of the great mysteries of nature. There is something funny about the disparity between one's own and other people's judgement of one's intellectual work. (Masson, 1985, p. 74, translation modified)

That curious disparity between self-assessment and the judgement of others is, however, the least of his problems in this period. His critical uncertainty also involved self-doubt, and that began even with the question of his physical health. Here, too, as in his intellectual echo-location, the chief human co-ordinates were these two, Fliess and Breuer. Just as Breuer was, it seemed to Freud, refusing to follow their hypotheses on the aetiology of hysteria to their logical conclusion, so he felt that Breuer was also withholding the correct, and possibly fatal, diagnosis of his own (actual? imagined?) heart complaints. Freud was now relying on Fliess to present a true statement of his condition, and, if necessary, to pronounce the death sentence he was half anticipating.

The distinction between the real and the imaginary has, in this case history, become a question of life and death. In a letter of 19 April 1894, Freud wrote to Fliess, "For the medical practitioner who torments himself every hour of the day to understand the neuroses, it is too painful not to know whether he is suffering from a well-founded or a hypochondriacal disturbance" (Masson, 1985, p. 67, translation modified).

*   *   *

Freud's resounding phrase "mysteries of nature" might serve as a rallying cry for the whole community of scientists and doctors in this photograph, dedicated as they were to investigating the natural world.

The *Naturphilosophie* on which the GDNÄ was grounded had asserted the unity of nature and the human spirit. At its first congress in Leipzig in 1822, Carl Gustav Carus had argued that metaphysical speculation was an inherent aspect of physical research. In doing so, however, he was also arguing against Kantian reason as a suitable instrument for gaining insight into the natural world. For nature, he asserted, cannot be penetrated by reason alone: "For here is the eternal cause that rational constructs always correspond only to a certain degree with observation of nature—and that in turn will only give evidence to a certain degree of being rationally rule-bound" (Engelhardt, 2007).

By 1894, this attitude, typical of the romantic age, had, for the most part, been replaced by nineteenth-century materialism and a commitment to strict determinism in explaining natural phenomena. Yet it is hard to exclude any discussion of origins. *Naturphilosophie* continues lurking, not just in the background of the Society as a whole, but in that of individual members.

Freud's own scientific career, for example, had begun under the inspiration of a neo-mystical lecture, "On nature" (Freud, 1900a, p. 443). This essay by the Swiss theologian, Georg Christoph Tobler, was generally misattributed to Goethe, who later explained how he was himself to blame for this. Because of a memory lapse, he had claimed it as his own early work (Goethe, 1989, pp. 11–13; 860–861).

Around the middle of the nineteenth century, mechanistic determinism by and large displaced *Naturphilosophie* and the man most responsible for that shift was Hermann von Helmholtz. He had demonstrated the mechanical nature of nerve impulses almost half a century before this gathering. The generations of neurologists visible in this photo fall under the shadow of his rejection of *Naturphilosophie* in favour of chemical, mechanical, and electrical forces.

Exner's "Project for a Physiological Explanation of Mental Phenomena", which was published earlier in 1894, was based on the Helmholtzian premise that nerve impulses are purely quantitative (Exner, 1894). It was, however, not well received by some in the GDNÄ (Hirschmüller, 1978a, p. 218, n. 571) and it was not everyone who accepted the idea of nervous forces as mechanical impulses, or nature as mechanism. Versions of vitalism, along with ideas of "intelligent forces", persisted, sometimes as variants of Darwinian evolutionary theory.

Among those in the photo (though blurred because he sits at the far left end of the front row and is, consequently, not identifiable with certainty), Max Kassowitz gave popular scientific lectures at this period, as did Helmholtz and Mach. They were converted into a book that Freud had in his library. Its title is programmatic: *World – Life – Soul. A System of Nature Philosophy for the Layman.* There were other examples of such eclecticism. The following GDNÄ meeting at Lübeck in 1895 would include a paper by Georg Eduard von Rindfleisch, entitled "On neo-vitalism", and one by Wilhelm Ostwald, "Overcoming scientific materialism" (Engelhardt, 2007). All in all, there was no unanimity as far as fundamentalist materialism is concerned.

Meanwhile, the concept "nature" remained a potential source of embarrassment or confusion. "Nature is perhaps the most complex word in the language", Raymond Williams notes, and points to multiple subliminal slippages between three common usages of the same word: (1) the essential quality of things, (2) the force directing the world, (3) the material (and human) world itself (Williams, 1980, p. 184). Freud's "mysteries of nature" could be understood, in the pragmatic sense, as meaning that the disorders of the mind form part of a natural order. Like the gynaecologist–artist Carus, Freud did not expect nature to yield its secrets to *a priori* rational enquiry (Ellenberger, 1970, pp. 207–208). The rules and reasons that dictated its conduct were themselves the form of the mystery.

In the *Interpretation of Dreams*, Freud presents his own dream of Goethe attacking a Herr M. In the dream associations, Freud brings together Goethe, Fliess's mathematical biology, and the origins of his own vocation as a natural scientist. In this account, he recalls the cry "Nature! Nature!" which heralds the onset of a patient's madness. It is a sexual conflict which has driven him mad (Freud, 1900a, pp. 442–443). In this context, the word "nature" implies sexuality and this is one of the keys to the dream.

However, the conjunction of sex and nature could hardly be considered a mystery, either in 1899 or in 1894. In Darwin, sexual selection is a basic principle of evolutionary success. One level of Freud's dream association seems little more than a mechanical association of words. But what of the non-logical connections of imagery that formed those associations? Do those connections take the form of neural pathways, or are they no more than abstract features of language? In this hermeneutical psychology, perhaps the real "mystery of nature" is how words relate to the body.

An 1890 issue of the French journal *La Nature* had published an illustration that might be taken as a parodic emblem of that relationship. It shows the back view of a woman, a hysterical patient of Dr Mesnet. Her blouse has been lowered to expose her shoulders on which two words appear, as if stencilled into her flesh. The doctor had apparently persuaded her to demonstrate the phenomenon of "*autographisme*". Her sensitive skin reacted to the touch of a finger writing on it by producing the words "LA NATURE" etched in livid capital letters across her back (Winter, 1998, p. 352).

* * *

Especially for the sufferer from an unknown heart disorder, who does not know whether he is a hypochondriac or a condemned man, it is vital to define the limits of the imagination.

This is a universal methodological preoccupation. It applies not only to science, but also to historiography or iconography. I look at the massed minds and bodies in this photograph, and imagine it as a vivid visual antithesis to the biographical stereotype of Freud's state of "*splendid isolation*" during the 1890s. Obviously, that state was subjective and it was limited to a specific intellectual problem. Freud was a pre-eminently social creature; he always had his family and friends.

The phrase itself, a political catchword that Freud quotes in English in "On the history of the psycho-analytic movement" (1914d), only became current in 1896. Although his own contemporaneous references to intellectual solitude start occurring in 1894, it could be assumed that the term was meant to refer primarily to a slightly later period, beginning around 1896. One could choose to date that "splendid isolation" from the lecture "The aetiology of hysteria", given at the Club for Psychiatry and Neurology on 21 April 1896. Its inauguration would then be aptly announced by Krafft-Ebing's notorious remark that Freud's account sounded "like a scientific fairy tale" (Masson, 1985, p. 184).

As is known, Freud reacted to that remark with indignation. Yet, strictly speaking, he had no good reason to be indignant. He himself would come to concede that his case histories seemed to read like short stories, and, to cite another commentator on the rules of natural observation, in his lecture at the 1894 Meeting, Ernst Mach had said, "The dramatic element should, as we see, no more be lacking in a natural scientific description than in an exciting novel" (Mach, 1896 p. 259).

In the photo, Krafft-Ebing looks well aware of his status. He is holding a wide-brimmed hat. Like Charcot, he was criticised for self-dramatising academic performances (Oosterhuis, 2001, pp. 94–95). Nevertheless, in his *Psychopathia sexualis*, he did not allow his own personality to prevent the objects of his study from speaking for themselves, thus acknowledging their autonomy, if not their self-diagnoses. His relationship with Freud at the time of that famous remark appears to have been equable (Schröter, 1997, pp. 180–182) and Freud would remain a regular recipient of reprints of the *Psychopathia*, bearing the author's dedications (Davies & Fichtner, 2006). From Freud's point of view, this could well have made Krafft-Ebing's apparently slighting comment all the more difficult to endure.

In response, Freud's implied "Götzian" riposte to the club and its members ("They can go to hell, euphemistically expressed", i.e., "they can kiss my a∗∗∗"), though performed on the private stage of a letter to Fliess, is also, in its way, an act of bravura self-dramatisation (Masson, 1985, p. 184).

It is not only according to Mach's version, or even Freud's own later judgement, but also in formalistic terms that Krafft-Ebing's fairy tale verdict could be considered justified. Freud's argument in that paper does indeed follow the narrative structure of a folk tale. There is an undiscovered treasure (the truth about the neuroses) but it is protected by a shape-changing guardian (the hysterical symptoms). The older brothers with their father's approval (previous researchers with their ideas of "hereditary taint") have failed in their quest. Then along comes the youngest brother armed with nothing but his mother wit (the "Breuer–Freud method" of enquiry) and discovers the golden key (unconscious sexual memories).

In Mach's terms, a scientific description is a type of linguistic mimicry, the real world extended into its narrative conceptualisation: "Description is a construction of facts in thought, which, in the experimental sciences, often founds the possibility of a real representation" (Mach, 1896, p. 268). Comparison enables communication and is the very essence of science, "the most powerful inner living element of science" (Mach, 1896, p. 254). His lecture at the conference had ended with a rousing comparison: in a hundred years time, the Meeting of Natural Scientists would, he predicted, be far more unified than it was in 1894. Branches of science that were now separate would come to share method and approach. As the founder members of the GDNÄ had dreamed, "the inner relationship of all research" would prevail (Mach, 1896, p. 274).

The individual scientist, like the object of science, is subordinate to fundamental laws that are beautiful. In their cause Billroth and Charcot, among others, had died. This faith substitutes Nature for God. It makes a subliminal appearance in a letter to Fliess on 6 February 1899, where Freud misquotes Shakespeare's "Thou owest God a death" (*Henry IV*, Part 1) as "Thou owest nature a death".

Mach's methodology of science echoes Büchner's lecture, in so far as it also treats aesthetics as a guiding principle. He speaks, for example of "the pure logico–aesthetic sense of the mathematician . . ." (Mach, 1896, p. 273) but, in dealing with the language of science, Mach entered another region—one that has relevance to historiography, too. Science prophesies, he stated, adding that cultural commentators and historians also prophesy. However, they do it, so to speak, backwards, seeking out retrospectively how to characterise past events and realise them through description. "Science has to complete partly extant facts in thought" (Mach, 1896, p. 269).

*   *   *

A photograph reflects the lived world. It is also a contrived reconstruction. That is especially evident in the case of formal group photos such as this 1894 gathering. The rows of participants face the camera like an audience at a theatre. Obviously, it is not the photographer for the Atelier Nina who is the object of their attention. They are anticipating seeing themselves in reflection, as actors in the drama of the future image that they are composing for the camera. It is for the camera's sake that they are expressing or acting out their intellectual preoccupations. Hence, with some exceptions, the serious faces. One or two do appear to be risking a cautious smile, though in most cases the beards mask any expression. Only one stands out, almost at the centre of the image—the figure of Alois Alzheimer, with his head cocked and an enigmatic smile visible beneath his moustache, as if he were prophetically amused by the paradox of fame associated with the progressive form of oblivion to which he would bequeath his name.

The number of connections and correspondences between members of this large group of related figures is, potentially, vertiginous. Freud provides a narrative, but one that branches out indefinitely as associations accumulate. The name of the photograph studio itself, the Atelier Nina, sets up one set of associations linking several of the participants.

In his only known subsequent reference to this event, his first letter to Ludwig Binswanger, Freud mentions having met Ludwig's uncle at the 1894 Meeting. Otto Binswanger, the brother of Robert Binswanger, sits in the front row, third from the left. This family relationship, which would only make sense for Freud in the future, meshes with a professional relationship that connected Freud, Krafft-Ebing, and Josef Breuer at the time. At that period, they had all been consulted about a patient, subsequently dubbed "Nina R". She was, at the time, in the care of Robert Binswanger, in the sanatorium Bellevue at Kreuzlingen.

In addition to neurasthenia, Nina R suffered crippling and prolonged period pains. In view of their severity, Robert Binswanger had suggested "castration" (ovariectomy and/or hysterectomy) as a radical cure. Breuer, more cautiously, argued that the cure might turn out to be more detrimental than the illness, and suggested instead treatment by periodic curettage (Hirschmüller, 1978b). An undated report on Nina R that Breuer sent Robert Binswanger also includes Freud's report.

Freud refers to Nina R's childhood onanism and her need to repress her sexual excitement. At such times, Freud states, she would suffer extreme anxiety, would philosophise and undergo "experiences of dying". Everything reminded her of the transience of all life and the unreality of the world. Freud's report on her concentrates on psychological factors: it makes no mention of heredity or degeneration. By contrast, Breuer's attached note, while stating that he has little to add to Freud's report, goes on to mention the hereditary taint on the patient's father's side.

Freud's own symptoms that he had listed in his letter to Fliess—tachycardia, arrythmia, terror of death, etc.—would soon be enumerated among the generalised symptoms of anxiety neurosis:

> Anxiety attacks accompanied by disturbances of the *heart action,* such as palpitation, either with transitory arrhythmia or with tachycardia of longer duration which may end in serious weakness of the heart and which is not always easily differentiated from organic heart affection; and, again, pseudo-angina pectoris – diagnostically a delicate subject! (Freud, 1895b, p. 94)

Freud's own uncertainty whether his condition was physical or mental illustrates the vagaries of description. That is encapsulated in the metaphorical aspects of heart conditions, as seen in Freud's own emphatic pun on them. On 22 June 1894, he wrote to Fliess, "I have renounced climbing 'with a heavy heart'—how full of significance the expression is".

Freud's scientific research into the neuroses at this period was fraught with several types of personal anxiety. How easy it is for self-observation to turn into hypochondria and how difficult it is to distinguish between the psychic and the somatic. The anxieties extend further, and involve more than an examination of his own "heart". Although "hereditary taint" may be another diagnostically delicate subject, it cannot be entirely dismissed when you are concerned with and about the nerves and minds of your own offspring. As witness a letter that summer:

> If the maid goes on holiday, you should take Mathilde in charge and guard her strictly, the affair is worth all your exertions, otherwise at the age of 14 she will surprise with nervousness that will end up in an institution. This is my greatest worry in relation to the children. (Freud to Martha Bernays, 21.6.1894, SFC)

That Mathilde's potential neurosis might strike at fourteen years old, that is, during puberty, is a calculation that keeps the sexual component in balance with heredity. The "hereditary taint" continues to feature in Freud's publications of this time, though it comes to look increasingly like a fig leaf concealing the less acceptable sexual factor—or as a tacit admission of his own diagnostic failure. "In some cases of anxiety neurosis no aetiology at all is to be discovered. It is worth noting that in such cases there is seldom any difficulty in establishing evidence of a grave hereditary taint" (Freud, 1895b p. 99).

* * *

For a description to be truly scientific, it should be cogent and coherent. Like Billroth's life and death, Charcot's was also portrayed by Freud as enviable. In his 1893 obituary, he describes him, like Adam, looking at things for the first time and fixing names to phenomena that had previously remained undefined. In an exemplary instance of theory following observation, he wrote, Charcot had reproduced hysterical phenomena through hypnosis and thus managed, through an "unbroken sequence of conclusions", to establish hysteria as a true mental disorder. It was that logical sequence, Freud continued, which had led to a scientific theory of the neuroses (Freud, 1893f, p. 23).

However, that "incomparably beautiful piece of clinical research" had by no means gained general acceptance among the participants of this 1894 gathering. This was primarily because of the chronic controversies surrounding the nature of hypnosis. These surfaced in discussions during the morning of Thursday 27 September. First, Jonas Grossmann spoke on "Suggestion therapy in paralyses with an organic basis", followed by Auguste Forel on "The relationship of certain therapeutic methods to suggestion". Friedrich Jolly (the distracted gentleman at Krafft-Ebing's left) objected to both speakers' equation of hypnosis with suggestion, and to what he saw as their undue optimism as to its therapeutic benefits. He went on to speak of the danger of inducing hysteria. His objections were backed up by Moll.

There is again no record that Freud participated in the discussion, and he never recorded any subsequent references to it. Others, notably Obersteiner and Krafft-Ebing, were, at the moment of this picture, at least as deeply interested as Freud in hypnosis. No comments of theirs entered the *Tagblatt* record either.

The previous week, Krafft-Ebing and Moriz Benedikt, as prominent specialists with opposing viewpoints, had been drawn into commenting to the press on a scandalous news item (Lafferton, 2006). In Budapest, a young woman, Ella von Salamon, had died, apparently under hypnosis, while taking part in an amateur experiment to test clairvoyance. The case gained international notoriety and Krafft-Ebing's commentary on it was relayed by *The Times* on 24 September 1894 and entitled "The fatal hypnotic case". He asserted that this was the first recorded case of death under hypnosis. However, it was not a medical experiment, he pointed out, and drew attention to the fact that the hypnotist was an amateur and in 1845 an Austrian law had been passed forbidding the practice of "magnetism" by anyone other than doctors.

In referring to it as the first death under hypnosis, Krafft-Ebing was, of course, disregarding what might really be termed a "scientific fairy-tale": Edgar Allan Poe's sensational narrative, *The Facts in the Case of M. Valdemar*, published in 1845. In this fictional account, the protagonist, dying under mesmerism, is held in suspension between life and death. Poe was intrigued by the notion that under mesmerism the soul seemed to be at the same time bound absolutely to the operator's instructions and released from the bonds of its own body (Poe, 1950, pp. 269–277).

The newspaper scandal was obliquely reflected in the discussions between Grossmann, Forel, Moll, and Jolly on 27 September. Moll and Jolly had spoken of "hypnoid states" of consciousness. But hypnosis remained a conceptual scandal, a confusion of the psychic and the physical, and arguments over its status and definition went far beyond the question of whether it was simply heightened suggestion.

In *Hypnotismus und Suggestion* published earlier that year, Benedikt (another of the significant absences from this photograph) had criticised Charcot for failing to throw any useful light on hypnosis because he had used hysterical subjects in his hypnotic experiments (Benedikt, 1894). Freud was, at this time, also concerned by the confusion of these two fringe conditions of consciousness. One of his great differences with Breuer that year was over hysterical splitting of consciousness. Breuer referred to them as "hypnoid states". Freud defined them as "psychic defence mechanisms".

Benedikt believed that electrostatic tensions on the surface of the body might one day resolve the ambiguous status of hypnosis by providing an objective physical correlate of the condition. Once these tensions could be accurately measured, this might bring hypnosis into the exact sciences. Yet biomechanics remains irrelevant to all but the most primitive forms of psychology, for measurement does not describe.

Questions of the boundaries of science hang over these discussions as they do over Freud's relationship with Breuer. What made their collaboration particularly problematic at this period was Breuer's continuing scepticism as to the scientific validity of descriptions of mental processes (Hirschmüller, 1978a, p. 66).

Mach's keynote lecture, "On the principle of comparison in physics", had offered a positivist slant on the philosophy of science, or, more specifically, on the function of description in scientific methodology. Mach was concerned with the nature of language and the fact that all science stems from the primacy of sensations. This means that it is based, in the end, on the evidence of our senses. According to Mach, the task of science is to produce adequate descriptions, of which there are two types. A direct description of phenomena transmits observed or sensual meaning; an indirect description incorporates the essential factor, concepts, which enable phenomena to be classified and compared.

Mach's examples from the history of science came from physics, mechanics, and chemistry. Psychology was not mentioned. Members of the Psychiatry and Neurology Section who attended it might have felt that his idea of description did not really concern their domain, but Mach himself believed in the ultimate unity of science.

In spite of Fechner's "psycho-physics", and in spite of Mach's own prediction of a future unitive scientific language, physics and medical psychology and the other branches of science were continuing to move in widely different spheres. Categories of knowledge proliferated. Even while Mach was speaking of "the inner affinity of all research" in 1894, Dilthey was formulating a new distinction, between human and natural sciences (Mach, 1896, p. 274).

The problem was reflected even in the name of the section in the photograph. Until 1876, its equivalent at previous GDNÄ meetings reflected a practical, clinical approach: it would have been the "Section for Psychiatry and Nervous Diseases". It was only in 1879 that this was changed to "Section for Psychiatry and Neurology" (Hirschmüller, 1991, p. 41). Neurology was a new discipline, but whereas "nervous diseases" clearly relate to psychiatry, how does neurology, as the anatomy and physiology of the nervous system, relate, conceptually or practically, to mental illness and treatment? In short, no distinction between nervous and mental diseases had been defined.

In view of this fluidity between what later became more or less fixed categories, it is interesting to compare the discussions of another section at this gathering, Ethnology and Anthropology. The title of one paper presented to this section by Dr G. Buschan was: "Influence of race on the extent and form of pathological changes in general and on nervous and mental diseases in particular". In this presentation, the new science of racial studies has teamed up with neurology. The report summarises the proceedings: "The Semites represent a large proportion of nervous and mental diseases, in particular diabetes, but are on the other hand relatively immune to infectious diseases (cholera, croup, typhus, lues) and tabes" (Kerner & Exner, 1894, pp. 250–251).

Although his name has become a unit of measurement, Mach himself remained sceptical about the value of measurement as scientific evidence. Benedikt was evidently less so, for, after Buschan's ethnological paper, he gave a demonstration of a "precision apparatus for cranial measurement" (Kerner & Exner, 1894). The apparatus appears to give post-phrenological credence to skull dimensions as (psychologically?) significant data. Buschan's discussion and Benedikt's demonstration could then be seen as mutually reinforcing. Scientific measurement and ethnological description combine to ratify a new class of phenomena. From another angle of retrospect, this looks more like the ingredients of a terminological—and, ultimately, social—witches' cauldron.[5]

*   *   *

Büchner's Woyzeck assumes that character and structure are given, but nature is indescribable or beyond description. Nature controls Woyzeck's behaviour. It makes him piss against a wall, thus depriving the scientific doctor of a specimen of urine produced on an exclusive diet of peas. Balanced between compulsion and free will, Woyzeck acts out the dilemma of natural philosophy. Clicking his fingers in despair, he is suspended between showing and saying, between "you see" and "how can I say", between parallel forms of demonstration. Nature is both reality and drama, acted out in the world and in lecture room and operating theatre.

The pseudo-Goethean essay that first inspired Freud to study natural science, *Die Natur*, speaks of nature as a play acted out in front of us: "She [Nature] is acting a play: we do not know whether she sees it herself, and yet she is acting it for us, who are standing in the corner" (Goethe, 1989, p. 11). The audience of that natural philosophical play is peripheral, the play goes on with or without it, but the drama of natural science cannot exist without its witnesses.

They are lined up here in this photograph, an audience of scientific observers. Their task is revealing secrets, getting behind the scenes. That, too, has been an impetus in this discussion of their photographed forms. Taking "behind the scenes" in its most literal sense, I have already conjectured that the stands visible behind the participants in the first and second arcade arches from the left might form part of the exhibition on the state of the sciences that was put on to coincide with the Meeting. Pursuing that possibility, we find a newspaper report on the historical section of this exhibition that goes into more detail. Among other things, it informs us that the exhibition included a heliographic portrait of Johann Heinrich Schulze and an account of his work.

The originator of this particular exhibit, Josef Maria Eder, Director of the Vienna College of Photography, claimed for Schulze the distinction of first discoverer of photography ("Wer hat die Photographie erfunden?" in *Neue Freie Presse*, 20 September 1894. Nr. 10803, p. 6. Also: Eder, 1917).

In 1727, a century before Niepce, Schulze wrote an account of his experiments on light sensitivity, using jars of a chalk solution of silver nitrate:

> I covered the glass with dark material, exposing a little part for the free entry of light. Thus I often wrote names and whole sentences on paper and carefully cut away the inked parts with a sharp knife. I stuck the paper thus perforated on the glass with wax. It was not long before the sun's rays, where they hit the glass through the cut-out parts of the paper, wrote each word or sentence on the chalk precipitate so exactly and distinctly that many who were curious about the experiment but ignorant of its nature took occasion to attribute the thing to some sort of trick. (Leggat, 1995)

Here, too, a demonstration is suspended, though in another way, between showing and saying—the images formed in the chalk precipitate are words and they are ephemeral. It would be another century before a way was found to fix a heliographic image.

Freud stands in the corner here among the massed ranks of natural scientists. His fixed stare brings the biographical documentation of his times into the picture. Against the background of the "deliria of dying" and dread that Freud had experienced during the months before this photograph, was it the gnawing problem of how to categorise his observations that was disturbing him? The mysteries of nature were in the world, but they also existed as images of his own psyche and his own neurosis. How to classify those representations—

are they only virtual, or are they real images like a shadow or a photo-graph? How is one to reconcile objectivity with radical self-reflection?

If the photo was taken on 24 September, was Freud mulling over Mach's notions of scientific description? Or, if the picture was taken the following day, was it Forel's plenary lecture on "Brain and soul" that was on his mind?

The photograph is not exactly dated. At any rate, a photograph is only a fixed image. The mind, whatever that might be, is something else.

CHAPTER FIVE

Freud & Co.

"You speak a language that I understand not:
My life stands in the level of your dreams . . ."

(Shakespeare: *A Winter's Tale*, III. 2)

The photo documentation of Freud's family was haphazard. There should have been a copy of this picture in some album or other, but in fact it turned up only after the death of Mathilde Freud's home-help and companion, Tini Maresch, among papers she left to the Freud Museum. It is the last record of a neglected member of Freud's family, but one who earned Freud's respect, even admiration—his eldest half-brother, Emanuel.

When the extended Freud family living in Freiberg split up in 1859, Jacob and Amalia, with their two children, left for Vienna via Leipzig, while Emanuel and his family, together with his younger brother Philipp, left for England. The *Manchester Directory* of 1861 picks up one of their earliest traces: "Freud & Co, importers of French and German Fancy goods, 26, Market Street".

Around two years later, Freud produced the earliest of his works to have survived. It is a letter he wrote around the age of seven to Emanuel. Although it was a response to a lost letter sent by Emanuel's son John, it was addressed to the father, not the son. Freud begins, "I was glad to receive the letter from your dear son, but I am very sorry that I did not understand any of it. Now I am trying to write a few lines to you" (E. Freud, L. Freud, & Grubrich-Simitis, 1978, Pl. 12).

It looks as if Emanuel's dear son John might have written to Freud in English. If so, that would have been a blatant exercise in linguistic one-up-manship. There had already been rivalry between the boys when they were still all together in Freiberg. Assuming Freud's letter was the response to such an assertion of the other boy's superiority, his words come across as both touching and skilful. He avoids any confrontation with John. Without pointless recrimination, he switches his attention instead to the friendlier father.

The knight's move. That might be a way to deal with this photograph, too. The sitters are obscure; if they are addressing us in any way, it is in an unknown language; the image is too dark and austere to yield more than the minimum of details and there is scanty outside evidence about their lives. The print itself offers no clues beyond their names. It was produced in the postcard format popular in those days, but not posted, and the back of the card bears only the handwritten inscription: "Emanuel und Bertha".

There are no other reliably identified photos of the old Emanuel or his children, so whoever wrote their names on the back would either have known them personally or been informed by someone who did. The only other attributed image of Emanuel dates from about forty years earlier. It is the famous group photo, and is most likely to date from 1878, which was the year of one of Emanuel's known visits to Vienna, and not 1876, as shown in the picture biography of Freud where it was first published (E. Freud, L. Freud, & Grubrich-Simitis, 1978, Pl. 36). Apart from the uncertainty about the figure identified as Emanuel, this picture of the extended Freud family also includes two or three unidentified children. The glowering, full-bearded young Freud stands at the back, behind his seated and still young-looking mother. Next to him, in profile, heavily side-whiskered and with a shaved chin, stands an older man next to Rosa, who has her hand on his shoulder. Maybe he *is* Emanuel. But we would then have to explain away a note written by Rosa on a letter inviting her to Manchester, where she says she met Emanuel as a child, and then did not see him again until 1883.

It is hard to see any resemblance, apart from the same mutton-chop style of beard, between the youthful figure in that group photo (who does not look forty-five years old, as he would have been at the time), and the worried old man in the flat cap in this photo, taken at least thirty years later. As for Bertha, no other adult photo of her has been found as a point of reference.

Questions of identification can sometimes be resolved by comparing pictures taken at various ages, but there is half a lifetime between that group portrait and this small, dark photo. It is hard to imagine the younger man in that group and this older man as the same person. Often, it is only a name that ratifies self-identity over time, as if identity were no more than a convenient legal fiction, backed up by self-deception. With no habits or memories to attribute to them, these two figures in this dark scene seem shipwrecked on the bare rock of the photographic present. A hypothetical despair hangs over them; they barely emerge from the blackness surrounding them.

The approximate date of this photo has to be deduced from the supposed age of the sitters. Emanuel was born in 1833, Bertha in 1859. The picture could, therefore, have been taken around the time of

Freud's last meeting with his half-brother, an unexpected visit of the eighty-year-old Emanuel to Vienna in May 1913 (Brabant, Falzeder, & Giampieri-Deutsch, 1993, p. 485). Many of his visits were similarly unexpected; he enjoyed such surprises and practical jokes. Freud often described him as lively and humorous.

Nothing of that could be guessed from the photograph. If they were not tethered to the names inscribed on the back, these shadowy sitters seem so much adrift from family or history that they could be dream figures. That sets the desolate mood, the sense we are looking at the dead, or, rather, the doomed living. Knowledge they will die seems written into their attitudes and expressions, their curious awkwardness and lack of confidence—the old man not sure what to do with his hands, the daughter leaning protectively against him but looking away from the camera. Even accidental blemishes in the photo, the creasing or the air bubble that mars his face, add to the overall sense of mortality.

This is all impressionism, pathos substituting the missing information. Photos of better-known subjects emerge from a background of historical chatter. This Emanuel and Bertha appear almost in silence and ignorance (ours), and the less we know about the subjects of old photos, the more their images are infused with death.

The challenge of such images is to overcome such emotions or emanations, and construct a story. Reading them can then become historiography, an attempt to rescue the lost from total oblivion.

In this case, the trail leads through (Freud's) dreams. Most notoriously, there is the distorted and condensed image of Emanuel that survives at the very heart of the *Interpretation of Dreams*, in the figure of the Dr M of the paradigmatic "Irma" dream:

> *Dr M. was pale, had a clean-shaven chin and walked with a limp.* . . . I thought of my elder brother, who lives abroad, who is clean-shaven and whom, if I remember right, the M. of the dream closely resembled. We had had news a few days earlier that he was walking with a limp owing to an arthritic affection of his hip. There must, I reflected, have been some reason for my fusing into one the two figures in the dream. I then remembered that I had a similar reason for being in an ill-humour with each of them: they had both rejected a certain suggestion I had recently laid before them. (Freud, 1900a, p. 112)

*   *   *

"Behold, Esau my brother is a hairy man, and I am a smooth man"

(Genesis 27: 11)

During the 1890s, echoes of the life of Emanuel (the real one) reach us primarily through references in Freud's correspondence. Only two actual visits of Emanuel to Vienna are referred to during this decade, in late May 1896 and in early June 1900, when he came with his son, Samuel (Masson, 1985, pp. 190, 417). As for the visit he paid to Freud's specimen dream on the night of 23–24 June 1895, like his other unexpected appearances, that was a sort of joke. However, unlike those that Emanuel usually played, this was a joke on him. He was forcibly disguised, condensed with a doctor having the manner of Breuer, his co-identity betrayed by his clean-shaven chin and his arthritic limp.

In Freud's dream associations he mentions a "certain suggestion" he had made to Emanuel and Breuer, and that they both rejected. Did he offer to pay back old debts? Such a refusal would have been guaranteed to irritate Freud. But the suggestion is left unexplained, to irritate the reader instead.

In the letter quoted at the beginning, the boy confidently addresses the thirty-year-old Emanuel as "brother". The Freud band of brothers spanned a wide age range, from Emanuel, born in 1833, to Alexander, born in 1866. Because he himself was already a father when Freud was born, Emanuel blurs father–son–brother relationships. As far as their mutual father is concerned, by the time of the specimen dream age had brought about the revolution of turning an old parent into a child, dependent on his children. In Freud's "revolutionary dream", he sees his debilitated, blind father enduring that very humiliation, and Emanuel also features in this dream narrative (Freud, 1900a, pp. 208–218).

As a historical figure, Emanuel is fated to remain tangled up in Freud's dreams. Yet, in the photo, he and his daughter must be reflecting on their own fantasies. Bertha's dreamy gaze or Emanuel's disillusioned stare in this picture speak of their own impenetrable world. They are not striking attitudes for the camera: they are acting themselves.

These two ageing figures against a dark background were among Freud's earliest enthusiasts, offering him encouragement at the time of his first visit to Manchester in 1875 and, subsequently, expressing their faith in the young man's ability and in the success of his future career. When he mentioned them, it was with affection. In 1883, he characterised his relationship with Emanuel as "intimate–friendly" (Fichtner, Grubrich-Simitis, & Hirschmüller, 2013, p. 489). This did not change greatly over the years. In 1900, he was still speaking of his brother with admiration for his physical and intellectual liveliness (Masson, 1985, p. 417). Their relationship was always harmonious enough for their differences to be dealt with amicably, in marked contrast to Freud's attitude to the other face of Dr M, Josef Breuer, where an old friendship would break down completely and end in bitterness.

Because blood is thicker than water? But both men are fatherly figures, and that would be an important factor in Freud's relationship to Breuer. On the other hand, Freud's relationship with Emanuel's younger brother, Philipp, was cool, even unfriendly. When Emanuel arranged to meet Freud in Dresden in December 1883, he told him he would be travelling with an English businessman, Mr Robinson—a typical practical joke of his, since Mr Robinson turned out to be their brother Philipp. Freud had not met him for several years, and was disappointed by the deterioration in Philipp's character. He judged him timid, mean, and petty-minded. But Emanuel continued to hold his sympathy as before. He was still "just as good, prudent, full of the joy of life, affectionate and understanding" (Fichtner, Grubrich-Simitis, & Hirschmüller, 2013, p. 513).

Of all these characteristics, the one most notably absent in the photo is "full of the joy of life". The darkness is closing in. Perhaps the photo even dates from 1914, the year of Emanuel's death, but the contrast with the description, and with the youthful figure in the 1878 group photo, brings back uncertainty about the identity of this melancholy couple.

Inscriptions are often untrustworthy. One published inscription identifies Martin and Oliver as children with their grandfather Jacob, in a photo taken in Manchester, where they never went at that age. "Martin" seems, in fact, to be a girl. The picture might actually be of Bertha with her brother Sam (E. Freud, L. Freud, & Grubrich-Simitis, 1978, Pl. 135).

Apart from the inscription, the evidence in this photo is far from compelling. It can be reduced to the physical characteristic that Freud, in his specimen dream, chose as Emanuel's signifier—whiskers and shaved chin. This style was in fashion from around the 1850s to the

1880s. By the time of this photograph, it was out of date, another remnant of the past, indicating the wearer's allegiance to a vanished era.

By the time Freud could have seen this photo—if he ever did—his memories of Emanuel had already taken on their own independent life, or after-life, analysed and distributed through the dream book, while the shadow of the man this photo shows, arthritic, perhaps disillusioned, either shuttled between the old Manchester business he could not entirely abandon and the lodgings in Southport which was his retirement address, or was already in his grave.

There is an idealising strain in Freud's relationship with Emanuel. He hardly said anything negative about him. But Martin Freud does mention Emanuel's overbearing nature. This could be a consequence of the age disparity, but if his observation was valid, it might possibly have something to do with the mysterious disappearance of Emanuel's son, John, from all family records. For Freud, it is as if Emanuel represented the benevolent shadow of their father, or as if Emanuel, as the *real* eldest son of Jacob, had consented to transfer his birthright (the father's blessing) to the younger.

There are hints that when Freud first travelled to Manchester in 1875, he suspected or imagined a benign scheme, hatched perhaps between Emanuel and their father, Jacob, that he might marry Emanuel's daughter, Pauline. Thus, he would have inherited the privileges of his brother's economic and social situation, for what that was worth. How much he was attracted by the daughter he does not say, but he was certainly attracted by the prosperity, culture, and science of Victorian England, by its liberalism, and by the idea of being a British citizen.

At university in Vienna, he was beginning to experience anti-Semitism for the first time (the word itself would be invented only a few years later, in 1879). The British Prime Minister of the time was Disraeli—baptised, true, but unmistakably Jewish. As for the scientific aspect, the England he first visited was the home of Darwin himself, still alive and working in the south. And Manchester, where he stayed with his brothers, was an impressive metropolis. It was Disraeli, in his novel *Coningsby*, who had called it "the most wonderful city of modern times". Girouard, glossing that quotation, adds, "For a newcomer the first distant view of Manchester and its smoking chimneys must have been as extraordinary as a first view of

Constantinople in the tenth century, or of New York in the early twentieth century" (Girouard, 1985, p. 258). If Freud had stayed in England, whether to study or to trade, the country could have offered him glittering opportunities.

In economic terms, his father Jacob's actual birthright seems to have been nothing but debts. Yet blessing is more a matter of confidence and status. It is earned as much as inherited.

What is curious about the sequel to Freud's visit to England is not so much that he turned down this possibility of a new life or career, as that he did not return for another thirty-three years. Lack of money or opportunity alone are inadequate explanations—in the interim he had enough money and leisure for many long holidays and Mediterranean excursions. Perhaps there was something to be proved as far as England and his family there were concerned. It might not have been only the unexpected appearance of Emanuel in Salzburg in 1908 that finally summoned him back, but also the fact of the Salzburg psychoanalytical congress itself, the first international gathering of those interested in, or practising, this new technique and treatment. The hopes he had of England, and the hopes his English relatives had of him, had finally been validated, now that he was an internationally recognised innovator. He could show his face there with pride.

His letters from England that year were high-spirited. On 7 September 1908, he wrote home from St Anne's on Sea, near Blackpool, where he was staying with his brother,

> I tell stories and discuss the whole day in English. All the rest by word of mouth. Of course in between we eat excellently. It is a long time since I felt such well-being. I have also changed in another way, I won't say how. (Tögel, 2002, p. 242)

Sea air, good food, and English conversation may well be exhilarating, yet there has to be more to this euphoria than just sensual or intellectual satisfaction. Perhaps there is a sense of achievement behind it, the moral satisfaction of having fulfilled his brother's and their father's expectations? Maybe it was the emergence of this carefree English self that enabled him to reveal himself in the new guise that the final sentence quoted above indicates, warning his family that on his return from England he would be "changed in another way".

When Freud first visited Engand in 1875, he promised to bring back for his friend Silberstein a razor, probably of Sheffield steel

(Boehlich, 1990, p. 128). What happened in 1908 is that he now submit-ted himself to the razor. High spirits might have played some part. His stay with Emanuel might well have infected him with his half-brother's love of springing surprises. Or (why not?) perhaps he decided to distinguish himself decisively from the bearded father and the lavishly side-whiskered brother? Whatever the reason, the fact is that Freud chose this place and year to have not just his chin, but his entire beard shaved, for the only time in his adult life.[6]

*   *   *

"Rose, on this terrace fifty years ago . . ."
(Alfred Lord Tennyson: "The roses on the terrace")

There is another reason, apart from the sombre lighting and serious faces of the sitters, for the sense of abandonment that fills this photo-graph. That is the familiar nineteenth-century narrative we read into the image of an old man with his middle-aged daughter. Her posture and unfocused gaze invite the conclusion that she might be unmarried and might remain that way. Something has gone wrong in her life, one imagines, or in the life of the family. Perhaps it was the father's failure as much as the daughter's.

When Freud visited Manchester in 1875, he was favourably impressed by the social standing of his relatives, but not by their wealth. Eight years later, he wrote to his fiancée about Emanuel's daughters: "The poor things, Pauli is as old as I am, Bertha 1^1/$_2$ yrs. younger, they have too little money to find a husband in Manchester" (Fichtner, Grubrich-Simitis, & Hirschmüller, 2013, p. 390). A little over a month later, he added that he could not borrow from Emanuel because he was saving for dowries for his nubile daughters (Fichtner, Grubrich-Simitis, & Hirschmüller, 2013, p. 489).

Marriage to a pauper was out of the question. This predicament was on Freud's mind at the time of writing, 1 November 1883, well into the second year of a long engagement and with no end in sight—that end being, of course, the prospect of financial security. His letter goes on to detail the bleak situation of Freud's sisters and his nieces and their struggle to make a living. The one sister left unmentioned is Rosa, and for good reason—Martha had already been informed a few months previously that she was involved in an affair with an acquaintance of Freud's named Brust.

Rosa had been among the first confidante of Martha's and her brother's secret engagement in the summer of 1882. In March 1884, she had become engaged to the lawyer, Josef Brust. But his subsequent behaviour puzzled Freud—he seemed to lack real commitment. The doubts were justified: the engagement was soon broken off. It was in the wake of this emotional upheaval that Rosa took up her half-brother's earlier offer, to take refuge with him if she was ever in trouble. In 1885, she went to Manchester, apparently with the intention of working and perhaps establishing herself there. In a later note on this episode in her life, Rosa describes her relationship to her half-brother in a very similar manner to her brother's description, as "a profound, sympathetic, harmonious friendship".[7]

Emanuel's benevolence survives only in these few testimonies, Bertha's qualities in no more than a few phrases from a letter to Martha Bernays:

> I enclose a letter from my niece Bertha from Manchester, a clever and good girl, 24 years of age, who is very dear to me, don't be frightened of the family vanity evident here, for to a large extent my family's hopes are on me and I expect that you will grow very fond of Bertha once you have seen her. (Fichtner, Grubrich-Simitis, & Hirschmüller, 2011, p. 150)

Even the single glimpse of Bertha afforded by this photo is more than we have of her mother, Marie Rokach, who is virtually lost to history. She enters it only as a faint echo, the sounding board of Emanuel's humour. This is recorded in the vignette of Emanuel's home life, among the associations of the "revolutionary dream":

> My associations then led me to England and to my brother's house there. He used often to tease his wife with the words 'Fifty Years Ago' (from the title of one of Lord Tennyson's poems), which his children used then to correct to 'fifteen years ago'. (Freud, 1900a, p. 211)

In the *Standard Edition*, the editor's footnote to the literary reference points out that there is, in fact, no poem of Tennyson with that title, and conjectures that it might be a reference to the ode "On the Jubilee of Queen Victoria", in which the words "fifty years"—but not "fifty years ago"—repeatedly occur, or that it might have been *Locksley Hall: Sixty Years After*, which is, however, ten years out. But if the phrase refers to the *first line* rather than the *title*, then the poem must be the following:

The Roses on the Terrace

> Rose, on this terrace fifty years ago,
>   When I was in my June, you in your May,
> Two words, 'My Rose,' set all your face aglow,
>   And now that I am white and you are gray,
> That blush of fifty years ago, my dear,
>   Blooms in the past, but close to me to-day,
> As this red rose, which on our terrace here
>   Glows in the blue of fifty miles away.
>   (Tennyson, 1919, p. 874)

Both this poem and "On the Jubilee of Queen Victoria" were not published until 1889, so Freud could not have actually witnessed Emanuel reciting it to his family. It must have been Emanuel himself who reported this teasing, perhaps on his visit to Vienna in 1896.

It may indeed be teasing. But it has the bitter aftertaste of lost time—"I am white and you are gray"—and who knows what other undertones. There is the question of his wife's absences, from his visits to Vienna, from letters, from the photo itself. The exclusivity of the father–daughter couple in the photo might extend beyond the image. When Freud's oldest sister Anna travelled to the USA in 1892, it was only Emanuel with his daughter Bertha who greeted them at Liverpool (Freud-Bernays, 2004, pp. 59–60). Why didn't his wife, or the elder daughter Pauline, or one of her two brothers accompany him?

It is curious that, apparently, none of Emanuel's four children married. John's already mentioned disappearance leaves that in doubt, but there is no record of him being married up to the time when he disappears from the records at the age of fifty-four. It is also curious that no further mention of him can be found in any of the extant correspondences. This might imply not a simple death or even a mysterious disappearance, but a falling out. He may have become unmentionable. Knowing his infant squabbles with Freud, seeing him later as a sharp British businessman, one can imagine friction between him and his possibly domineering father. On Emanuel's journey to Vienna in 1900, he was accompanied by Sam. By 1906, "Freud & Co." had mutated into "E. Freud and Son". That singular "Son" was, in all likelihood, Samuel, not John.

Photographs isolate a momentary subject and the viewer extrapolates the isolation, creating a universal narrative of loss. But a highly specific and ultimately unknowable family nexus of affections, antagonisms, over-attachment, and resignation marks the faces of the sitters of this double portrait. Rescuing these lost characters from oblivion, the photo shines a spotlight on one moment of their lives. It is an illusion that this moment can be extrapolated with any confidence. The view we get remains as frozen and hieratic as the distant rose in Tennyson's poem.

Moreover, the sparse evidence of Emanuel's life by no means fits the image in front of us. How have the years transformed the head of "Freud & Co.", that active and social man, into this sad figure? Something is wrong here. We also have to imagine Emanuel standing up after this photograph, loosening up after the strain of posing (perhaps worsened by the pain of arthritis), joking with his daughter and the unknown photographer.

*   *   *

"I must have left the carriage while I was in a sleeping state."

Examples of such somnambulism, Freud adds, "are to be found in the experience of a neuropathologist. We know of people who have gone upon railway journeys in a twilight state . . ." (Freud, 1900a, p. 457).

Twilight falls across old photographs, making them intrinsically melancholy objects. This fact is our problem when dealing with them as historical sources. The mood infects the observer and fogs our vision. We should be looking *past* these protagonists, forever tensed for the click of the shutter, and imagine their other selves breathing a sigh of relief afterwards, relaxing into their real life, their everyday attitudes which even the best portraits (perhaps these *least* of all) will never recapture.

Even so, the evidence of the image has to be taken into account. If the photo happened to have been taken in late summer or early autumn 1914, that is, after the start of the First World War, their defensive attitudes would have been well justified. Emanuel had by then lived over fifty years in England and, according to both Freud and his son Martin, had become the model of an English gentleman. But his name and the name of his business was German and in the early months of the war there was an outburst of anti-German feeling in

England, attacks on German shops and businesses, the Defence of the Realm Act (DORA), and, from late August on, the rounding up of "alien enemies" into concentration camps.

One of these aliens was Freud's daughter, Anna, who was on holiday in the south of England when the war broke out. If she had not managed to leave the country in the nick of time, her only refuge would have been with Emanuel.

If we conjecture this photo was taken after August 1914, that is, after Emanuel's original mother country, the Austro-Hungarian Empire, was at war with his adopted homeland, there would be reason enough, in addition to the ordinary woes of age, for him to appear apprehensive, even depressed.

But *suicidally* depressed? That question may be asked because of the strange manner of his death. It was reported in the *Southport Guardian* on Wednesday 21 October 1914:

> On Saturday afternoon, just as an express passenger train from Manchester to Southport passed Parbold station, it was noticed that one of the carriage doors had opened and an elderly man lay on the line. He had apparently fallen out of the compartment in which he had been travelling alone. He was dead when picked up. He was identified as Emanuel Freud, aged 82, and residing at 21, Albert Road, Southport.

Emanuel was actually not eighty-two, but eighty-one years old at the time, that is, he died at the same age as his father, a fact which did not escape his numerically superstitious half-brother, Sigmund. Although residing in Southport, Emanuel was not registered as a resident there: the ratepayer at 21 Albert Road and presumably his landlady there was Mrs Worthington Roberts.

Given Emanuel's age, he might have mistakenly opened the door out of forgetfulness and under pressure of a natural need, perhaps thinking he was entering the train corridor or opening a lavatory door. This hypothesis would be strong enough to support the most probable verdict of accidental death. Yet a shadow of doubt lingers on.

The twilight of his unmarried daughters was depressing, too. Apparently, Pauline ended up "stone deaf and became mental" while Bertha herself died "due to a fall down the stairs of their house".[5] The pathos of these fates and this photograph is, in part, an effect of the paucity of evidence. The sitters stare at us like condemned captives,

pleading for their undocumented lives. More evidence, more information, would signify a sort of reprieve.

Under normal circumstances, there should have been an official
Board of Trade inquiry into such an incident as caused Emanuel's
death, but no trace of one has been found. Philip Atkins of the
National Railway Museum library told me the failure to investigate
might have been a consequence of the war. Yet, the very fact that
Emanuel fell out of a train throws an uncanny spotlight back across
his own past and that of his brother. Over the years, the Freud
brothers had shuttled back and forwards across Europe to meet
each other in Manchester, Leipzig, Vienna, Salzburg, Harwich, and
Berlin. Emanuel travelled to Europe, ostensibly on business, but it
looks as if pleasure and family meetings were often his prime motives.
Trains carried Freud to holidays with his family in the mountains
or south to his beloved Italy at least once a year. Across Europe, the
ever-expanding network of railways mapped out a nerve system,
transporting human impulses to their source of attraction. This was
psychic utility on a massive scale: tons of steam traction engine power
and thousands of miles of steel rails, all in the service of the pleasure
principle.

It was in a train from Vienna to Aussee, on the night of 23–24 July
1898 (exactly three years after the specimen dream), that Freud dreamt
the "revolutionary" dream in which Emanuel features, both explicitly
in the associations and implicitly in the latent content.

Apart from his appearance reciting "fifty years ago", Emanuel is
also implicit as an English representative of a free society, as witness
of the 1848 revolutionary year, and as the goal of the railway journey
on which Freud was involved in an anti-Semitic incident (E. Freud,
1960, pp. 78–79).

Reflected or distorted in that dream, the train (more precisely,
the closed first-class compartment in which Freud is travelling) is a
magical space. The outside intrudes into the inside. It is (in the dream)
"as though thinking and experiencing were one and the same thing"
(Freud, 1900a, p. 210). But when Freud awakes under pressure of the
need to urinate, he finds no hole in the floor of the compartment to
meet his natural need. Was the dream in part a fantasy substitute for
that non-existent perforation?

Freud's florid dream on the journey to Aussee intersects Emanuel's
real exit from his compartment between Manchester and Southport

only in imaginary space. But the trains were certainly real and the trains of thought they set in motion criss-cross the stories and queries behind this photograph. Was it pressure of his bladder while asleep that impelled Freud to construct a delirious history of nineteenth-century revolutionary movements, culminating in the rebellious vision of their blind old father urinating? Or was it, as Freud was more inclined to think, the inflated ambitions expressed in the dream that aroused the need to urinate? Cause and effect push and pull like the pistons of a steam train.

Which was the first cause, megalomanic dreams or—as Strachey endearingly translates *Harndrang* (i.e., "bladder pressure")—"the desire to micturate"? Just as the seven-year-old Freud had avoided a confrontation with John, the older Freud deftly sidesteps the question. "But in any case it will do no harm to leave the point unresolved" (Freud, 1900a, p. 218).

What pressure of bladder or fantasy impelled Emanuel out of the moving compartment? Or what combination of debility and delusion led to Bertha's fall down the staircase over two and half decades later? The photograph starts up trains of thought that will never arrive anywhere. A destination or resolution would have to be death for the stories. It is only the uncertainties—about the facts and figures, about their relation to us and to each other—that keep this image alive in my imagination.

CHAPTER SIX

Portrait of an alien enemy

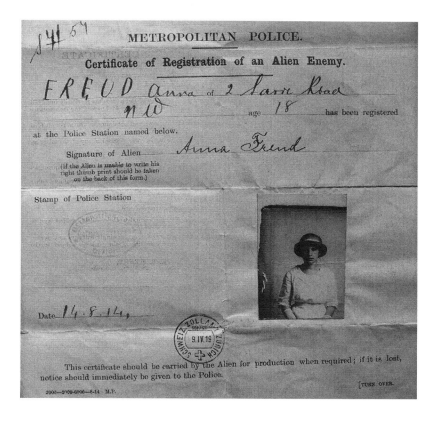

Being-in-the-world

"... but until now I always imagined that being-in-the-world [*Aufderweltsein*] was actually something hostile and the good and beautiful aspect of it only the people who liked you" (Anna Freud to Lou Andreas-Salomé, 26.12.1921) (Rothe & Weber, 2001, p. 12).

W hen a photograph like this one is found attached to identity papers, two dimensions intersect. The document grounds the portrait in a specific historical landscape. In this case, both portrait and landscape are captured at a particularly dramatic moment. This photograph of the young Anna Freud appears, in fact, on two documents, the document depicted here—"Certificate of Registration of an Alien Enemy"—and a permit allowing the holder to travel from London to the port of Falmouth from noon 16th to noon 17th August. Both were issued at the Albany Street Police Station, London, on 14 August 1914. Her ship to Genoa, and her one chance of escape from a hostile country, was due to leave Falmouth at midnight, 16 August.

War between Great Britain and the Austro-Hungarian Empire had been declared nine days previously, on 5 August. Since that ship was almost certainly her last opportunity to return home, her documents had to be put in order instantly. Getting hold of an identity photo was the first prerequisite. These are commonplace nowadays, but Anna would have arrived in England without a passport and she left without one, passports being unnecessary at the time. The British government's decision to register enemy nationals, taken on 8 August 1914 under the Defence of the Realm Act, would mark the beginning of a new phase in its relations to citizens and to foreigners in the country.

A. J. P. Taylor's account of pre-war lack of regulation sounds elegiac:

> Until August 1914 a sensible, law-abiding Englishman could pass through life and hardly notice the existence of the state, beyond the post office and the policeman. He could live where he liked and as he liked. He had no official number or identity card. He could travel abroad or leave his country for ever without a passport or any sort of official permission. . . . For that matter, a foreigner could spend his life in this country without permit and without informing the police.

Unlike the countries of the European continent, the state did not require its citizens to perform military service. (Taylor, 1965, p. 1)

In the documents that the state now began issuing in 1914, the photographic image would become an instrument of classification and control. This haunting portrait of the eighteen-year-old Anna Freud epitomises that paradigm shift. Its ragged and improvised appearance shows a photographer and sitter caught between two worlds.

Later rules of identity photographs would forbid hats or such lighting effects as the heavy shadow that falls across the right side of her face. The now standard blank background is already in place, but not yet perfected: the squares of a screen or large window behind the sitter can still be made out. Whether this was part of the Albany Street police station interior, or whether that of some jobbing photographer's studio, at least the staff issuing the document were tolerant of what would come to be considered deviations from a strict norm. For the time being, these rules had not yet taken hold. But the fact that in the few days before her departure Anna had to get hold of no less than four documents in order to leave the country indicates the instant inflation of bureaucracy since the declaration of war.

The other two documents were *Provisorische Reise-Legitimation*, issued by the Austro-Hungarian consulate in London, and *Aliens Restriction Order 1914*. They might help explain Anna's expression in the photograph. If it appears sullen, that could well be an effect of official and officious impositions, and an after-effect of all the rushing around that had been necessary—to the Austro-Hungarian consulate in the City, to the Albany Street police station, to the photographer, and wherever else she had to go in order to gather together these various scraps of paper with their vital signatures and rubber stamps.

Comparing this official photograph to earlier pictures of Anna Freud, we see her here for the first time emerging as a woman. In the well-known photos taken a year earlier, in the summer of 1913, in her *dirndl* walking in the Dolomites, she is still a girl, an impression reinforced by her being on her father's arm. It is not only that she is a year older here. She was also on her own and independent for the first time in her life.

It seems that the trip to England was her own initiative, maybe assisted by an English friend, Mabel Pring. Whatever her future career—and at this point she seemed destined for teaching—English would be useful. Her holiday included a course at a ladies' academy in St Leonards, near Hastings on the south coast, as well as a stay with the Pring family in Arundel, further along the coast.

After arriving by ship at Southampton, she went first to Arundel. Other archive photographs show her with members of the Pring family, which was a large one—two sisters and three brothers are featured—and this at least must have felt familiar to her, as the youngest of six children. None the less, however much the Prings and others might have made her feel welcome, she was only eighteen years old and alone in what had suddenly become a hostile land.

Internal or covert hostility was nothing new to her. As the youngest child, she had always had to fight for attention. Her childhood rivalry with her older sister, Sophie, had been a long existential struggle between the wish to be like her and rebellion for the right to be unlike her. She had also grown up with anticipation of anti-Semitism as a constant. What was new in England was that hostility was now officially recognised and approved, and she was its designated object.

There is a discordance between the portrait of this innocent young girl and the title assigned to her—"alien enemy". When Anna found herself in the same situation a quarter of a century later, again in England and ex-citizen of a country at war with the UK, the phrase had switched to "enemy alien".[9] In the 1914 variant, "enemy" is the noun itself, not the adjective. Thus, hostility becomes the bearer's primary distinguishing characteristic, as far as officialdom was concerned. In that respect, Anna's defensive–aggressive expression in the photograph could be considered fully justified. The country she had landed in has changed, and that change has altered her. She finds herself assigned this alarming new identity, and an unpredictable, dangerous future.

It has to be added: the sitter's mood and moodiness are over-determined. Although probable, there is no certainty that the photograph was taken exactly at the time of acquiring those documents. In a photograph of Anna with the Pring family, as well as in other photos of the same period, she wears a similar challenging or sullen expression. It could also be read as a generic characteristic of adolescence, which is often a state of being at war with the world. If so, it was a phase that may have lasted well into her twenties. When Anna's brother-in-law, the professional photographer Max Halberstadt, photographed her in 1922, she wrote, "But he complained bitterly about the expression that I showed on it, which was as stupid as it was bad-tempered . . ." (Rothe & Weber, 2001, p. 38). Whatever the reasons may be for her brooding expression, the fact of the mood alone is what most of all brings the portrait to life.

Halberstadt was Sophie's husband, so who knows what that might have meant for his portrait of her. But she could not then have had the same motive for suspicion that her younger self had in this photograph, her official alienation, nor another possible motive, anticipation of anti-Semitism.

After the war, Loe Kann commented on Anna's expectations:

> When Annerl was here she remarked on the decency that met her everywhere – the Embassy did not spit at her for being a Jewess, although she thought they would refuse her on that ground; from the main Police-station to the small police station, courtesy met her everywhere. She repeatedly remarked on that fact. (Loe Kann to Sigmund Freud, 20.8.1919, FML)

Loe Kann, previously Ernest Jones' common-law wife, was looking after Anna, and (Freud hoped) protecting her from some of the

dangers now threatening his daughter. Loe had been in analysis with
Freud during 1913–1914. She had, by that time, transferred her affections to "Jones II", the young American millionaire Herbert "Davy"
Jones. In June 1914, Freud was one of the witnesses at their wedding
in Budapest. She and her husband returned to England and became
unofficial guardians to Anna during this critical period.

Loe, who was a Dutch citizen, was able to communicate with
Freud via Holland after war had been declared, and while she was
supporting Anna in her efforts to return home. At this time, Loe's
loyalties were split. Her violent hostility to the Austro-German alli-
ance had to be suppressed in Anna's presence. This was something she
only admitted to Freud after the war:

> Also that my Jewishness disappeared to all practical purposes, that I
> felt more English (and Davy more French) and both of us more anti-
> German than we could ever have dreamt of. Right in the beginning
> (when Annerl was still with us) we had to mind our p's & q's: the
> horrible Belgian campaign war was in full swing: we did not want to
> hurt her feelings – but we had already drifted wide apart: we hoped
> & feared for 2 different sides! – And at that time neither her personal
> friends nor ours were involved yet! (Loe Kann to Sigmund Freud,
> 20.8.1919, FML)

The address that appears on Anna's official documents is 2 Sarre
Road NW. The *Rates and Electoral Registers for 1914* show that this
ordinary terraced house in a lower middle-class area of West
Hampstead was officially occupied at the time by Theresa and Arthur
de Tiel. They were Jewish acquaintances of Loe Kann. Years later,
Arthur de Tiel would be godfather to Herbert Jones' son by his second
wife, Olwen. In a much smaller war, her "last war", since it broke out
the year of Anna's death, that son, also called Herbert Jones, died a
hero's death in the Falklands (Wilsey, 2002, p. 93).

On 13 August, the Austro-Hungarian consulate issued her travel
document to return home (*Provisorische Reise-Legitimation Für die
Reise nach Oesterreich-Ungarn*). Because she was subject to the *Aliens
Restriction Order* (Section 22), which limited movements of aliens to
within five miles of their registered address, she now also required a
British *Alien Travelling Permit* to Falmouth, her port of departure. She
obtained that the following day and left England two days later.

After the voyage via the Straits of Gibraltar to Genoa, Anna finally reached Vienna on 26 August 1914. Freud wrote to Loe and Herbert Jones, thanking them for returning his daughter to him:

> In this miserable time, during this war which is impoverishing us as much in our ideals as in material goods, I have not yet had an opportunity to thank you for the so skilful and purposeful way that you were able to send my little daughter back to me and for all the friendship that lay behind this. She is well, but I think she sometimes feels nostalgia for the land of our enemies. (Freud to Herbert & Loe Kann Jones, late August 1914. In: E. Freud, 1960, p. 305)

The letter of thanks does not mention the reason why he had first invoked Loe's assistance, even before the war broke out, which was to counter another, more intimate, peril that was threatening his daughter.

Jephthah's daughter

> "And he said, Go. And he sent her away for two months: and she went with her companions, and bewailed her virginity upon the mountains."
>
> (The Bible, Judges 11.38)

An identity photo should do no more than reflect facial features. Insight into character is not demanded. But it is that excess—the fixed gaze and sulky, wide mouth—that makes this portrait so intriguing.

She has been harassed by circumstances. In addition, the sitting itself, the very fact of having to have her picture taken—or stolen—is reason enough for revolt. This was not a voluntary sitting; the photograph was demanded by bureaucracy and police. They should at least see that the bearer of the document is not subservient. More than that, they might even wonder what sort of girl or woman this was. Despite her feminine dress and long gloves, it is noticeable that the left glove is not level with the right but has slid down towards her wrist, and that the linen dress is creased. Neither is she sitting up straight, as a conventional young lady might be expected to do: her posture is slightly slumped, with rounded shoulders.

Is it the viewer or the sitter herself who is questioning her femininity? This was something that concerned both her and her father at the time she left for England, and the question became critical on her arrival, where she was met by Ernest Jones, who was now free of his involvement with Loe Kann and on the lookout for a new wife.

On 17 July 1914, Freud wrote to Ferenczi,

> Annerl telegraphed yesterday that she arrived well in Southampton and was greeted by Ernest Jones. I used this occasion to make my attitude towards the matter clear to her, because I do not want to hear anything more of it and do not want to lose the dear child to an evident act of revenge, even apart from everything else that speaks against it on rational grounds. I think Loe will also be on guard like a dragon. (Falzeder & Brabant, 1996a, p. 52)

Even though he had assured Freud of his approval of Loe's marriage to Herbert Jones, Ernest Jones' "revenge" would have been for the analysis that had supposedly estranged Loe from him. Jones had also assured Freud that Loe would deceive herself and others to protect her morphine habit, that she had tormented him during their relationship, and that Freud should be sceptical about any accounts she gave of it or of him. But Freud and Anna were, for the time being, both charmed by Loe Kann. Consequently, Jones' comments about Loe could only backfire. Hence, Freud's extreme suspicion of his motives at this time.

After a few days' consideration of Jones' reception of his daughter, Freud wrote to him on 22 July:

> I thank you very much for your kindness with my little daughter. Perhaps you know her not enough. She is the most gifted and accomplished of my children and a valuable character besides. Full of interest for learning, seeing sights and getting to understand the world. She does not claim to be treated as a woman, being still far away from sexual longings and rather refusing man. There is an outspoken understanding between me and her that she should not consider marriage or the preliminaries before she gets 2 or 3 years older. I don't think she will break the treaty. (Paskauskas, 1993, p. 294)

That an eighteen-year-old girl should not yet consider marriage is understandable, but what did Freud mean by her not considering "the preliminaries"? Did that imply the custom of courting, or any close male friendship at all? As for "outspoken understanding", the adjective was evidently translated literally from the German *ausgesprochen*, and Freud simply meant "explicit". However, Jones might well have taken the word in its English sense, as "blunt, forthright, and unwelcome". Whether he took it in its German or English sense, he obviously got the message. Thirty-nine years later, he was still protesting the honesty of his intentions at the time to Anna (Young-Bruehl, 1988, pp. 67–68).

The same day that he wrote to Jones, Freud also sent a letter to Ferenczi, commenting on the situation:

> The little one should only learn how to assert herself, and she will probably be adroit enough to get out of the way of a declaration that can only lead to disappointment. She feels quite sure of herself. (Falzeder & Brabant, 1996b, p. 7)

It was as if Anna and Jones were being subjected to a test. Both were made fully aware of the rules and what was expected of them and then left to their own devices. It was immediately evident that Anna's chastity was not threatened. As her father had stated, she "did not claim to be treated as a woman". For his part, on 27 July Jones replied to Freud's description of Anna with some highly ambivalent praise of the father–daughter bond:

> I had already fully appreciated what you write about her. She has a beautiful character and will surely be a remarkable woman later on, provided that her sexual repression does not injure her. She is of course tremendously bound to you, and it is one of those rare cases where the actual father corresponds to the father-imago. (Paskauskas, 1993, p. 295)

No further intervention was necessary. Jones restricted his attentions to offering a helping hand if required, to reporting to Freud on the Pring family with whom Anna was staying in Arundel, and to taking both Anna and Mabel Pring on an idyllic river trip up the Thames near Windsor one day. For his part, Jones was accompanied by a friend, a professor of English called Martin. Anna ended her enthusiastic report on this outing with the sentence: "But I would not have accepted [the invitation] if you had not written that I could" (Anna Freud to Freud, 26.7.1914 [Meyer-Palmedo, 2006, p, 133]).

The treasure of Anna's innocence was protected as if by a dragon, and the dragon was not Loe, as Freud had written a few days previously, but, in Jones' words, Anna's own father-imago. She was bound in a web of affection that she had no intention of breaking.

If Freud was fully aware of the strength of his bond with his daughter, his initial outburst on hearing of Jones' supposed advances seems, on the face of it, excessive. But he could take nothing for granted. His two other daughters had both sprung surprises on him as far as choosing partners was concerned. Also, he did have good reason to suspect Jones' intentions, and not only on the basis of information he might have received from Loe during the final stages of her recent analysis.

Jones had written to Freud on 9 January 1914 that his practice was thriving and that he would soon be able to marry. Freud wrote back on 16 January:

> But will you do me the personal favour of not making marriage the next step in your life, but to put a good deal of choosing and reflection into the matter since there is no need for you to repeat a story like that of Jephthah's daughter. (Paskauskas, 1993, p. 256)

The response perplexed Jones. Why was Freud asking "as a personal favour" that he should defer his marriage plans? In the previous sentence, Freud had expressed satisfaction at having predicted Jones' professional success. By contrast, the advice that followed seems to predict the failure of any imminent marriage. Jones was obviously concerned that Freud had been influenced against him by Loe Kann's accounts of their relationship during her analysis.

However, Jones did not query Freud's curious comparison between his prospects of marriage and the Hebrew general Jephthah's sacrifice of his own daughter. In the Old Testament, Jephthah vowed to offer up the first creature to greet him on his successful return from battle (Judges 11.31). In Freud's version, Jephthah's rash vow relates Jones' prospective marriage to a blood sacrifice, but the explicit theme of the story itself is the father–daughter relationship and a pledge of self-sacrifice and perpetual virginity.

Freud's analogy itself seems to have had its immediate origin not in the Bible, but in Byron. While Anna was planning her visit to England in the summer of 1914, to help her practise her English—and her poetical talents—Freud gave her Byron's *Hebrew Melodies* to translate, including "Jephtha's daughter". This poem speaks in the first person, the daughter proclaiming her willingness to die for her father:

If the hand that I love lay me low,
There cannot be pain in the blow!

And of this, oh, my Father! be sure –
That the blood of thy child is as pure
As the blessing I beg ere it flow,
And the last thought that soothes me below.

(Spreitzer, 2014, p. 248)

Freud praised his daughter's translations of these poems, and they deserved his praise. Her childhood and early adolescence had been disturbed by jealousy of her sister, and by eating disorders, and her intellectual gifts came as a sort of compensation and pleasant surprise. On 17 May 1914, Freud had written to Abraham,

> It will interest you that we recently discovered that my little one translates English poets very beautifully into German verse. As a test I set before her some of Byron's Hebrew Melodies, and cannot deny that her version pleased me almost more than that of Gildemeister. It is a very fine little creature. (Falzeder, 2002, p. 241)

That last sentence (in German, "Es ist ein ganz feines Tierchen") admits several translations ("a splendid little animal", "a very refined creature", etc.), but all of them convey the message that whatever praise he might bestow on her, it is still counterbalanced by a keen awareness of her immaturity. The affectionate term "little animal" leaves her human self in abeyance. In the light of that phrase it is possible to look again at this photograph and discover an aspect of Anna's expression that seems almost feral—stubborn resistance, an animal suspicion of the world and what it offers.

As the youngest child in a large family Anna struggled for attention and was used to being patronised and teased. In the Pring family, she took on the same role, it seems, for on 26 July 1914 she wrote to her father, "I am on tremendously good terms with everyone in the house and am terribly teased by the brothers." (Meyer-Palmedo, 2006, p. 132).

Even after her siblings had left home, she could lay no claim to the exclusive attention of her father. The adult world was still inaccessible. By leaving home, she was able, paradoxically, to gain that attention. First, the Jones danger, and then the outbreak of war worked to her advantage. To be aware of his concern and anxiety must have been a source of gratification, albeit still a secret one.

The break in communication after the outbreak of war meant that she was really on her own—she could not consult him now about what to do next. Before Britain had entered the war, Ernest Jones had offered to escort her home. He was now advising caution, and that she should stay in England until it was once again safe to leave. The other Joneses, Herbert and Loe Kann, were less enthusiastic about a possibly indefinite extension of their responsibility for this alien enemy. But, like Ernest Jones, they had to treat her with the respect due to a free agent.

The certificate and photograph register a turning point. Faced by several possible futures, one of which was to stay with her Manchester relatives whom she had not yet visited despite Emanuel's pressing invitation, she chose to return home. If we continue reading the photograph with that in mind, we might make out, besides the defensive querying of the world, traces of a challenge thrown at it—she has proved, under duress, that she is able to take decisions independently. It is likely she has gained self-respect and maybe she even feels she has gained her father's respect.

Clearly, she is a long way from being able to count on that respect. It remains contingent on her situation and behaviour. A year later, on 12 July 1915, she would begin a letter to her father: "My dear Papa! – I almost think that I will have to go back to England again and undergo all sorts of curious experiences to get you to write me a long letter again." (Meyer-Palmedo, 2006, p. 132).

In England she asserted her freedom of choice—by returning home.

The face in this photo has not yet found itself, or its way, and that might be one reason why the portrait moves and disturbs the viewer. Indeed, the empathy it awakens goes beyond the purely personal and touches an intellectual predicament shared by us all. Her unresolvable relationship to her father is ours, too; in fact, it is the question faced by an entire culture. How can one live with this man? But, on the other hand, how could one imagine life and thought without him?

"... naked I"

An identity photo is a husk: it serves only the purpose of physical recognition. But this photograph exceeds its official function; a strong sense of character shines through Anna's features. This corresponds in some way to Anna's own sense of herself, her own experience of identity, as she expressed it in a letter to Lou Andreas-Salomé on 24 May 1925:

> As I said, the only certain and unchangeable thing is one's own self. This has always been a strong conviction of mine: that I have always been the same, that from my earliest years I have had the same sense of self. But perhaps not everyone feels this to be so clearly unchanged. (Rothe & Weber, 2001, p. 190)

That sense of self (*Ichgefühl*) takes us into the concealed landscape of her subjectivity. Its contours can only be deduced from her own words, above all from her own poetry, which begins around the time this photograph was taken.

The second document on which the photo appears is the "Aliens Permit: Travelling", permitting Anna to travel to Falmouth where she would embark on the ship sailing to Genoa on 16 August at midnight. It was either on that ship home, or remembering the voyage some time later, that she composed a prose poem entitled "On the Boat", describing the experience of travellers escaping from a hostile land:

> Behind them lies the island they have just left, filled with a warlike mood and unconfirmed wild rumours, lie days filled with tension, alarm and exhausting tasks; in front of them lies their own land from which they have for weeks heard as good as nothing, the crippling uncertainty about the fate of their loved ones and the war with all its horror and atrocities. But in between they are rocking endlessly for idle days in the blue sea and the sun, sky and water surround them with endless beauty. (Spreitzer, 2014, p. 186)

In this dialogue between internal anxieties and external world, that beauty alone does not signify peace, since there is no place in sea or sky on which the traveller's gaze can rest. It is only towards evening that the mood turns from impatience to acceptance:

> And he brings back from this great journey the feeling of an immense helplessness that slowly turns to tired acceptance. Only in the evening, when great golden stars appear in the sky, does this acceptance become joyful. (ibid.)

This prose poem reaches beyond description or autobiography (the protagonist is unnamed and male—"the traveller"). England, her voyage back, the war itself, are transmuted into features of a symbolical drama. They represent the need to escape from the wild emotions spurring the unquiet self. The desired end, finally achieved in the evening, is self-surrender, a realisation of one's own limitations culminating in joyful submission to fate.

Anna's original poems begin to be dated only in October 1918, the month when her psychoanalysis with her father was to begin, and, obviously, a critical period in her life. But a number of the poems, including this prose poem, are undated. Although it is impossible to say exactly when they were produced, all of them share a continuity of theme and tone: they all seem to emerge from the same phase of her life, the same sense of self (*Ichgefühl*). This was evidently a period of intense self-questioning and searching for a purpose. Something of that same mood comes across in this identity photo.

Anna was translating before she began writing her own poems. She had already begun translating poetry in the months before coming to England, and it is likely this was as much practice for her art as for her English. Her father set Byron (one of his favourite poets) as an exercise. She also translated poems from a small volume Herbert Jones gave her in May 1914—*Bassae and Other Verses*—his own work, but published anonymously by Lakeside Press in 1911, and she translated a number of poems by Rudyard Kipling.

Although "On the Boat" is a version of the voyage she embarked on a few days after the photograph, her ordering and inner distancing of the experience does argue for a later date. But not much later. Spreitzer points out, that the typewriter used for this piece and the translations was different from the one used during her documented period of poetical activity from 1918 to 1922 (Spreitzer, 2014, p. 185).

In old age, speaking of her time as a teacher during the First World War, Anna stated, "In those days I read a lot of poetry, and wished I could write poems that would have meaning for others, not only myself. (There is a difference, believe me, I gradually learned!)" (Coles, 1992, p. 15). Although the chronology remains imprecise, around the time of her employment as a teacher Anna Freud may already have been trying to work out, through her poems, whether or not she had a poetic vocation, but it was probably only at the time of her psychoanalysis that she began consciously working on the relationship between fantasy and expression. "Beating fantasies and daydreams" (1922), her first psychoanalytical work, culminates in a discussion both of the motive and mechanism of writing down fantasies. That discussion, and its acceptance by a community of others, indicates that her psychoanalysis was succeeding where her poetry had failed.

The mechanics of the photograph itself and the expression of the sitter are both subject to a question of *exposure*. Here we see Anna well dressed, with hat and long gloves, but her eyes are vulnerable. Also, her poetry exposes a longing to be untrammelled, free of duty and anxieties. In the poem "Dreams" (*Träume*) at the very beginning of her analysis in October 1918, this expresses itself as the thwarted desire to walk the world barefoot:

> Harder than shoes pressing on feet, / fears, force and opposition weigh on your senses; / unfeeling, rejected by things, / you turn your desires inwards. (Spreitzer, 2014, p. 105)

The poetry failed as a form of writing down, because it could not establish a foothold for fantasy in the real world. That is clear in another poem, "Error" (*Irrtum*), written the same month:

> I have, / instead of depicting the world faithfully, / drawn an image of my own self, / consequently, because I made people out of myself, / I was fearful of hurting them, / so that I should not inadvertently cut into my own flesh and so that I should not wantonly / shed blood of my own blood. (ibid., p. 107)

The emotional exposure of these poems is too unmediated to face a hostile world in its own right. Introspection or dreaming were worthless unless they found a form of expression that transformed them or raised them above the intimate desires in which they originated.

At some time in the early 1920s, Anna Freud abandoned her creative writing (*Dichtung*) and devoted her life to science (*Wahrheit*). Probably, there was no exact date or single moment that marks her renunciation of poetry. However, one undated poem, "End" (*Ende*) gives it concise expression:

Too long you have been brooding on your senses, / dreamed the dream so often that it stands there stale, / so that you have been left behind by what you have begun, / what you yourself created, despises you. /

Abandoned by the darkness and by the light, / rejected, useless, strength and light spent, / no action and no dream left to you, / what will you, naked I, do with yourself? (Spreitzer, 2014, p. 127)

That final question, lacking an answer in the poem, looks purely rhetorical, but the answer has been given, both in her life and in the story of this photograph. What she would do with her naked self is to return it to her father and to his protection, and to devote it to his creation, psychoanalysis.

CHAPTER SEVEN

"I'm staying there"

The first thing I noticed about the original print of this photograph is that it was fading into a beautiful golden sheen. Its subjects are dead, and now the supposedly preserved moment is following them into extinction. The natural world, or a bath of weak hypo, is having its revenge on art. The bleaching image is acting out its own doom.

In cinematography, fading or overexposure are often used to represent dreams or distant memories. Anyone acquainted with that technique is likely to read this image as unreal. Yet, in spite of chemical deterioration, the brown-tinged, century-old sunlight still picks out most of the details. In theory, the place and the children could be identifiable. That, at least, was my hope when I found the photograph among material bequeathed by Lucie Freud (née Brasch), the wife of Freud's youngest son, Ernst.

I assumed it related either to the Brasch or Freud families. However, there was no other external clue, no inscriptions or documentation. I guessed it must be around the turn of the century, give or take a decade, and the children's clothes indicate the Austrian or Bavarian countryside. It was not so much the cryptic activities of the children as the atmosphere that attracted me to the image. Certainly, I wanted to find evidence and understand what was going on, but no historical data could completely explain the effect of the picture.

A little boy is seen standing alone in a fenced garden. Some older boys have stopped nearby to watch what he is doing. His activity is unclear. In his left hand he is holding a stick or flat lath and pointing at it with his right hand. He is concentrating intently on the stick, as if reading it. Since he is of pre-school age, this must be a game and, like many children's games, probably an imitation of an adult activity. That might account for the amusement of the boy leaning over the fence, laughing perhaps at the little child's unwittingly comic performance.

Late childhood laughing at early childhood? The pre-adolescent disavowing the shame of infancy, which Yeats, in his "Prayer for My Son", called the "ignominy / Of flesh and bone"? (Yeats, 1950, p. 239)

There remains another relevant question, apart from identifying the boys. Why did the unseen witness, the photographer, choose to snap this particular scene? Were the older boys just passers-by caught just as the small child was being photographed? Or are they the intended subjects just as much as he? The impression is that this tableau was spontaneous and unposed, but the camera is not centred on the infant and the dominant position of the boy in the hat indicates he might not have been incidental.

Aleksei Parshchikov, a poet who once earned a living as a photographer, came up with the quip: "Who was the first photographer?— Perseus" (Parshchikov, 1996, p. 135). In this analogy, the image is an actual object, Medusa herself, petrified by her own reflection in the warrior's shield. Yet a photographic image is really nothing in and of itself, because it is never a present moment. A photograph always looks back. Even with today's digitally time-coded imagery, once the shutter has been clicked the image signifies a moment already lost. Whatever it may be, it is not set in stone.

I suggest an alternative mythic counterpart: Eurydice, condemned by Orpheus' fatal backwards glance to remain in the underworld, from which she was about to emerge. Furthermore, she is condemned never to emerge into daylight *because* he looks back at her.

The way we look at a photograph decides what we will see. We decide a certain photograph is historic. In consequence, the moment of the photograph turns its back on us the instant we turn towards it and try to drag it into the light of our day.

Also, there is something orphic about decoding photographs, especially this one. It seems to be full of mysterious allusions. Despite the apparent clarity of the composition defined by a strong diagonal axis, the brightly lit slatted fence leads the eye away into an indistinct distance. At the same time, the fence curves round and encloses the garden on the right. This precise division of space into inside and outside, and the enclosed situation of the innocent-looking infant next to a tall flower (a lily?), bring to mind the *hortus conclusus*, the paradise garden of medieval tapestries. This, in turn, refers us back to cryptic, isolated memories of early childhood.

However, the little child here, although enclosed, is not isolated from his surroundings. The key aspect of this garden is that the boys outside are reaching across the fence.

Given its provenance, there has to be a strong probability that the photo features a Freud. Since the infant and the boy in the background remain unidentifiable, the boy in the feathered cap becomes a prime suspect.

As a point of reference, there is that framed collage of family photos in the dining room at Berggasse, to which I referred in the first chapter. The Freud children are its main theme. Since the latest picture included shows Mathilde aged eighteen in 1905, it is likely the selection was put together soon afterwards as a record of a phase of family history that was just ending, or had already ended—a decorative archive, recording a stage of family history, the end of the collective childhood (Engelman, 1976, Pl. 50).

The children in that framed archive posed in a studio, dressed in their best clothes. In one of the photos, the boys are in Tyrolean costume against the painted background of a mountain, which seems to be a fanciful representation of the Dachstein, one of the most dramatic of the peaks that formed the background of several summer holidays. A similar photo forms the frontispiece of Martin Freud's *Glory Reflected*. In the photo facing page 49 of that book, we see them in a rowing boat on Thumsee, in 1901. In the front of the boat, we can just make out nine-year-old Ernst wearing a feathered hat.

In fact, most middle-class Austrian children dressed in *Lederhosen* and traditional Tyrolean *Tracht* on their holidays, as Martin Freud recorded in his memoirs:

> We Freud boys followed the example of all city visitors on holiday in the Bavarian mountains and wore the leather shorts and the costume that goes with them. This makes a holiday in the Bavarian and Austrian mountains unique: because it is not usual in other parts of the world for visitors to copy what amounts to peasant dress. (M. Freud, 1957, p. 93)

If Lucie Freud preserved childhood pictures of the Freud boys, it is likely they would include her future husband, Ernst. The boy leaning over the fence here certainly bears no resemblance at all either to Martin or Oliver. The specific problem is that this boy must be around twelve years old. No other photos of Ernst at around that age are to be found. Also, in all the other childhood photographs he is dutifully and unsmilingly staring straight at the camera. Nowhere is he seen either in profile or smiling. There is only a profile pencil sketch in the Freud Museum archives dated 10 August 1911, probably a self-portrait when he was twenty-one. Although serious and mustachioed, the face does at least show that nose, chin, ear, and overall structure could well correspond to the boy in the feathered hat in this photograph.

This is some way from a positive identification. But, as far as reading this picture is concerned, even that would still leave the main question unresolved: what is going on here? The little child stands in a garden involved in some private game. The older boy (provisionally to be known as Ernst) is leaning across a fence, laughing, perhaps teasing the child. This is all that can be made out, whoever the other participants might be.

As I was looking through the envelope of photos from the Lucie Freud bequest, the first thing about this picture that caught my attention was simply the radiance of a fading image. Then I sensed something else. The spontaneity of the older boy's lunge over the fence is counterbalanced by an impression of stillness surrounding the action. It is the relationship between these two aspects of the image, immediacy and formality, that creates its specific effect, as if this picture came out of a confusion of genres, a snapshot whose composition contradicts its apparent artlessness.

One excessively famous photo, Robert Doisneau's *Le Baiser de l'Hôtel de Ville, Paris* (1950), exemplifies a certain pact that viewers make with a snapshot. In that photo of lovers kissing on a Paris street, the effect hinges on the unrehearsed reality of the instant. When we find out that the lovers were actually hired by the photographer, we feel tricked. The photograph's air of spontaneity told us that this was a world of chance captured in action. We wanted those lovers to have been living in their own separate world and not to have been complicit with their own image—or with our interpretation of it. We were in search of innocence and were innocent ourselves. We wanted to be duped.

Therefore, I should be wary and assume there is a lot of artifice and self-consciousness in this little scene.

I suggested the little boy is playing a game and that consequently his gestures may have a magical significance. This is a peripheral deduction, but it is curiously echoed by an accidental illusion within the image. While the child's left hand holds the lath, his right forefinger that is pointing towards the stick seems—impossibly—to extend far past it, forming the horizontal axis of a cross that reaches all the way to the edge of the picture. This can only be an effect created by the coincidence of his forefinger and some horizontal rod behind him.

Even if that cross is an illusion, what is the function of the stick he is pointing at and why is he doing so?

The photo is full of pointers—the stick, the infant's right finger, the pointed fingers of arms hanging over the fence, even the fence itself, which draws the gaze towards the misted meadow in the distance. As there is no future in the photo, the act of pointing takes on its own enigmatic significance. This is a world of allusions rather than meanings.

*   *   *

> and made to think of the small pale
> Face that seemed to sink into the pond: –
> O childhood, o fleeting likenesses.
> Where do you go? where do you go?
> ("Childhood": Rilke, 1966, p. 141)

In Doisneau's *Le Baiser de l'Hôtel de Ville,* the kiss translates as love lighting up the workaday world. Indifferent passers-by are there to convey that message. Yet they are the real subjects (unless the photographer hired them, too?). Only their interesting indifference rescues the image from formulaic banality.

Childhood is as tainted a word as love. Yet, whatever it may represent in and for this photo, it has to be the sense or direction of these allusions. Perhaps image and magic overlap here in the little boy's game. His sticks might be evidence of magical thinking, instruments for controlling the volatility of the confusing world.

In his final years, Tolstoi would revert to memories of his distant childhood and remember especially what he called the game of the "green stick". His elder brother, Nikolai, had announced to the others that there was a green stick hidden in the garden at Yasnaya Polyana and on it was inscribed a secret which, once known, would bring to an end all human misery and everyone would henceforth live in harmony and happiness. In his last years, Tolstoi chose to be buried at the place where the green stick of his infancy was supposedly hidden.

After Lou Andreas-Salomé and Rilke had visited Tolstoi in 1900, Lou left Yasnaya Polyana with her thoughts full of the enigma of childhood and its fear of growing up. In her diary, she wrote,

> Something that is already being lost speaks out of every new arrival, a glance back, a period of time, and that makes one afraid: in part one is proud of it, in part however one senses how being grown up will be new and terrible and death for so much that will never return.
> (Andreas-Salomé, 1999, pp. 57–58)

Another possible scenario for the photo, in parallel to the pre-adolescent's version, could be around the little boy's antipathy to growing up, if, as conjectured, we imagine the older children encountering the little boy in the garden and taunting him. In his concentration on the stick, the infant might be avoiding them, aware that he is being baited. In his eyes, those older boys are intermediaries between him and an off-scene adult world.

In fact, that adult world is already represented here, invisibly, by the camera lens and the photographer behind it.

Taking this as a Freud family scene and the boy in the hat as Ernst, then the camera operator is likely to have been one of the two family photographers, either his uncle, Alexander Freud, or his older brother, Oliver. The actual identity is less relevant than where he stands in relation to the children, in terms of age disparities. Oliver was only two years older than Ernst, but the camera would make him an honorary adult.

According to this hypothetical scenario, both the child's magic and the boy's mockery relate to the spectre of adulthood stalking this closed garden. It is a real spectre. An inferred adult eye is looking through a keyhole/lens into this encapsulated world of childhood.

As soon as the adult eye enters the scene, the locus of reality shifts. Once the image is experienced as a child's world seen by an adult, the scene is no longer an event, but already a memory.

Freud has a psychological "uncertainty principle" to account for the quirks of childhood memories:

> This is often the way in which childhood memories originate. Quite unlike conscious memories from the time of maturity, they are not fixed at the moment of being experienced and afterwards repeated, but are only elicited at a later age when childhood is already past; in the process they are altered and falsified, and are put into the service of later trends, so that generally speaking they cannot be sharply distinguished from phantasies. (Freud, 1910c, p. 83)

This boy in a hat who might be Ernst, this unidentifiable child playing with a stick—whatever historical message I had thought they might convey, I am left with the impression of figures in some badly fixed memory/phantasy, now drummed into "the service of later trends".

* * *

It can be assumed that Sigmund Freud was not the photographer. His observations of children never extended to photographing their activities. His library did include Darwin's *The Expression of the Emotions in Man and Animals* (1872) and Bourneville and Regnard's *Iconographie photographique de la Salpêtrière* (1876–1880), two pioneering works of the scientific use of photography, so he was well aware from the outset of its potential application in studies of behaviour in general, or infant development in particular. Later, the infant studies of his daughter Anna at the Jackson Nursery in Vienna 1937–1938 and the Hampstead Nursery in the 1940s would be comprehensively photo-documented by the photographer–analyst, Willi Hoffer, but there is no evidence Freud himself ever handled a camera.

His unnatural science depended on maintaining the distinction between idea and image. That, and his abstention from photography, could be seen as intrinsically anti-authoritarian. Photography brings with it the double danger of interfering in the object of study at the moment of photographing it, and, by freezing that object in the photograph, of objectifying it.

Freud did not interfere in the Berggasse nursery when his children were growing up, and, by and large, did not impose his will either on his children's choice of partners or career. He clearly played no part in Ernst's choice to become an architect. At the time, he wrote to Pfister on 15 June 1911, "I don't know whether I am supposed to have given my consent". Possibly, he made this comment because architecture was so far outside his range of experience. That, according to Ernst, was partly his own reason for choosing the profession. It was his escape from the magic circle of the family. Pankejeff, the Wolf Man, reported that Ernst had, in fact, considered becoming a painter, but was dissuaded by the "iron necessity" of economic realities, and, presumably, lack of faith in his own abilities.

Into photographs of children we project auguries of their future. Confidence brings achievement in its wake, Freud wrote in a short study of Goethe, and that confidence is grounded in the mother's unconditional love (Freud, 1917b, p. 156). It was a quality he recognised in himself, too, and he told the Wolf Man that, of his boys, it was his youngest son, Ernst, who came the closest to him in character and temperament (Gardiner, 1971, pp. 144–145). Ernst was designated the lucky child of the family (*Glückskind*) and German for "luck" overlaps with "happiness". Let it be imagined that some sense of luck is carried in the light that saturates this scene.

So much for the atmosphere—sunlight, summer holidays, the countryside. The radiance is general, even generic. Childhood memories are rich in sunlight and summer holidays, as if memory itself were light sensitive. But how much of that light is reflected off adults?

A large proportion of Martin Freud's memoirs deals with summer holidays. These were the periods when the children saw most of their father, and *vice versa*. Unlike in Vienna, the family on holiday was self-consciously together, and their daily life justified not by timetables and work, but the duty of pleasure. One anecdote illustrating the infant Ernst's commitment to the enjoyment of holidays would enter the family folklore.

When Ernst married Lucie Brasch, Freud alluded to that incident in his letter of congratulation on 2 April 1920:

> Let everything become and remain as sunny as you have always wanted. From earliest childhood you felt the attraction of sun, warmth and beauty, already at the age of $2^{1}/_{2}$ years old on leaving Lovrana. Since then you have made your own life much more independently than your older brothers, and always to our satisfaction and to your own success. Let all the privileges which you have so far enjoyed remain true to you! (Schröter, 2010, p. 301)

The "departure from Lovrana" refers to a remark made by the infant Ernst at the end of a holiday on the Adriatic in 1894. As the carriage took them away from the town, he kept turning round, repeating what would become a family catch phrase: "I'm staying there" (*"Ich bleibe da"*).

In a letter from Rome on 20 September 1912, Freud wrote to Martha that he would "do it like Ernst" and announced his intention not to cut his holiday short. He went even further, announcing his ultimate intention to return and live out his retirement in the glorious south. He really wanted to stay there.

The child is father to the man. Alternatively, the man's child lives out the father's wishes and aspirations. Ernst's attraction to the south and the sun—and independence—were not the only qualities that his father approved of and shared with his son. Although, for practical reasons, Ernst decided against art as a career, he had chosen instead a craft that gives adequate scope to artistry. Here was another familiar quality, that ability to adapt and compensate for loss, that his father, too, had shown when he abandoned research science to become a medical neurologist.

Years later, Freud even extrapolated that family talent into a racial characteristic. In the 1930s, after Ernst had emigrated to England, he managed to duplicate his lost German holiday cottage on Hiddensee by acquiring a substitute in the East Anglian village of Walberswick, named Hidden House. On hearing of this, Freud commented: "It is truly Jewish not to give anything up and to find oneself a substitute for what is lost" (Schröter, 2010, p. 438)

That remark of 1938 was clearly influenced by his current work on Moses and the Jewish character. But the theme of loss and restitution goes back a long way. In his earlier works on art ("Delusions and dreams in Jensen's *Gradiva* (1907a), *Leonardo da Vinci and a Memory of his Childhood* (1910c), "Creative writers and daydreaming" (1908e)), Freud had posited artistic creation as a sort of pseudo-Darwinian adaptation, allowing childhood fantasies to survive through modification into adulthood. Although he did not focus on this aspect again, his works inspired by the First World War ("On transience" (1916a), "Thoughts for the times on war and death" (1915b), "Mourning and melancholia" (1917e)) are concerned with the necessity of reconstructing what has been destroyed or lost. In the background of the cultural problem was a personal concern; the real prospect of the loss of his sons in the war. One incident in 1915 had brought that home: Ernst's narrow escape from death in a bunker on the Isonzo front. He had only just left the bunker when it was bombed and all his companions inside were killed (Falzeder & Brabant, 1996b, p. 86).

In mourning, fixation on the lost object is followed by substitution. The melancholic (i.e., the depressive) fail to detach themselves and are drawn into a vortex of misery. Art offers one technique of diverting the energy previously invested in loss, reassigning it to production.

A few weeks after the bombing of the bunker, on 18 November 1915, Freud wrote to Lou Andreas-Salomé that Ernst had received the first architectural commission of his career. It was to design a monument to his comrades killed in the bunker. But Welter (2012), who has made a systematic study of Ernst Freud's architectural work, finds no evidence that this commission (assuming it was more than just a soon-forgotten promise) was ever executed.

* * *

Uncertainties about the identity of the boy in the hat never affected my experience of the image. Associations can have an effect, even if none can be attached to any known memory or event. Maybe here it is *because* they cannot be attached to any known incident that they create such a curious impression. Ernst's smile contrasts with the seriousness of the boy behind him, whose eyes seem to be judging him, as if he already represented the adult world. The concentration of the infant on his own game excludes everything else. There seems no comprehensible connection between the parts that compose the snapshot. Each emotional segment is an ideogram that lacks a syntax—no sentence emerges from the separate elements. If the photo speaks like childhood memories, what it says remains incoherent.

Perhaps that is because it is so self-contained. None of its pointers lead out of the picture. The hands over the fence point downwards, into the infant's garden. Do they indicate he has dropped something and should look down? As for the infant who is the centre of attention in the picture, he continues paying no attention to anyone else.

The focus remains on him and his game, and the reason why this little figure in his Sunday best fixes our attention is that he stands alone in an enclosed space. The other boys, looking at him, act as our representatives in the picture, asking our questions: what is he up to? What is it that the child has?

Freud once commented on the fascination of narcissistic women, cats, and little children—self-contained creatures still unalienated from mother love. And he wondered for many years about a recurrent memory-image of himself as an infant, crying over the disappearance of his own mother, while his half-brother Philipp opened a cupboard. It was a scene that had been available to his consciousness since around the age of sixteen. Only in his self-analysis in 1897 did he finally, after twenty-five years, interpret the cupboard or box as memories of his old nurse, supposed originator of his sexual life, who had also disappeared. She been a thief and had been imprisoned, or boxed up, as Philipp might have said. The cupboard/box he opened for the little boy was empty. The woe in the dream was motivated not simply by the mother's disappearance but by foreboding. It denoted the birth of a sibling and the impending loss of the sole possession of his mother's love.

From the limp position of the older boy's arm, it seems as if he had been stretching it out and let it drop a moment earlier. The photograph juxtaposes the gaiety of his expression and the seriousness of the little boy. The infant seems to be concentrating on holding together the objects of his imagination, aware how fragile they are and how threatened they are by interruption from the adult world. The older boy may have forgotten, or suppressed, that world of magical thought, those early memory-fantasies of imaginative gratification. Observing that little child playing, locked in a perpetually receding dimension, the older boy reaches out as if trying to recapture what is lost in his own past. That lost element is not fantasy—he may well be capable of far greater flights of imagination. It is the security that pervades his imagined past. Now that time and death have impinged on his world, it is as if the image of the infant stands for the idea of grace in a dystopic universe.

This radiant garden is suffused with imminent woe and the boy's game can be interpreted as a magic spell against melancholy.

*   *   *

> Strictly speaking – and why should this question not be considered with all possible strictness? – analytic work deserves to be recognized as genuine psycho-analysis only when it has succeeded in removing the amnesia which conceals from the adult his knowledge of his childhood from its beginning (that is, from about the second to the fifth year). This cannot be said among analysts too emphatically or repeated too often. (Freud, 1919e, p. 183)

Documentary sources for the childhood and adolescence of Ernst Freud are sparse. Martin Freud's memoir, *Glory Reflected*, has comparatively few references to his youngest brother: five years difference in age and differences in temperament separated them. In Freud's correspondence with colleagues, the children, "the rabble", earn mention only occasionally, often in connection with sickness. In 1900, for instance, Ernst's liveliness shines through an account of his behaviour during high fever, as "inexhaustible energy" and "manic vivacity and wildness" (Masson, 1985, p. 417). At the time of the photograph (continuing to assume the boy in the hat is him), he would have been entering adolescence. Around that time, he began reading poetry and sharing that inclination with Anna. She was closer to him than to Martin, the "family poet", who had anyway by then accepted his own lack of talent (Masson, 1985, p. 377). In 1915, his father called Ernst a "Rilke fan" (Pfeiffer, Robson-Scott, & Robson-Scott,

1963, p. 35). Lou Andreas-Salomé, who knew Rilke better than anyone else, even spoke of a similarity between Ernst and Rilke (Pfeiffer, Robson-Scott, & Robson-Scott, 1963, p. 51). There is a romantically gloomy photograph of 1917 that shows Ernst cheek to cheek with another artist, his cousin Tom (IN 873, FML). Isolated in low light against deep shadow, they seem to be whispering together the secret language of their generation.

Although Ernst was at the front and missed meeting Rilke when the poet visited Berggasse on 20 December 1915, he eventually managed to meet his idol when he came to Vienna on leave in 1916 (Pfeiffer, Robson-Scott, & Robson-Scott, 1963, p. 39). Childhood is no less central to Rilke's poetry than it is to Freud's theory. To be as enchanted by Rilke as Ernst and Anna were implies a profound fascination with visions and versions of childhood.

The older boy in the photograph is barely out of childhood himself. Whether he was already reading Rilke cannot be known. Each growing child experiences the dark side of existence: boisterous activity may do no more than temporarily divert attention from that insight. Commenting on Ernst's feverish high spirits in 1900, his father said it reminded him of tubercular patients. And in the snapshot, the one boy's amusement is counterbalanced by the seriousness of the other boy looking over his left shoulder and half obscured by it. His unwavering stare creates unease.

For the infant, the concept of time means, in practice, no more than the daily cycle. The older boy, seeing in the infant what he used to be, has internalised time and needs to somehow live, not only with the prospect that he will suffer irreversible loss and change, but also with the knowledge that this might already have happened.

To describe childhood would mean recapturing an aura or evoking a mood poetically, not in the idioms of history or science. But this photo of a child at play is not about childhood itself, it is an *image* of childhood and the camera is our intermediary between fact and conjecture. Ernst Freud's sparsely documented early life and his father's spectacularly documented contemporaneous theorisation are the noises off, backgrounding the picture.

Regarding the earliest memory/phantasies (of his nurse and his young mother and the empty cupboard) that Freud was trawling in October 1897, he had to play devil's advocate to his own interpretations: "A harsh critic might say of all this that it was retrogressively fantasied instead of progressively determined" (Masson, 1985, p. 270). At that point, his mother's word and witness rescued him from a shadow-land of liminal impressions. His version of the cupboard memory was submitted to the *experimenta crucis* of factual corroboration—her independent memories of the nurse who disappeared.

No witnesses of this photo incident have come to light, or any further documentation to corroborate or identify the scene.

In the chapter "Childhood memories and screen memories" in *The Psychopathology of Everyday Life* (1901b), Freud concludes that one's self-image in apparently remembered infantile scenes is evidence that the scene has been subsequently revised, for a genuine visual memory would not include the observer. It is, consequently, a screen memory with a coded message:

> Thus the "childhood memories" of individuals come in general to acquire the significance of "screen memories" and in doing so offer a remarkable analogy with the childhood memories that a nation preserves in its store of legends and myths. (Freud, 1901b, p. 48)

This comparison between the way childhood memories are "re-written" and the way historiography has developed over the ages is elaborated in *Leonardo da Vinci and a Memory of his Childhood*.

> It was inevitable that this early history should have been an expression of present beliefs and wishes rather than a true picture of the past; for many things had been dropped from the nation's memory, while others were distorted, and some remains of the past were given a wrong interpretation in order to fit in with contemporary ideas. . . . A man's conscious memory of the events of his maturity is in every way comparable to the first kind of historical writing [which was a chronicle of current events]; while the memories he has of his childhood correspond, as far as their origins and reliability are concerned, to the history of a nation's earliest days, which was compiled later and for tendentious reasons. (Freud, 1910c, pp. 83–84)

In Freud's "remarkable analogy" between screen memories and legends or myths, he is appealing to images and idols and pre-literate records, therefore to iconography as a branch of historiography. There is no direct way of corroborating the associations aroused by early images, no *experimenta crucis* of factual accuracy. The emotional message persists, though no single fact about the scene can be established with certainty.

However, I have taken it for granted that the scene has not been set up like Doisneau's kiss series or a Victorian allegorical photograph. It is fading, and still in the world of chance and change.

Also, it still teems with allusions. The two boys in the foreground are both pointing. If we look again, we notice an unattached arm at the edge of the picture. There is a disembodied left hand, also pointing, and it links the picture with the world outside the frame. Whatever elements of memory and fantasy may be spun around the image, it remains part of an outside world. There is a historical situation, too, even though we cannot read it through this picture.

"... the child should know ..."

Examined closely, this photograph reveals a *mise en abyme*—a miniature picture within the picture, the small image reflecting the larger one. In her right hand, the little blonde girl is holding a blonde doll. Its dangling legs are exactly in line with her own legs. Her grandmother's right hand clasps both the girl's legs and those of the doll. The expression on the face of the doll can just about be made out. It looks uncannily similar to the girl's. Its left hand is raised as if to ward off a blow.

The photograph itself has an ominous atmosphere. Two small figures in an empty park or garden, overhung by dark foliage.

In many ways, this is the antithesis of the previous photograph, the little boy playing in a sunlit garden. For lack of any reliable information, that other photo could only resolve itself into general memories and fantasies of childhood. But the figures here are identifiable and this picture is rooted in a precise time and context. Like the strong lines of perspective formed by the wall and path, it concentrates on those two figures isolated in the foreground, the infant all in white and the old woman in deep mourning. An implicit question is being asked: what gets transmitted from age to youth, from generation to generation? Although only two figures are visible, there are actually three generations represented here. The invisible one, the link between the two sitters, is the photographer herself, the active element in this picture.

According to the inscription the photo was taken on 14 September 1924, when the child was "two years, one month and three weeks old". She is Angela Seidmann, and the woman in black is her grandmother, Freud's sister Mitzi. In all probability, the photographer was Mitzi's daughter and Angela's mother, Tom Freud. Tom was a writer and talented illustrator of children's books. (Walter Benjamin, who collected children's books, and her artist relative, Lucian Freud, both respected her work.) From the age of fifteen onwards, she had stopped using her registered name, Martha Gertrude Freud, yet nobody seems to know where her nickname came from. That it was male is easily explained: according to her cousin Anna Freud, she disliked being a woman. Since she once had a governess from Leeds and had studied in England, perhaps she took the name from "tomboy"?

Questions of heritage and upbringing and family bonds hang over these two figures in the deserted garden. The grandmother is holding the child with one hand and a black bag with the other. Her expression gives nothing away. Her granddaughter appears to be looking at some-thing out of the picture. Neither is smiling. The visible scene, as the photographer has constructed it, is a serious and formal pattern.

Later pictures show Angela happy and high-spirited. Anna Freud would call her "a little elf" (Heller, 1992, p. 131). In terms of family traits, that lightness might be traced back to her maternal grandfather, Moritz Freud. He was a fantasist, Freud wrote at the time of Mitzi's engagement to him, but should bring "lighter blood" into their "pessimistic self-tormenting" family (Fichtner, Grubrich-Simitis, & Hirschmüller, 2013, p. 464). Freud's casual and sometimes cutting remarks about his sisters have been enshrined in the folklore, often through Jones' biography. Tom's older sister, Lilly Freud-Marlé, in her memoir of their father, pleads for a more nuanced account of the relations between Freud and both Moritz and Mitzi (Freud-Marlé, 2006, pp. 45–48). Lilly presents her and Tom's beloved father as a highly cultured autodidact: "... during his hard apprentice years, he related, hunger for knowledge impelled him 'to devour' ships' libraries" (Freud-Marlé, 2006, p. 276). Because of his frequent travels as a merchant (trading, among other things, in jute), at the birth of his first daughter, Margarethe, he was in Egypt, when Lilly was born he was in St Petersburg, and at Tom's birth in Greece. As he had educated himself on board ship, he later set about educating his children, not through ship's libraries, but by travel:

> Moritz Freud often used to take one of his daughters with him on his travels, so she could read and grasp the living book of life with its many-coloured illustrations, its large and small letters. That was father's education for his children. (Freud-Marlé, 2006, p. 277)

Reading between the lines, we see a much loved and often absent father—as good a basis as any for producing an idealising attachment in his daughters. Tom was even closer to her father than her sister. She became his favourite companion on his journeys abroad (Murken, 2004, p. 80). Clearly, she loved her father deeply and was distraught when he died suddenly in 1920.

It was hardly a matter of chance alone that she met her future husband, Jakob Seidmann, on the first occasion that she left the house, a month after her father's death. Reporting the fact, she wrote, "Daddy would have been so happy ..." (Murken, 2004, p. 87).

Since he died two years before Angela's birth, whatever the girl might have inherited from him could only have reached her through the byways of genetics or through inflections of her mother's and grandmother's voices and habits.

In the photograph, Mitzi is in deep mourning and this is over-determined, marking not only the loss of her husband Moritz four years previously, but also—more recently and perhaps as griev-ously—that of her youngest child and only son, Theodor, drowned on 13 July 1923 at the age of nineteen. The boy had lived in the same house as Tom: he had been a friend of her husband Jakob, and he had played with their daughter Angela (Murken, 2004, p. 88). But since she was born on 21 July 1922, less than a year before his death, if she had any memories of this lost uncle they could hardly have been anything other than abyssal. Whatever else was left of him or his father could only reach her as echoes.

High trees hang over the figures in the picture and determine its mood, but there is a curious and complete absence of shadows. The dead, when they return, notoriously cast no shadows, yet they exert a constant pressure on the living. Mitzi's prolonged mourning, and Tom's record of recurrent depression are both woven into this picture. Both the visible and the unseen woman are still mourning their respective losses—losses that fill the air the child breathes.

*   *   *

The album containing this photograph is bound in brown leather with the name "SIGM. FREUD" tooled in capitals into the spine. It bears the epigraph "Berlin 1928" in Freud's hand on the inside front cover, which may well be the date when it was given to him. The photos begin around 1925 and the last photos are of the plaque ceremony in Pribor in 1931. In general, the photos are arranged according to family groupings, with a strong Berlin slant, since two of Freud's sons, Ernst and Oliver and their families, were also living in Berlin during the 1920s. The entire album page shown here is devoted to the family of Tom Freud, her husband Jakob (Jankew) Seidmann, and their daughter Angela.

In this page, the couple are seen standing in a street holding their daughter. The angle and lines of perspective replicate or reflect those of the photo in the park. Three generations feature in these two photographs, but, in a photograph on the first page of this album, a fourth generation appears: Angela stands with her great-grand-mother, Freud's mother Amalia, who was celebrating her ninetieth birthday in 1925, an occasion on which the child was delegated to give her a card designed by her mother (Murken, 2004, p. 89). Since she looks the same age there as on the other page, it is likely that all these photos date from around 1925.

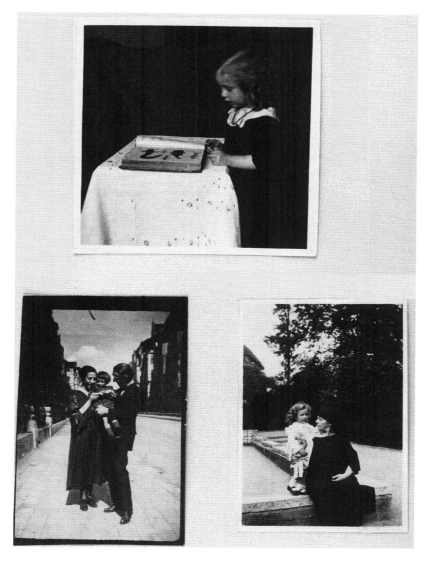

In the photo at the top of the album page, we see Angela (alone, still with her long hair) reading a book. Or, since she is too young to be reading such a weighty tome, probably just looking with rapt attention at the page of pictures in front of her. It shows drawings of fishes, and may be a popular scientific work rather than a children's book. Perhaps her mother was using it as a basis for her own fish drawings, since fish played a significant role in her texts and pictures.

In her book entitled "David the Dreamer" (1922), the protagonist is shown in a little boat next to a huge goldfish and a small seahorse. In "The Fish Journey" a year later, a large goldfish leads the hero, Peregrin, in his little boat to a paradise where fish and boy live together in harmony (Murken, 1981, pp. 176–8). That book was dedicated to her drowned brother, Theodor.

The children of writers and artists (or fantasists?) may have particular difficulties disentangling the image of who they might be from their parents' representations of them. Tom surely had some understanding of this: she renamed herself at the age of fifteen. Her subsequent career was based on sensitivity to a child's needs. But a child also grows up to need distance from the parent, and such insight and empathy might then prove an infringement of a certain necessary solitude.

In the two early books mentioned above, both the protagonists, David and Peregrin, appear in little boats. The initials TF (Tom Freud) appear on the bow of David's boat, indicating the drawing was done before 1921, when she married Jankew Seidmann. The marine theme continues in *The Magic Boat* (1929), and here the boat on the cover picture bears the initial TSF (Tom Seidmann-Freud). This is the motherly magic boat that carries the children in the book on their grand adventure. There is another, even more curious boat in "The Boat", one of the stories in "The Book of Fulfilled Wishes" (1929). It looks like a floating, trepanned head with its scalp removed. An eye and an ear appear on its bows, and it contains a child as passenger (Murken, 1981, pp. 184–186).

Fantasy vessels project an after-image on to the photograph. The old woman and child are positioned on the sharp corner of two lines of wall, as if on a ship's prow. Tom's photo casts her mother and daughter adrift on an empty sea.

*   *   *

A boat represents adventure, and a house stability. These apparent antitheses are reconciled in Tom's two delightful "Books with Changing Shapes"—"The Wonder House" (1927) and "The Magic Boat" (1929). Both books offer excitement ("for turning, moving and changing"). On the opening page of "The Magic Boat", there is a lively "new Wonder House" inhabited by an extended family: "Here in this house live grandfather and grandmother, father and mother, Kathrine and Sabine, the children Tobu and Hobu and baby Lookattheworld" (Seidmann-Freud, 1929, p. 1).

When a tab at the foot of the page is tugged, the faces in the windows change. A young woman carrying a tray in an upstairs window is replaced by a white-bearded old man with a cigar.

Did Anna Freud notice this oblique tribute to her father when she opened the book? From 14 September to 26 October 1929, Sigmund Freud was in Berlin, staying at Schloss Tegel, for a medical consultation with Dr Schroeder about his oral prosthesis. Anna was accompanying him, and Tom must have given her a copy of the brand new book when they met. On the page facing the house in Anna Freud's copy of the book is a dedication: "For Anna 30.9.1929".

It was less than three weeks later, on 19 October, while Freud and Anna were still in Berlin, that Tom's fragile world fell apart. It is easy to say, retrospectively and knowing her history of depressions and suicidal tendencies, that something like this was inevitable. It is even possible to play the game of fatality with this photo and read an oracular prognosis into its bleak shadowless illumination, like an overwhelming lack of affect, or to see the doll's arm raised as if in a mockery of futile self-defence against grief to come.

Tom's husband ran a press that specialised in Hebrew scholarship. It had gone bankrupt and he committed suicide. Tom went into a deep depression and was consigned to a sanatorium. Left alone, Angela had to be looked after. Since Sigmund and Anna were in Berlin, it was on their initiative that the child was taken into the care of their friends, Hans Lampl and his wife Jeanne.

*   *   *

These events were four years in the future as far as the Angela and Mitzi of the photograph are concerned, but they are now irrevocably part of that aura of surrounding time which makes old photographs uncanny.

Photographs may be the most real and accurate of records possible, yet they are cut off from the flow of time and alienated from networks of lived intentions and emotions. They create a space that the imagination fills with the pseudo-time of memory. Like Tom's "Wonder House" "for turning, moving and changing", photographs are externally fixed, yet internally mobile.

In the year of this photo, Freud published his own version of wonder: "A Note on the 'Wonderblock'" (*Notiz über dem 'Wunderblock'*, generally translated as "A note upon 'the mystic writing-pad'" (1925a)). Its question was also one of time and motion. How can memory traces that persist derive from perceptions that are fleeting? Using the example of the *Wunderblock*, a self-erasing writing instrument, Freud illustrated how the perception–consciousness system might function according to a mode of intermittent activation—perception traces being continually registered and erased. If perception and consciousness are indeed intermittent, this hypothesis might also explain how the body experiences time.

*   *   *

Through her father's death and her mother's breakdown, Angela became everybody's and nobody's charge in the family and wider circle of friends. Alternatively, it could be said that her abandonment infused her with a symbolical and moral charge. She stood for the atavistic demands infancy makes on adults.

One way of looking at Tom's work is to see it as a response to those demands. By vocation, she was as much an educator as an artist. Her concern was with what needs to be passed down from generation to generation and with what might be unique to each individual. Her earlier works are educational in the wider sense of encouraging imaginative activity.

Tom's last books, the "Play Primers", were aimed at developing the specific skills of reading, writing, and reckoning. Barbara Murken speaks of these books as a special genre, and they differ greatly in their nature from the earlier picture books for which she is best remembered. As primers, they are closely linked to school obligations and social constraints—the necessity of adapting and limiting the free play of imagination. This seems to contradict Tom's apparently libertarian ethos. In fact, their title, by combining *play* and *primer*, gives voice to that contradiction.

In her draft notes to the primer "Hurrah, we are reading! Hurrah, we are writing!" (1930), Tom wrote, "The old school imposes only a constant running after goals, struggling against others for 'ability' to do what the almighty adult demands" (Murken, 1981, p. 187). Tom's mission was clear. It was to do away with the old school and reconcile play and learning: ". . . the child should know that it is not stupider or more intelligent because it can or cannot solve all the tasks or questions it has been set. It is as if it plays a game to the end or not . . ." (Murken, 1981, p. 190). Given that competitiveness and achievement are inherent in traditional education, and growing up in general, this remark demonstrates the extent of her ambition, to change the established order by changing the attitudes both of children and their teachers.

Imagine that the low wall in the park where Angela is standing is the barrier surrounding a playground. The child is being held in balance between two areas of activity, two ways of growing up.

*   *   *

Tom's last picture book, "The Book of Fulfilled Wishes", which Barbara Murken considers her finest and most accomplished work, was turned down by her regular publisher, Herbert Stuffer, and was brought out only in 1929 by Müller & Kiepenhauer. It sold no more than sixty-two copies in three years. But while Tom was in the sanatorium, Stuffer wrote a final letter to her, telling her of the success of "The Magic Boat". In its first three months, the book sold 4,606 copies (Murken, 1981, p. 182).

After that first bout of overwhelming depression, Tom was by then back at work on the "Play Primers". She had started work on them before her husband's suicide. There is no way of knowing whether they were just done for money, or how much inner satisfaction the work gave her. It seems that Jankew had kept from her the full extent of his business difficulties. Nevertheless, lack of money was nothing new to them and financial problems, among others, had certainly been weighing the couple down. That, and its effect, are evident in the poem "Sweet death", which she wrote in 1929:

> The memory of sleepless nights has gone
> and of difficult days
> because of the hideous social circumstances
> and the lack of money.
>
> (Murken, 2004, p. 78)

It has to be asked whether Tom could really have worked whole-heartedly on the "Primers", even before her husband's suicide, much less after it. For all the effort to make them child-friendly, they are in the end what they say on the cover, school primers, that is, agents of the all-powerful adult world. There is little room here for the flights of fantasy her other work displays. And for all her own fascination with mathematics, the supposition remains that financial pressures must have contributed largely to their creation.

Tom's return to work on them in the sanatorium did not turn out to be a sign of recovery. The fact that she felt forced to finish them during her depression could well have contributed further to her inclination to end her life. Apart from the drudgery itself, there may also have been a gnawing realisation that these "Primers" represented a conces-sion, or even a defeat, in her advocacy of the child and its imagination.

*   *   *

If Tom composed the enigmatic scene in this photograph, she is also its pervading absence. The two thoughtful figures are holding each other, but each seems isolated or lost in their own thoughts. I cannot help viewing it as an illustration of abandonment.

During the winter of 1926–1927, Tom was in Vienna and had several conversations with Anna Freud. Afterwards, Anna wrote, "For a long time she had a certain tendency towards suicide, in her youth she once came very close to it . . ." (Murken, 2004, p. 90). If she was constantly resisting that tendency, then it is evident that her husband's suicide must have broken her resistance. More than that, it probably gave her both impetus and permission to submit to it.

Almost three decades later her publisher, Herbert Stuffer, sent Angela a manuscript he had found, which Tom must have written in the sanatorium. She wrote that she was abandoning her own work, her "Wonder House", "bequeathing" it to her readers:

> Now 1000 children are sitting and turning and tugging and observing the happy people who live in the full house. . . . and I am lying here worse than dead and sadder than can be expressed and more impov-erished than those who are cold and have no art. (Murken, 2004, p. 98)

There was a last barrier against suicide—her daughter. How could a loving mother (and all the evidence is that Tom was that) abandon her only child?

Tom had an answer to that: "The child does not need me, she will be better off without me" (Murken, 2004, p. 96). There is a perverse logic here. Tom had, after all, devoted her life and work to teaching children, including her own, to develop their own imaginative self-reliance. By abandoning her, she was putting her daughter—and her own educational theories—to the most extreme practical test. Obviously, this was not a *reason* for her suicide, but it might well have formed some part of the reasoning that permitted it.

Herbert Stuffer wrote that Tom's "Play Primers" were really aimed at precocious children:

> Based on experience with the upbringing and the first lessons of her own little daughter, she created them . . . for such children as already show an interest during the pre-school years in text, letters and numbers, that is, show an aptitude for reading, writing and reckoning. (Murken, 1981, p. 187)

Angela was more than just a guinea-pig for Tom's project. According to her mother, she was a colleague and collaborator: "The child helps too . . . we do everything together" (Murken, 2004, p. 91).

Out of her own unhappiness, Tom had imagined another way of bringing up children, an education founded on empathy for their way of thinking. Her daughter was part of her project. She imagined a child freed of its parents.

*   *   *

Even by her suicide on 8 February 1930, Tom did not totally abandon Angela. While she was in the sanatorium, Freud and Anna had assumed responsibility for the girl, assigning her to the temporary care of the Lampls. But Tom had an inkling that Anna might be contemplating adopting the child herself. There had been a plan under discussion to bring the child to Vienna (Tögel & Schröter, 2004, p. 60). At some point, Tom left explicit instructions with the lawyer, Arpad Eisinger, forbidding Anna from becoming her daughter's guardian (Molnar, 1992, p. 60).

A tangle of motives lies behind Tom's counter-plot, some imponderable blend of personal antipathy towards Anna with hostility towards child psychoanalysis. In 1926–1927, Anna had recommended that Tom should undergo psychotherapy, though she seems to have

had no great hope of its success, owing to Tom's known suicidal tendencies. This suggestion alone might well have aroused Tom's antag-
onism. But it seems their formerly cordial relationship was already
foundering. Anna wrote at the time, "Previously she possessed great
natural warmth and goodness, but there is little trace of that left now"
(Murken, 2004, p. 90)

The two cousins confronted each other across a divide. It is impossible now to determine all the causes of the conflict, though it is easy
to see that they would have had more in common when they were
younger. Like Tom, Anna had herself been a self-tormenting girl, and
she, too, had been artistically inclined, as evidenced by the melancholy poetry she wrote between the final years of the war and the
early 1920s, and which I quote in the previous chapter. However, Tom
had lost her father and Anna had found her way to hers. In their
respective work for children, Tom championed the child's imagination
and Anna wanted to strengthen its superego. Tom must have seen
Anna's form of child-care as active intervention, or guidance by the
"all-powerful adult". In death, as in life, she took her stand on behalf
of the child's freedom. That, at least, is one way of viewing her final
act of will.

*   *   *

After Tom's suicide, there was a period of confusion about Angela's
fate. Vienna, with its endemic tuberculosis, was not a good place for
a frail child such as Angela, Freud wrote. He and Martha were
evidently too old to care for her: Anna was, in fact, too preoccupied
with her own work. The child's abandonment was a mute reproach
to all involved. The moral confusion even infected Freud's grammar.
He suggested "a reliable country education" ("ein verlässliches
Landeserziehung") for the child. But the German grammar is in-
correct: the neuter adjective *verlässliches* does not agree with the feminine noun. Did he mean to add the word "Heim" (meaning here
"institution"), then dropped it, perhaps out of repugnance for the idea
of sending her to such a "home"? (Molnar 1992, p. 274)

In the end, Angela's aunt, Lilly Freud-Marlé, adopted her. The
family lived in Hamburg, then moved to Prague, where they were
living until the eve of the Nazi invasion of Czechoslovakia. Here, at
the age of only sixteen, Angela began her independent life. Her foster
parents and their son would flee to England. But just two weeks

before the invasion, Angela decided to leave them and to emigrate instead to Palestine with the Youth Aliya.

It was a courageous decision. Some of her daring might be traced back to her childhood experiences, some to the times themselves. There are many similar examples of children taking bold decisions independently of their parents, who, in the face of unprecedented circumstances, could offer no guidance. (There are certain parallels here with the fate of her cousin Eva, discussed in the final chapters.) Angela would adopt the Hebrew name Aviva. These decisions seem to echo both her mother's change of name at around the same age and her father's involvement in Hebrew scholarship (Murken, 1981, p. 169). However, if we see this early independence of mind as a posthumous vindication of Tom's educational theories, then it has to be stated that this was an ambivalent inheritance, having been acquired at the exorbitant price of her parents' suicides.

Her grandmother, Mitzi, meanwhile, had returned to Vienna after Tom's death, since she had no further affective ties in Berlin. After the Anschluss in 1938, she and her sisters were first subjected to the preliminary persecution of being deprived of their living quarters, and then, after deportation to the camps in 1942, of their lives (Tögel, 2004, p. 42).

This "future in the past" is the dark filter through which we are nowadays obliged to look at this photograph.

* * *

On the fourth and fifth pages of Tom's delightful "Magic Boat" (1929), there is a series of red and black drawings and a loose square of red film. In one of the pictures, a boy is seen lying prone with outstretched arms on a red sofa. When the coloured filter is placed over the image, the sofa disappears and he appears suspended, as if flying in mid-air. The red film allows the reading child to view the fantasy behind the fact.

On the ninth page of the book, we find a large grid with each of its squares containing a picture—a chaotic variety of animals and objects, birds, fishes, houses, cars, etc. Between the pages there is a loose template, a square card perforated with an asymmetrical pattern of square holes. When this template is placed over the grid one way, it reveals only pictures of birds; when it is turned through ninety degrees, only animals appear in the slots. Another turn reveals only fishes, a final twist only children. Flipped over, the card offers four further categories of image: nothing but houses, nothing but flowers, nothing but fruit, nothing but vehicles.

Through play and manipulation of images, children could learn how to create order out of the chaos of unlabelled perceptions. Tom's "Books of Changes" captivated readers by demonstrating how discoveries emerge from games. After Tom's suicide, Annie Jacker would write in the *Berliner Zeitung am Mittag* on 11 February 1930, "Her little blonde orphaned girl has inherited a treasure as her legacy, which, if things go right, will raise all the children in the world" (Murken, 2004, p. 99).

CHAPTER NINE

Portrait of a refugee

. . . fortunately to Barcelona

T his photo of Oliver Freud was taken in early 1943. He was fifty-two years old, a refugee newly arrived in Barcelona, and waiting for visas to travel on via Lisbon to the USA. Probably this is a contact print copy of one of the photos taken for those visas. It could be a rejected version. It is expressive, perhaps too expressive for an official document. On the other hand, identity photos in general do tend to bring out one particular expression—they make the sitter look guilty—and, from a border guard's perspective, any refugee *is* guilty, and of a crime against nature, because he wants to renounce what is officially seen as his "natural identity": his nationality.

It is an identity photo, like the portrait of Anna examined in a previous chapter, and, consequently, it shares a number of characteristics with that or any other example of the genre. In some ways, Oliver can be seen to be reacting in the same way as his sister did. But he is not an alien enemy, as she was twenty-nine years previously, or even an enemy alien, as his brother Martin had been pronounced three years previously in England. He is simply a man in a trap.

Until the visas he needed came through, Oliver was well and truly trapped, and that can be read into his tortured expression. At that moment, he was at the mercy of the various consulates and foreign offices that had control over his fate. The photograph represents their power and the camera is its instrument. Obviously, he has to face it dumbly, with apparent resignation, but we could deduce other feelings, as with Anna: above all, mute revolt against his circumstances.

In one respect, he should have been relieved. He had just escaped from Vichy France and reached the comparative safety of a neutral country. It was his second attempt to get out. Yet this is still the face of a hunted man, or, at least, of one who has not yet shaken off the threat he has just escaped. However else we might choose to interpret this portrait, it would hardly be in terms of happiness.

Yet "happiness" or "good fortune" (*Glück*) comes into the picture, restrospectively. In an interview ten years later, Oliver would use the word "fortunately" (*glücklich*) to describe his escape across the Pyrenees:

> An adventurous flight across the mountains, mostly night marches, and resting in prepared shelters or "*abris*". One was a charcoal burners' hut in the middle of the woods. Another was some sort of cattle

stall where there were all kinds of animal noises underneath me. It was dark. I couldn't see the animals. One could only hear them. There were calves and young cattle and ducks and hens, and in the end I got through fortunately to Barcelona. (Eissler, 1953, p. 54)

"... *und schliesslich kam ich glücklich durch nach Barcelona.*" Or should it be "luckily", or "successfully", or just "finally"? Alternative translations circulate like atoms round the nucleus of some hypothetical final reading. Whichever of them one might choose, in this retrospective account Oliver certainly shows himself to be conscious of his good fortune in having escaped. By no stretch of the imagination can that feeling be detected in this photo.

The same word, *glücklich*, occurs in another, more paradoxical context, in Oliver's (undated) draft autobiography. Here, it applies to the fact that his daughter Eva, who had remained behind in France, survived the persecution of the Jews. In the context of her subsequent tragic fate, the word can only look ironic. But that is not how Oliver uses it. The implication must be that, however she died, at least she did not die at the hands of the Nazis. That alone, like each phase of his own escape, each evasion of the enemy, counts as good fortune.

In Oliver's description of his own flight across the Pyrenees there is no mention of the fear he must have felt. In that respect, the Barcelona photograph speaks for him, retrospectively, of the inevitable fatigue and anguish. His report of his flight is dispassionate, almost dreamlike. Rustic details replace emotions—a forest hut, a cattleshed, the animal noises that lingered in his memory years later. It is reminiscent of some sixteenth-century Dutch "Flight of the Holy Family to Egypt"—except that in Oliver's word-picture there is no wife and child. He had had to leave them behind. The *passeur* (person smuggler) who was to take both him and his wife over the Pyrenees could only manage one at a time, on the pillion of his motorbike, from Perpignan, where they were waiting for him, to the mountain village where the actual crossing began. Oliver went first. When the *passeur* returned for Henny, they found that German forces had suddenly appeared at the frontier. It was over two weeks before it was safe enough again for her to attempt the crossing and join him.

These recent events are the background of this photograph. It might have been taken during that interval when he was waiting for her, and found himself entirely alone for the first time in twenty years.

If so, that might be one further determinant of his tormented state of mind at that moment. Another would be that Eva, his eighteen-year-old daughter, had absolutely refused to come with her parents and had been left behind in Nice. The parting had been painful; he had left in tears. The photograph is the aftermath. It is only 1/25th of a second, some time in February 1943, and at least a month later. But that split second can give us a cross-section of those moods and memories.

The refugee trail across the Pyrenees was already well trodden. During the later 1930s, thousands of Spanish republicans had trekked northwards into France. With the fall of France to the Germans in June 1940, the tide reversed. In September 1940, among many others, Heinrich Mann, Franz Werfel, and Lion Feuchtwanger, together with their wives, had all fortunately or successfully crossed the mountains on foot. Two weeks later, Walter Benjamin, having also successfully crossed and then been threatened with forcible return to France, had committed suicide in Port Bou.

It was all a question of timing. Any photographer knows that, and not so much the shutter speed as the moment chosen. The reason why Oliver had ended up crossing the mountain alone, and why Eva had refused to come at all, was because a previous attempt at leaving the country, in November 1942, had failed.

As early as 1940, Roman Vishniac, another photographer and refugee (and more experienced than Oliver in both careers), had warned him to get out quickly. Vishniac had spent years photographing the Jewish culture of the east european *shtetls*, a world he knew was vanishing. He was temporarily in Nice, waiting to emigrate, and in the interim Oliver let him use his darkroom. Oliver's family had been living in France since May 1933 and felt protected by their recently acquired French nationality. He had a thriving photo business in Nice: he was happy where he was. Vishniac, who had watched the Nazi régime from close up in Berlin and been interned by the Vichy government, read the signs better.

Timing can be a matter of good or bad luck. It seems that Benjamin, characteristically, turned up in Spain on the one and only unlucky day. A day earlier or a day later he might have avoided the legal trap he fell into (Arendt, 1969, p. 18). In Oliver's first attempt at leaving Vichy France, on 14 November 1942, the question of luck and timing was less clear-cut. Afterwards, Eva would condemn her father for missing the train out and their last chance of escape. He himself would claim that by missing that train he had saved their lives.

On that first occasion, they had had all their papers in order, transit visas for Spain and Portugal and entry visas to the USA. Naturally, Oliver studied the train timetables for their journey from Nice to Madrid via Pau. He worked out that, after they had changed trains at Pau, their next train to the Spanish border would arrive there in the early afternoon, leaving them no choice but to take an overnight train to Madrid. On arriving in Pau, already tired after an eighteen-hour journey from Nice, Oliver decided on the spur of the moment to avoid the discomfort of that night train. They would instead stay a couple of hours longer in Pau, writing postcards, and then leave by the next train, thus arriving on the Spanish side of the border in the evening. They could then spend the night at some hotel and, rested, travel on more comfortably by the next day train to Madrid.

Accordingly, they left Pau at nightfall. Half an hour from the border, a French official who had boarded the train warned them urgently to leave it at the next station. The previous train, the one they would otherwise have taken, had, he said, been subjected to a German inspection. Fourteen refugees, all with their exit papers in order, had been removed from the train and transferred to lorries, presumably for transportation to concentration camps. To avoid the same fate, Oliver and his family left the train at the penultimate station before the border, high in the Pyrenees, in "deep night and fog" ("*tiefe Nacht, und Nebel*"). They spent the night in a farmhouse and the next day returned to Nice where, for the time being, they resumed their previous lives (Eissler, 1953, pp. 47–49).

In this (Oliver's) account, his refusal to take the first train from Pau saved their lives. Why, then, was Eva, according to one account, enraged by her father's failure to take that train (Weissweiler, 2006, p. 410)? Did she not know of, or not believe, the French official's warning? This even contradicts her fiancé's account, and her father's subsequent explanation: that she had been so horrified by their narrow escape from arrest that she decided it was less of a risk to stay behind in Nice than to try again. Her anger, whether rational or irrational, is also part of the background to her father's expression, but far off and out of focus.

This is a passport format photo. Whatever hidden anguish might be read into it, what the face expresses most immediately is the sitter's awkward legal situation. The family had already obtained entry visas for the USA for their previous, failed attempt at emigration. These were still valid, but they were now useless because the next ship from Lisbon to the USA was due to sail only after they had expired. Meanwhile, their previous transit visas for Spain and Portugal had already expired.

In Barcelona, the Spanish authorities would only grant an exit visa once Oliver could show a new US entry visa stamped in his passport. However, the Americans would not renew the entry visa without first seeing the Spanish exit visa stamped in the passport. This was the bureaucratic vicious circle framing the object of this portrait.

The man trapped in the flashlight might look sad, but he, too, had his share of luck and the survival of the photo itself is proof of it. The picture, in itself no more than an instant and disposable identity, will let him free, it will open his passport to a new life in the USA.

"why the cuckoo continually calls out his own name"

In fairy tales and in the Freud family, it is the third and youngest son who turns out to be the lucky one. According to the pattern, the two elder sons will fail in their quest for fortune. This is how Martin and Oliver have generally been presented in the historiography in contrast to the lucky child (*Glückskind*) Ernst, although Paul Roazen, at least, has questioned this consensus, and tried to present a more positive image of Oliver (Roazen, 1993, pp. 167–196). The problem is that he has always been seen through his father's eyes. Freud started off with high hopes for his clearly intelligent son and these hopes were deceived: in a letter to Eitingon on 13 December 1920, he speaks of him as "my secret hope until he became my greatest worry . . .".

It is Freud who sketched the first draft portrait of Oliver, in the *Interpretation of Dreams*. On holiday in Obertressen near Alt-Aussee in 1896 when Oliver was five years old, he had dreamt one night of climbing up steps for six hours to reach the Simony Hut, an alpine shelter on the Dachstein mountain. Freud explains that the previous day Oliver had been taken for a walk near the mountain. He kept asking if the surrounding hills were part of that mountain and became more and more despondent when told they were only foothills. His subsequent dream, of climbing up as far as that imagined Simony

Hut, was included in the book as an example of undisguised wish fulfilment (Freud, 1900a, pp. 145–146).

If dreams, or the wishes that produce them, persist, that fortunate mountain crossing into Spain was over-determined, being both forced flight (in reality) and fulfilment of a childhood fantasy. In Freud's account, the fantasy is taken to be simple compensation for their failure to reach the Simony Hut, but it was surely more than that.

In the account Freud writes, "The children made repeated attempts at seeing it [the Simony Hut] through the telescope – I cannot say with what success" (Freud 1900a, p. 127). Freud is implying that the children may not have gained any certainty that this hut really existed. They could see the huge and incontrovertible reality of the mountain, but were told only that somewhere on its slope there was a refuge for climbers. Oliver's fantasy of reaching it would mean that its reality could be proved.

Did his faith in his father waver, since he had seemingly broken his word to show it to them? One reading of the dream might be that it repaired the damaged image of a father who had failed to deliver on an assumed promise, to take him to the mountain the previous day. The dream presented at breakfast was, in effect, the gift of the promised land, a blessing bestowed by the son, restoring his father to the heights where he belonged. Where they all belonged. Recompensed for their long climb, the whole family would be magically reunited in their alpine refuge.

His father was unable to elicit much of the dream, or whether the magic of the hut's name took on visual form or not. All he could discover from his son's account was that they had to climb up steps for six hours, a figure the boy had already been told.

In Freud's references to Oliver in his correspondence, the theme of numbers starts becoming ominous from 1899 on. On 3 July that year, he wrote to Fliess, "Oli classifies mountains here, just as he does the city railroad and tram lines in Vienna" (Masson, 1985, p. 358). Or, a few weeks later, "Oli is again practicing the exact recording of routes, distances, names of places and mountains" (Masson, 1985, p. 364). This sets the tone for how Oliver would be represented from then onwards in family references (and subsequently in the historiography): a whiff of mockery tempered with underlying concern.

When Freud was undergoing treatment in Berlin in 1929, he visited Oliver at his new home in Tempelhof. In a letter to the family, he wrote that the journey there was "forty-one minutes according to Oli's assertation!" Set against his earlier high hopes based on Oliver's mathematical prowess, the reference to that extra minute over the round figure—and the exclamation mark—tell another story.

But there is certainty and reassurance in numbers, and Oliver did find his way into a profession where "exact recording" is axiomatic. He became a civil engineer, specialising in foundation and underground work. Because of forced emigration, his actual career lasted less than two decades. At one time, he worked down Romanian mines, at another on the foundations of the Berlin Opera House, but what he considered the most fascinating project of his life as an engineer was the construction of a second railway line for the strategic Jablunka tunnel under the Carpathians during the First World War.

During its construction, Freud travelled to Mosty, the site of the tunnel, at Easter on 23 April 1916, to visit him. In his interview with K. R. Eissler for the Freud Archives, Oliver recalled their meeting:

> ... I remember a long hike through the woods towards a mountain crest, but I am not sure that we came up to the summit then; a visit to the town of Teschen, where we passed at the place where all my father's books had been printed – the big Prohaska printing plant; and last not least, he accompanied me on my inspection tour inside the half-finished tunnel, where we had to climb over several ladders. I tried to show him some features of our delicate work, and to explain the methods of progress in this treacherous mountain. (Eissler, 1953, p. 3)

The tunnel was a tube of stone masonry floating in continuously moving clay, and Oliver's task was to maintain its course and correct any deviations. The work was a struggle against insufficient manpower and inadequate equipment; against geological, meteorological, financial, and administrative difficulties, against wartime privations, and it had to be completed by a deadline of spring 1917. All of which his father probably learnt, but whether he was impressed we do not know. His visit had an ulterior motive, to reconcile Oliver to the failure of his short-lived first marriage to Ella Haim, and to urge him to undertake proceedings for divorce.

Their hasty wartime wedding was conducted in Vienna on 19 December 1915, while Oliver had two days' leave from work on the tunnel. The following day, the couple met Rilke on his only visit to

Freud: he was in Vienna agitating to commute his posting to an obscure north Bohemian barracks for administrative service in the capital. Unlike Ernst and Anna, Oliver had no poetical inclinations and was not a Rilke fan. Ella Haim was a medical student and had made it clear that she would prioritise her studies and career over marital cohabitation. The arrangement quickly turned out to be unsatisfactory, or the couple just as quickly fell out of love, or both. In the Eissler interview, Oliver was unwilling to discuss this abortive marriage.

Literally abortive: its failure became evident when Ella underwent an abortion on 29 March 1916 and, a few days later, announced her "renunciation". Perhaps Oliver's unwillingness to talk about it was because his second wife, Henny, was present during the interview. On being asked, he curtly dismissed it as the great mistake of his youth.

Tunnels and mountains. The railway tunnel into Spain which Oliver's family failed to enter on their first attempt to flee the country is now permanently closed. It has been converted into the Canfranc Underground Laboratory for research into the neutrino, an elusive subatomic particle lacking any electric charge and able to pass unimpeded through normal matter. As for the six hours of imagined climbing up the slopes of the Dachstein, it converts into sixty kilometres crossing the Pyrenees in 1943, the length of Oliver's journey from Perpignan to Gerona, and which he invokes mainly in terms of numbers in his interview. In normal times, as he pointed out, taking the train through the tunnel, it should have taken three hours, and that includes the normal formalities of the border crossing. Instead, in those extraordinary times, it had taken him five days and nights (Eissler, 1953, p. 54).

Two worlds exist side by side. The refugee has crossed over into a parallel time scheme and a parallel reality, its dimensions measured by another scale. The photograph, too, is evidence of that unreal state where to be yourself is criminal. The grim portrait photo could be transposed on to an outlaw poster—Wanted Dead or Alive.

It has to be assumed, that the inner and outer worlds are both in conflict and in collusion. Like everyone else, Oliver was fighting for his own life against destructive forces: inner anxieties and obsessions that drain vitality, indifferent or bloodthirsty enemies guarding the borders. Judging from this face, his battle was hard fought. This is the image of a man who, for good reason, has little faith in the world.

When Freud spoke of a mother's unquestioned love infusing the son with faith and confidence, perhaps he should have added that this love needs to be unquestioning. It seems that Oliver had his mother's love. Yet it might have been partly grounded in her sense of his weaknesses, and he could well have been aware of this.

When Martha learnt of his successful flight to Barcelona, her first thought was for Eva, and why she had been left behind. Against this reproach, Henny argued that, for her part, she had, in fact, wanted to stay behind with her daughter. Martha reassured her: she had done the right thing by staying with her husband, for, as she wrote, she could not imagine her son surviving alone.

Faith in reality is integral and elusive as neutrinos. It passes right through the ordinary matter of mind, drives that can be deduced or states that can be described. Traces in the photo's expression may be thought to provide evidence by default of a broken relationship or a loss of connection, or the expression may be seen as posing obscure questions. How do figures connect with the human world? How can we be sure words mean what they say?

In the spring of 1896, some months before the Dachstein dream, Freud wrote to Fliess that Oliver had asked him why the cuckoo continually calls out its own name. How words and things hang together is a good philosophical question and it is a pity Freud did not say how he answered it. But he did say he hoped Fliess's son would be quicker than his "to find out the secret of name giving" (Masson, 1985, p. 184). In that light, Oliver's question might be taken as evidence of retardation, or as a sympton of (neurotic?) anxiety. In his early years at school, Oliver was attracted by the dead languages, Greek and Latin. He abandoned them for science. As an adult, he attributed his eventual choice of study to an unconscious wish implanted in his childhood by his mother, at a time when he was particularly fascinated by trains. He should study engineering, his mother suggested, and then he could build railways when he grew up (Eissler, 1953, pp. 10–11).

Unlike words, numbers are unambiguous and their progress is linear. His mother's suggestion might well have chimed in with his own growing scepticism about his elder brother's poetry—or the unregulated nature of language in general. On his holiday in Obertressen that year, his father records Oliver's perplexity when faced by signposts sporting variable spellings of a local feature of the landscape.

Was the place really "Bärnmoos", "Bernmoos", or "Beerenmoos"? That means, should you expect to find bears (*Bären*) or berries (*Beeren*) there (Masson, 1985, p. 195)?

The place did have multiple meanings: it was already a numinous site in the family's mythic geography. They wove their own lore around that curiously named scenery. Oliver's daredevil older brother, Martin, later remembered a risky climbing adventure on "Beerenmoos" with his cousin; his father recalled its sensuously cool water; his mother imagined building a summer house there (M. Freud, 1957, pp. 55–57; Sigmund to Martha Freud, 12 July 1897, SFC). Unlike the Simony Hut on the Dachstein, there could be no doubt of this place and its reality in their lives. Why was its name so unstable? Oliver's eventual conclusion—"it's all the same" (*"das ist alles eins"*)— comes as a decision and a dismissal. He will accept the words, but only at the cost of disillusion with language.

Anna remembered that at some point during his later childhood, Oliver would occasionally have bouts of silliness, when he would distort words and talk nonsense (Anna to Sigmund Freud, 10 July 1921). There are hints of speech impediment at some period of his life, which may refer either to hesitancy due to reticence or to a slight stutter. His reluctance to speak of himself might be considered another symptom. When, in 1953, Eissler asked him for biographical details, his immediate response was, "Well, there is actually not much to say" (Eissler, 1953, p. 6).

In fact, there turned out to be a lot to say, and his saying began with his explanation about why there was not a lot to say. It was because he did not leave his parent's house until the outbreak of the First World War, with the exception of various holiday trips. One thing he had inherited from his father was his wanderlust. It was on a trip to Egypt before the war that he had met Ella Haim. (That he chose not to speak of this in his interview justified Eissler's suspicion that Henny was an inhibiting presence.)

After his youth, the nature of his travelling changed. During the war, he travelled with the army, from the Carpathians to Poland to Italy. After the war, much of his travelling took the form of economic migration, following work to Romania, to Saarland, Duisberg, and eventually Berlin. Here he settled for several years, only to be forced to emigrate to France in 1933. The flight across the Pyrenees was only the latest in a series of forced and unforced migrations.

The photograph shows an unstable subject in an unstable world. Let that account in general for his mood in this Barcelona portrait— any mood, however momentary, will be growing out of lifelong predispositions and the world around. In the background, the viewer has to imagine a social and psychological landscape of endemic unease.

This act of photography, it must be remembered, was far from innocent. The camera itself that took the picture, this instrument of political authorities on which his fate depended, in part determines his guarded, hunted expression. And there is that other, previously mentioned, aspect of his sitting for this portrait in February 1943: that, until a few weeks before the photo was taken, he himself had been a professional photographer.

On failing to find work in engineering after his first migration from Germany to France in 1933, he had turned to his lifelong hobby to make a living. His grimace for the Catalan photographer's camera, therefore, takes on an ironic edge. He is looking back at his alter ego and the agreeable life he had as a photographer in Nice, and from which he was now irrevocably separated, by time and the mountains.

In the summer of 1897, the Freud family returned to their alpine "holiday paradise" at Obertressen, Altaussee, the house in sight of the Dachstein. Freud himself continued working in Vienna, visiting them only at weekends. Before one such visit, on 24 June, he wrote to Martha, "Oli should not pull such faces. I will bring photographic paper".

It is only possible to guess why Oliver might have been pulling faces, or whether his mother had been unable to buy him "photographic paper", or whether that paper was intended as a threat to record his faces on film. We do know that from an early age, Oliver was already involved in photography, like his uncle Alexander. It was during these June weeks that Alexander, as the family "court photographer", was taking a photograph that, by its subject alone, qualifies as a melancholy object: of Sigmund and his sisters around their father's grave.

Both Oliver and his uncle were hobby photographers, and both were precisionists, obsessed with accuracy and passionate about timetables. Such character traits seem relevant to an interest in photography, since it traditionally demanded patience and dedication, technical ability, and even some knowledge of chemistry. But by the late 1880s, roll film, Kodak cameras, and popular photography had all arrived and a well-developed sense of order and a love of accuracy were no longer required. That still leaves the question of what obscure, and perhaps universal, desires are satisfied by freezing a moment of time and estranging a scene from its lived reality, and what might be the aim and gain in possessing that static visual memento.

Oliver was six years old, and, at that age, the past as such has no attraction. He already had a nature turned towards his future (and his future was a number):

> Recently my son Oliver aptly demonstrated his trait of concentrating on what is immediately ahead. An enthusiastic aunt asked him, "Oli, what do you want to become?" He replied, "Aunt, five years, in February." (Masson, 1985, p. 136)

What Oliver's early turn towards photography brought him might be the opposite of history or nostalgia. Perhaps he saw it as an effective separation from the past. Let it be framed, preserved free of confusion, closed off and surviving in indefinitely suspended animation. Or—another perspective, as viewed through a glass darkly, that is, through the telescope at the holiday house in Obertressen—let the photograph be the future, the fantasy we have to bring into existence.

"... the change in her vati"

Pictures fade into words. On its reverse, this little portrait has a smudged ink inscription which adds another dimension to these readings of its haunted expression. Written in Henny's handwriting, it states, "Oli in Barcelona 1943. [I am?] so sorry that Eva [could?] not see the change in her vati".

At first sight, this is baffling, and not just because of the illegible words. Being in English, the inscription was presumably written after the couple had settled in the USA. But what could Henny have meant in wishing Eva could see the change in her father? Surely no daughter could possibly want to see her father looking as drawn and tormented as Oliver does in this photograph?

The only way I can make sense of it is by assuming that Henny was contrasting Oliver's haggard expression here with some other, happier portrait taken around the time of the inscription. There is, in fact, such a photo, of Oliver in Pennsylvania a few months after their arrival in the USA, looking cheerful and rejuvenated, and on the back Henny has written "Pour Eva".

As for Henny being "so sorry" her daughter cannot see him, perhaps she is hinting that if Eva could see his sadness, she might change her (low?) opinion of her father. The comment draws us back into the triangle, and tangle, of emotions surrounding their departure from Nice.

According to testimonies gathered by Pierre Segond, Eva's problem was primarily with her mother, not Oliver. A close friend, Hélène Larroche-Dub, even went so far as to describe the relationship between mother and daughter during the period 1939–1940 (when she was living with the family) as a "terrible tension" and "unbearable" (Beddock & Segond, 1994, Part 2).

Oliver appears to have kept to himself as much as he could: Hélène Larroche-Dub thought he was crushed by his wife. Yet he could hardly remain a totally passive bystander in that conflict between mother and daughter. He would be forced to take sides and, as far as Eva was concerned, the side he took in the end was not hers. His tears when they parted were insincere, she wrote soon afterwards to a friend. In her self-dramatising account of the split, both parents were happy to have abandoned her. And since there is no earlier record of any problems with Oliver, this paternal betrayal must have seemed all the more bitter. Her mother's first letter from Barcelona, which Eva took as proof of her indifference, was full of praise for the city's cultural pleasures. And at that point, as she wrote, her father had not even bothered to write to her at all (Weissweiler, 2006, p. 411).

Oliver's face in the photo may bear the imprints of his recent escape. It may depict his entrapment in a bureaucratic vicious circle. It may reflect his severance from his recent past. But the inscription and its implications draw attention to another angle. Among the pressures bearing on him at that moment, one of them is a sort of emotional equivalent of the official *impasse* in Barcelona. Oliver had just left his eighteen-year-old daughter Eva behind in France; they had parted on bad terms; their estrangement was a counterpart to the lack of visas, and a correlate of his hopeless expression.

The legal situation needed only a little international goodwill to fix it and Oliver was lucky enough to encounter that. With the help of a

friendly official at the French consulate and a Portuguese-born representative of the American Joint Committee in Barcelona, he was
eventually able to extricate himself from that grotesque double bind
(Eissler, 1953, p. 55).

Family strife needs more than just a bit of goodwill or luck to
resolve it. Henny's claim that she had in fact wanted to stay behind
with her daughter, however well intentioned it might have been, is
suspect. By all accounts, she spoke French with a thick German accent.
Since she could hardly conceal her foreign identity as Eva could, this
would have been a massive hindrance to her survival in occupied
France. And given the "intolerable tension" between the two women,
it is hard to know whether to take her claim at face value, or just
see it as retrospective self-justification. Whatever doubts about her
decision she might have had at the time or subsequently, Henny was
finally forced to choose between husband and daughter. Her photo
inscription indicates how she attempted to reconcile herself with the
consequences of that choice.

Between its lines the same restrained desperation appears as in
Oliver's picture on the reverse. Perhaps, knowing the hopelessness of
her own relations with her daughter, Henny's inscription is enlisting
the photo as a sort of go-between in the relationship between father
and daughter. It is as if she were at least hoping for reconciliation
between those two, even if complete family harmony remained
impossible. That hope could be condemned as naïve, or justified as an
effect of thwarted love and self-denial. As in any family nexus, there
is no final objective viewpoint. The inscription does not resolve the
tormented image.

"sic ="

In the typewritten transcript of the interview with Eissler, Oliver's
account of the parting from Eva appears as follows:

> Our daughter, who was with us the first time on our failed flight,
> would absolutely <u>not</u> accompany us under the difficult circumstances
> and finally we decided to ~~hold her back / sic~~ leave her behind.
> (Eissler, 1953, p. 52)

The underlining is typed. The crossing out is in pencil. Two years after
that interview, Oliver was sent the transcript with instructions that he

pencil in his amendments (K. R. Eissler to Oliver Freud, 21 November 1955, LoC). To judge by the original text, it seems that Oliver must have stumbled over the final verb in that account, as indicated by the secretary's "/sic =", and then corrected himself. On receiving the transcript, he firmly crossed out his initial version of the verb. In theory, a final transcript should have replaced this amended typescript, but this version lingered on in the archives and with it this item of evidence.

Might Oliver really have felt that he had "held her back"? The fact of Eva's absolute refusal to join her parents is not an answer; it is part of the question. Why did she not accompany them in January 1943 when she had taken part in their first failed attempt to leave the country only two months earlier?

Oliver avoids speaking of her possible reasons. In his later accounts of their departure, and in the face of criticism from relatives and friends, he insisted that they had all been guided by reason and by concern for Eva's safety. The Pyrenees crossing they planned was highly dangerous, whereas Nice remained under relatively benign Italian occupation. Eva, unlike her parents, was entirely assimilated into French culture, a perfect Frenchwoman. She had a wide circle of friends and acquaintances and, above all, a reliable, older fiancé to look after her, and, moreover, one who was in the Resistance, a specialist in forged identity papers which would enable Eva to live under cover. Furthermore, the tide of the war was already turning with the Allied victories in North Africa, and there was good enough reason to believe she could hold out until the end of hostilities, when the family could be reunited. But all these good reasons may be taken as post facto justifications of a forced situation.

Was there no alternative? Eva "absolutely" refused to go with her parents. Yet, in her letter to her friend on 28 April 1943, she reproaches their apparent indifference, as if they had abandoned her (Weissweiler, 2006, p. 411). She was eighteen years old: it could be reasoned that in this awkward age between adolescence and adulthood, the extent of her own agency and that of her parents was shifting and undefined. She wants to assume responsibility for her own life, yet can still blame her parents for not having sheltered her from the consequences of her decision.

Elsewhere, Oliver invoked a consensus: "Following the advice of good friends we finally decided to leave her behind . . ." (Weissweiler, 2006, p. 410). Here it is fairly and squarely the parents' decision to leave without her. But the alternative verbs in the interview—hold back or leave behind—argue ambivalence as to the degree of agency and responsibility. Did he now accuse himself of having resigned his own responsibility by not arguing harder with her, by not insisting to the limit that she accompany them? In short, was he right or wrong to have conceded his daughter her freedom? By the time of the Barcelona photo, was he perhaps already regretting his decision (or his collusion with his daughter's decision) and asking himself whether or not he had, in effect, "held her back"?

None of these hypotheses can do more than represent those events schematically. Narrative does not replicate thought processes, it simply sketches outlines. Only a photograph can be accurate by saying nothing. And in general, there is a danger that this striving for accuracy (of dates, of situation, of interpretation) that infects this historical sketch might begin to appear mimetic of Oliver's own painstaking pedantry.

Under interrogation, his photo has been forced to speak for his actions and behaviour in Barcelona. But when images are converted into words, the unsaid always overshadows them, as effects of character unconnected with the specific circumstances, or as a free-floating anxiety continuing to haunt his portrait.

"a painstaking reporter"

Like both his brothers, Oliver found himself in his sixties bearing witness on behalf of his father's biographer. At Ernest Jones' request, Oliver had corrected various small printing errors and wrong names in Jones' biography of Freud. He began his interview with Eissler by telling him of a recent contact with Jones: "I wrote to him, I believe just 14 days ago, – or was it last week? – no, 14 days ago I wrote him a long, detailed letter . . ." (Eissler, 1953, p. 2).

This memory ritual—remembering a figure, then questioning it, then reaffirming the first guess—is a form of orientation and self-confirmation. If exact dates and numbers verify experience, it is important to know where one is situated in relation to them in time and space.

Both of Oliver's interviewers, Paul Roazen and K. R. Eissler (who otherwise agreed on very little) were similarly concerned by Henny's presence during their respective interviews. Both seem to have felt she might be inhibiting Oliver. Eissler even awkwardly suggested to her that he would prefer to be alone with her husband. But Henny objected, just as awkwardly, that she too was benefiting from the occasion: ". . . it is a quite extraordinary thing for me that my husband speaks about himself for an hour" (Eissler, 1953, p. 36). So she stayed.

At the end of the interview, Eissler suggested that Oliver return to continue some other time. At that point Henny intervened, and here it is as if she were almost contradicting her earlier wish to hear her husband speak of himself:

> Mrs Freud. It is bad when he begins from that, very bad when he begins with your question, 'Your life', 'Tell me about your life'. And we vowed never again to tell the horrible stories!
>
> Eissler. O of course!
>
> Mrs Freud. And he is so painstaking! It will take time!
>
> Eissler. Thank God! Yes, I mean an archive needs a painstaking reporter! (Eissler, 1953, pp. 59–60)

Henny's outburst looks like her revenge on Eissler for having wanted to be rid of her. Her quotes ("'Your life', 'Tell me about your life'") parody his mode of questioning. She then twists the "life" that Eissler wanted to hear about into "the horrible stories" (literally "murder stories"—"*Mordsgeschichten*") they refused to tell.

At the same time, is she speaking *ironically* of Oliver's painstaking thoroughness? Or is her voice even affectionate and approving? Any interpretation of tone of voice has to be conjectural, since my quotations are from a transcript and the actual taped interview in the archive of the Library of Congress remains closed to researchers until 2057. Whatever the tone, there is an emotional awkwardness about her objections that seems to have been characteristic of her.

Witnesses in Nice report that she came at things from a different angle to her husband and daughter, and that impression is reinforced by other accounts of her behaviour, such as Freud's reports: "For all her weaknesses and her clumsiness she remains always generous and touchingly affectionate". Or, after Freud's otherwise mild dog had bitten a hole in her dress: "She behaves clumsily with animals as well . . .". It is as if she were constantly missing the point and probably herself aware of it (Freud to Family, 25 and 28 September, 1929, FML).

The algebra of family life is complex, and Oliver, reticent as he was, appears in general to have tried to remain neutral or to withdraw from its tensions. But perhaps he was forced to find some way of balancing his wife's deprivation, a sense he may have had that she felt excluded, either from his parents' circle or from the relation- ship between him and his daughter. He himself was involved in that quasi-exclusion from the Freud family inner circle. He became distant from, or even at odds with, his brothers, for example when he had needed to borrow from the family to buy his photo business in Nice and in 1935 was subjected to the humiliation of an enquiry by Martin, the family financial expert.

In the period between the failed and the successful flight, his own family relationships must have come under even more extreme strain than during the previous two or three troubled years of Eva's early adolescence. In the end, it looks as if Eva either actively wanted to escape her parents or felt herself squeezed out. Between the mother's intrusiveness and the father's withdrawal, where was there a space left in the parents' relationship for the daughter to grow into, after she had emerged from childhood? This was not a theme either parent would speak of, at least not to others, and a slip of the tongue alone, in a language that was still foreign to the speaker, is fragile evidence.

Therefore, I can only leave this tentative thought muffled in mythological guise, and too hesitant to count as a firm suggestion. By staying behind, could Eva have played the part of Iphigenia, abandoned as the price of a fair wind for her father, that is, to preserve his marriage?

In another of her interview interventions that so annoyed Eissler, Henny interrupted her husband while he was speaking of Eva's subsequent life in France. In a whisper, she challenged his estimate of how long Eva had survived after their departure. Meticulous as ever, Oliver again stopped and reviewed his own calculations.

Henny's interruption had at least spared him from completing an unfinished sentence that could only end with the final consequence of his daughter's sickness. Instead of verbally and symbolically putting her to death, Oliver was able to turn his attention back to the pitiful brevity of her life:

> Oliver Freud. She was 18 years old at the time and a few months later she took a job in an office and during the following 2 years she earned

her living, until, as you surely know, towards the end of the war an illness

Henny Freud. (whispers) She only survived a year and a half, not years!

Oliver Freud. One and a half years? Not two?

Henny Freud. November '44

Oliver Freud. And this was January? This was January '43, that's right!

Almost two years!

So, at the end of January we met this leader, this smuggler, in Perpignan . . . (Eissler, 1953, pp. 52–53)

Henny was, in fact, right. Oliver's statement that Eva had lived two years without them was exaggerated. On the other hand, her own figure of eighteen months was an underestimate. Oliver and Henny had parted from Eva in mid-January 1943. She died on 4 November 1944. Eva's survival alone was, thus, around two months short of two years.

In this minor dispute over the length of their daughter's life, both parents were momentarily taking the measure of their memories. Out of love and pity, Henny wants to face the clarity of bitter truth, and that entails self-inflicted pain. Perhaps a different combination of the same motives impelled Oliver to hold on to the lost image by stretching the truth.

Seemingly overcoming his ingrained exactitude, Oliver stubbornly confirms his first rough estimate. Implicit in the exclamation marks, there is a note of triumph and gratification as he repeats, yes, she survived "two years", only adding "almost" (*beinahe*) as a sop to his congenital penchant for accuracy. At that moment, he is no longer such a pedant. Brushing aside his wife's objection, he grants his daughter, if only retrospectively and in fantasy, another two months of life.

In Oliver's mental arithmetic, these two months are only implicit in the subtraction of the real figure from his estimate. But, at another point in the interview, the same figure emerges in his estimate of his own time spent in Barcelona: "Then it took almost two months, a continual battle against international red tape, until we had all the papers in good enough order to be able to travel on to America" (Eissler, 1953, p. 54).

This echo resounds and invites Ernst Mach's question: what do these measurements actually measure? Perhaps Oliver's calculation of how long his daughter survived should really be applied not to an objective chronology, but to an emotional one.

The break-up of the family and Oliver's "fortunate" crossing of the Pyrenees came almost exactly two months after the failed flight with Eva in November 1943. But if Eva actually severed her emotional ties with her parents at, or just after, the failure of that first attempt (as her fiancé had implied), then Oliver's estimate of two years from their parting to her death emerges as a figure accurate enough to merit the triumphant exclamation marks with which the secretary punctuated the Library of Congress typescript.

These devious calculations engage in a dance around that other figure, the tortured lover of precision captured here on his temporarily thwarted flight to freedom. Only on gravestones is life reduced to exact numbers. These figures that Oliver estimates to measure his own past are, by contrast, imprecise and perverse, co-ordinates of an aura that cannot be put into words. They are outlines, preserving a curious form of life. Like the photo itself.

CHAPTER TEN

Her critical eye

A photograph is an image you look at, but sometimes the image looks back at you. Painters of Russian icons leave the eyes until last, because the moment the eye pupils are painted in, the icon comes to life. In this family scene, round a table on a verandah, the woman on the right is gazing thoughtfully across the table at the older woman. She, in turn, is gazing thoughtfully at the child. The child, turning her back on the table, is looking searchingly at us. It is the child's gaze that brings this picture to life.

In Andrei Rublyov's *Trinity*, there are three angels seated around a table. Every item and gesture in that icon, even the bowl on the table, is charged with symbolical significance. Without exegesis, who nowadays would realise that the bowl on the table alludes to the passion of Christ (Hamilton, 1983, pp. 137–139)? But this photo is no icon: it is neither symbolical nor allegorical. It is a profane image rooted in the disorderly world of perception. What it signifies is a historical narrative.

I wrote that the girl is looking at us, but in the historical narrative she was obviously looking at the photographer, and he was, in all probability, her father, Oliver Freud. Her gaze, therefore, relates in the first instance to him and in the second instance to her future audience. This little girl, Eva Freud, is the child of an amateur photographer who has been photographing her all her life. She knows what is going on, that her image is being taken and that it will be given back to her later in another form, as herself seen by others. What this photo of her captures is a precocious moment of self-awareness.

She is also looking out of the picture, and in that sense she *is* looking at us. That is, the viewer stands in the place of her future reflection, and she is interrogating it.

I first came across this image well over twenty years ago, when I was editing Freud's diary notes for the 1930s. On 13 April 1930, Freud noted that Martha Freud had returned from a visit to Berlin. Looking for some photo to illustrate this entry, I found two copies of this photo. The loose copy had an inscription on the reverse, in Henny Freud's handwriting: "Mrs. Freud in Berlin/Henny Freud"; the other was stuck in a photo album and someone, perhaps Martin Freud, had written underneath it: "Martha Eva und Henny Freud ca. 1930". It seemed reasonable to assume that it was taken during Martha's visit to Berlin in 1930, so I used a small reproduction as a marginal illustration for that diary entry (Molnar, 1992, p. 66).

Long before I recently went back to the image, it had already returned to haunt me once, and this was because of the marginal caption I used for the picture in that publication—"Martha Freud in Berlin, with her daughter-in-law Henny and her favourite grand-daughter Eva"—not realising I was arousing eighty-year-old family affections and rivalries. Out of the blue, Eva's contemporary and one of her last surviving cousins, Sophie Freud, wrote to me that she had always thought *she* was the favourite granddaughter.

I had based my comment on remarks in Freud's letters. But, as Sophie pointed out, she and her family hardly feature in his corres-pondence because they lived round the corner and visited him at least once a week. To compare degrees of love is a judgement of Solomon, that is, it involves the threat of infanticide, and it seems I had done just that to Sophie's own remembered childhood by arousing a dormant rivalry.

During their childhood, Sophie lived in Vienna and Eva in Berlin, and they seldom met. Years later, as teenagers, their paths crossed. In 1941, while she and her mother were waiting for the opportunity to leave the country, Sophie found herself living for a time in Nice and going to the same school as Eva. Eva and her family had been living in Nice since 1934 and she was by then completely assimilated. Sophie was an outsider and, on her own admission, less mature than Eva, and she did not manage to get close to her cousin.

In her socially precarious situation, Sophie was more sensitive than Eva to the advance of anti-Semitism under the Vichy regime. It had begun gradually. In 1940, the Vichy government removed penalties for anti-Semitic defamation and excluded Jews from public office, teaching, running newspapers or cinema (though First World War combatants were excluded). In early 1941, a General Commissariat for Jewish Questions was established.

Of the effects such legislation had on schoolchildren and teachers, Sophie wrote in her diary,

> They don't miss one opportunity to disparage Jews. Eva supported me a little. But it does not touch her. She does not feel like a foreigner and who knows, maybe not as a Jew. She is quite a nice girl, but terribly full of herself. (Sophie Freud, 2007, p. 223)

The entry refers to Eva's attitude in a specific situation, and it is that of a girl who had managed to integrate herself into a foreign society, and was now confronted by a "country cousin", possibly reminding her of what she herself had been, or might have become. It also raises the question: was the little girl in this photo already "full of herself"?

She was an only child, a difficult part to play. It means being the welcome or unwelcome focus of adult attention. How do you escape it? In the photo, she is the focus of her father's camera, and she has turned her back on her mother and grandmother. There is a sense that this moment was a lull in the conversation between the two women. Whatever the topic, the talk was literally over her head. Noticing that, I also noticed something incidental that had not caught my attention previously. Henny's inscription on the photograph excludes her daughter.

The inscription was in English, consequently written after Oliver and Henny's emigration to the USA. Perhaps it was intended just to note the occasion of that visit of Martha's to Berlin, without reference to the child or even to Henny, if her own name is taken simply as a signature. Perhaps. In the photo itself, the mother and child form a unit. The mother's right arm seems at first to be curved around the child's shoulders. Closer examination, however, shows the arm to be resting on the table just behind Eva's back. But there is an intriguing concealed symmetry. Henny's left hand on the chair arm displays a large ring, which is probably the signet ring Freud had given her. By this time he was distributing these rings, previously exclusive to members of the secret committee, to relatives and friends as well. Also, as if to reflect her mother's insignia of psychoanalysis, there is a tiny white band on Eva's left-hand ring finger.

This may be pushing visual signs to the limit, even to the verge of vanishing into the grain of the photo. Regardless of whether that band is a ring, a plaster, or just a blemish on the print, let it be taken to refer to this historical circumstance: that Eva is remembered because she inherited the Freud name, and that she was born into the house of psychoanalysis. The midwife who delivered her was Else Fuchs, Henny's sister and a future analyst, and one of the doctors in attendance at her birth was Freud's principal Berlin disciple, Karl Abraham.

Eva was born on 3 September 1924, and, five weeks later, at the first meeting of German psychoanalysts in Würzburg, Karl Abraham's pupil, Melanie Klein, presented the case of a six-year-old child ("Erna's history"). At the end of her presentation, Abraham announced "that the future of psycho-analysis rested with child analysis" (Sayers & Forrester, 2013, p. 150).

Eva would grow up at a time when children were increasingly under observation. And what are you looking at when you look at a child? If that look had been 1920s analytical, it might have been looking, as Karl Abraham was, for infantile origins of adult behaviour. Writing to Freud on 7 October 1923, he announced,

> I have something pleasant to report in the scientific field. In my work on melancholia etc., of which Rank has the manuscript, I have assumed the presence of a basic irritation in infancy as a prototype for later melancholia. In the last few months Frau Dr Klein has skilfully conducted the ψα of a three-year-old boy with good therapeutic results. This child faithfully presented the basic melancholia that I had assumed . . . (Falzeder, 2002, p. 471)

But if the look is historical, it wants less of the child and more of the child's world. It might be looking through its own adult eyes at this world, or attempting to look through the child's eyes. Somewhere along the line, it, too, is likely to encounter the melancholia Abraham assumed and Melanie Klein found.

At the time of Martha's visit to Berlin in 1930, Henny and Oliver Freud were living in a second-floor modern apartment in Tempelhof. This is obviously not the scene of the photo. Martha stayed in a hotel and during her stay she also visited her other son who lived in Berlin, Ernst and his family on the Regentenstrasse, and other acquaintances such as the Eitingons on the Altensteinstrasse in Dahlem. Any of these places might have been its background—if it were not for another photo which contradicts both Henny's inscription and my own previous acceptance of that date and a Berlin location.

After the death of Sophie Freud's brother, Anton Walter, his children donated some photos to the Freud Museum. One of them shows exactly the same scene, with the same background and table, but with Sigmund Freud, Martha, and her sister Minna all sitting around it. There is no record of these three ever having been in Berlin together at this period. I could only conclude that Henny was mistaken. After all, her inscription was written many years later.

The likeliest alternative location now seems to me to be Schneewinkel, near Berchtesgaden, the house the Freuds rented during the summer of 1929. It was a traditional alpine house, and that tallies with the wooden shuttered windows seen behind the table, and it stood by a meadow in the middle of thick forest, with a view of the mountains. "It is like in a fairy tale," Freud wrote (Meyer-Palmedo, 2006, p. 501, n. 4).

He was finishing off *Civilization and its Discontents* at the time when Oliver and his family visited the house in July. We know Oliver was photographing as usual because Freud commented after his departure, "To be added is that Oli has sent very successful photos of house and children. It is true, as a photographer he torments you a lot, but it comes out well" (Meyer-Palmedo, 2006, p. 502). The torment would probably refer to more formally posed photos than this example, but the use of that word stands as a reminder of Freud's own antipathy to being photographed in his old age.

If Schneewinkel is the actual location, then it is possible to imagine Freud somewhere off-scene, writing in his study nearby, or even standing next to the photographer. At any rate, he can be included among the adults looking at Eva, and here her effect on him must be mentioned, since it was so extraordinary.

When he met her for the first time in December 1926, she was only two years old and he wrote, "The strongest impression of Berlin is little Eva, an exact repetition of Heinele, square face with coalblack eyes, the same temperament, facility in speech, cleverness . . ." (Meyer-Palmedo, 2006, p. 451). Being in his eyes "an exact repetition", a *revenant* or double, Eva has to be categorised as uncanny as far as he was concerned. The effect persisted: a year later he was calling the similarity "more and more overwhelming" (Meyer-Palmedo, 2006, p. 484).

Heinele, the son of his daughter, Sophie, who died in 1920, was the love of Freud's old age. His enchantment with the boy was comparable to a love affair in its intensity, and, even more so, in its consequences. When Heinele died of tuberculosis in 1923 at the age of four and a half, Freud fell into a depression, as if that child stood in for all children and for life's possibilities in general. Two months before meeting Eva, on 15 October 1926, he had written to Ludwig Binswanger of his indifference to life and to his other grandchildren. As is the way with broken love affairs, recovery often comes through the rediscovery of the lost love in another incarnation.

What Eva's scowl in the photo might signify, or at whom it is directed, can only be the subject of supposition. But it is certain that the child bears a heavy affective burden.

In 1923, Sándor Ferenczi, who was Melanie Klein's first mentor, published a brief article; "The dream of the learned baby". Ferenczi referred the theme to the familiar iconography of the infant Christ. The wise child at the breast implied that it was wise to adult sexuality. In search of wisdom, the observer examines the child for insight into the roots of sexuality, and perhaps even for evidence of its impossible knowledge of the other side of sexuality—death.

In 1928, Freud was presented with a strange variation on the theme of the wise child. Ernest Jones' daughter had died at the age of seven. In a grief-stricken letter to Freud, Jones mentioned that, at the age of five, she had had an accurate premonition of her death at the age of seven. Not to be outdone, Freud replied that Heinele too had spoken of his own imminent death. "How do these children know?" he asked (Paskauskas, 1993, p. 128).

The question was left hanging and it hangs over this photo. There is a premature death in sight (in our sight, not hers). She looks as if she were trying to find something out from the adult she is facing. The wisdom of the child is attributed. This was something Ferenczi came to a few years later, in his paper on the confusion of tongues between adults and children. Whatever knowledge we impute to children must be differently conformed, they understand and use language in an entirely different sense. It is not another language, it is another world, and there is no way back to it. Looking at the photograph, the viewer tries to work out what the child might be feeling or what she intends to do. There is a difference about what each wants to know from the other. The child seems to be looking for missing factual information about the world. The adult, though well aware she or he is looking at a vulnerable being in need of protection, seems to be looking for forgotten wisdom, a lost experience of the world.

As far as Freud's new attachment to Eva was concerned, he took consolation in the fact that she was stronger than Heinele had been. Even so, his letters reveal anxiety about her health, occasionally expressed as doubts about her parents' ability to look after her properly. Freud seems to have viewed both Oliver and Henny as somehow inept, he obsessive and withdrawn, she physically and emotionally clumsy. Goethe's deadly Alder King ("Der Erlkönig") was prowling the forests of the imagination: the infant needed more protection than these parents were able to offer.

When she was no longer an infant, and Freud was already dead, that theme recurs in Martha's question to Henny; why they, the parents, had allowed the eighteen-year-old Eva to take control of her own life and stay behind in Vichy France when they fled the country. A parent's primal duty is to protect the child from premature death, which, for Martha, meant protecting her from herself or the consequences of her own actions.

As for those wise children like Heinele who foresee their own imminent death, Freud's question as to how they knew might imply the possibility of their having some insight, inaccessible to adult consciousness, into their body's visceral processes. The child lives differently with its body, closer to its own mortality, and this is part of the mystery the lay observer senses. For the analyst, researching the genealogy of the drives, the child is something like the missing link for evolutionary theory.

Eva was growing up during the "child development wars" between Anna Freud and Melanie Klein. When she first visited her grandparents, at their summer home on the Semmering in 1927, Anna Freud was just about to leave for the Tenth International Psycho-analytical Congress at Innsbruck. Here, she would clash with Melanie Klein and her followers, among other things over the date when the Oedipus complex emerged. Was it five years or so, or around three years old?

Eva was the same age as the real and theoretical children they were discussing and she, too, was the object of observation. Not theirs, but her own mother's, who kept a diary recording her development from her second year onwards. Henny was by training an artist, but had an interest in what was going on in the psychoanalytical movement of the time. Her sister became an active member of the Berlin Psycho-analytical Society, and she herself attended some of its meetings. Henny's observations are unsystematic, with much emphasis on language acquisition. As far as the child in the photograph is concerned, the contents of the diary are irrelevant, because unknown to her. What might well have affected her was the fact, and her awareness, of being under observation.[10]

In a certain light, to be seen is to be known, and, in terms of power relations, to be known is to be dominated. An infant is exposed, totally visible to its parents. Anna Freud and Melanie Klein came into conflict over the nature of those "parents". For Anna Freud, they represented the real father and mother internalised: for Melanie Klein, they were, even in the young infant, phantasmic forces of an already developed superego.

Eva must have been a wise child. She took to acting early, and that is neither hiding nor revealing one's own self. It demands control over what is shown, and an awareness of difference. Henny's diary even records her daughter's very first piece of acting: at the age of only fourteen months, Eva wrapped a nappy round her head and stated that she was a farmer's wife.

That was only an incident, but it had a counterpart a few years later. After her first term of school, at Christmas 1931, her class put on a show for parents and pupils, and Eva, wearing a headscarf, acted with great success, we are told, a chattering farmer's wife (H. Freud, notes for 9.9 1926 and 20.12.1931).

In the child wars that Anna Freud and Melanie Klein were fighting, the question of precocity was the key theoretical issue. In Freud's theory, the onset of the Oedipus complex would be in the fourth or fifth year. Melanie Klein judged it to occur much earlier. Freud tried to remain neutral, but could not help being drawn into the debate.

Jones had written to him on 20 June 1927, before the Innsbruck Congress: ". . . you say that you find Melanie Klein's views about the super-ego quite incompatible with your own. I would seem to be suffering from a scotoma, for I do not perceive this at all". For Freud, it was not the timing as such, but the implications to which he objected. He responded on 6 July that he was obliged to contradict Frau Klein on one point: ". . . that she posits the child's superego as being similarly independent, as that of adults, whereas Anna seems to me to be right in stressing that the child's superego is still the direct influence of the parents". Their respective approaches to child treatment were, in consequence, fundamentally different. Anna wanted to exert an educative influence on the child. For Klein, this was entirely incompatible with a real psychoanalysis.

Jones was a partisan of Klein, but he was understandably unwilling to go head to head with Freud. It was evidently in his interest to suffer "from a scotoma".

In ophthalmology, "scotoma" is a partial loss of vision. That term cannot be found in Laplanche and Pontalis's classic dictionary, *The Language of Psychoanalysis*, although René Laforgue, a founder member of the French Psychoanalytical Society, had helped introduce "scotomization" into the vocabulary of psychoanalysis during the 1920s, to refer to the hysterical blanking out of unwelcome impressions.

Because of Laforgue's later relationship to Eva—and his own subsequent oversights—it is worth giving a brief history of that term. At first, Freud had appeared to concede its validity, for example in *Inhibitions, Symptoms and Anxiety* in 1926. But when he returned to it in "Fetishism" (1927e), it was to polemicise against it on the grounds of a conceptual flaw. Impressions, Freud insisted, are repudiated but remain active instead of being totally eliminated as they are in the eye's blind spot. He left it at that, but Laforgue continued into the 1930s to argue that "scotomization" should substitute "repudiation".

Laforgue's notion of the blind spot would become an adjunct to his developmental theory of the perception of reality. In spite of the misleading title of his English article on that topic in the *International Journal of Psycho-Analysis* ("The ego and the conception of reality", 1939), Laforgue was not concerned with the philosophical concept or conception, but with the psychoanalytical idea of reality. His "reality" was an internalised construction or image of the world. Given his later interpretation of Eva's behaviour, this is worth bearing in mind.

It is even possible to treat Laplanche and Pontalis's omission of the term as a practical demonstration of "scotomization", for, during and after the war, Laforgue would become an embarrassment to French psychoanalysis. This was because of his attempts to set up a working relationship between the Paris Psychoanalytic Society and Matthias Goering's pro-Nazi German General Medical Society for Psychotherapy. After the liberation, he would be investigated for suspected collaboration. No case was proved against him, partly because his efforts to establish links with Berlin had failed. In his defence, he was known to have successfully protected numerous Jews and French Resistance fighters at the property where he was living in the south of France.

Eva was not among them. He had invited her, he claimed, and she had refused to leave Nice. He classified her refusal as symptomatic of her neurosis.

When Eva's parents had left her alone in Nice, Laforgue was one of the small number of people assigned to look after her. This meant they should be available for help and advice in times of need. But in Laforgue's case, there was a little more to it, since she was supposedly in analysis with him. "Supposedly", because the documentation of

Eva's life in Nice fails to unearth any unequivocal witness statements. Nobody could say for sure. After all, apart from the analyst, who witnesses psychoanalysis? Some, including her fiancé, were in doubt that she had done any analysis. Most of her friends knew nothing about it. Only one friend, Anne-Lise Stern, was prepared to affirm: "Besides, she was vaguely in analysis with him [Laforgue]". ("*Elle était d'ailleurs vaguement en analyse avec lui.*") But what is a "vague" analysis?

Around 1990, when I first saw this photograph, very little seemed to be known about Eva. In Freud's diary notes for the 1930s, she features a number of times, and in July and late August 1939 she twice visited him in London. In the very last diary entry Freud made, on 25 August 1939, he recorded, "Eva to Nice". Her death and his are contiguous in the annotation of that entry. Freud's doctor Max Schur noted the tenderness of the farewell to her, prefiguring his own imminent and final farewell.

While annotating the diary, I was concerned by the general vagueness about Eva's life, and, since it is her early death that watermarks her biography, by the vagueness as to its cause. In a 1945 letter, Martha Freud attributed it to "a terrible illness (brain tumor)" (Molnar, 1992, p. 263). In her biography of Anna Freud, Young-Bruehl reported that Eva "died of influenza" (Young-Bruehl, 1988, p. 279). Roudinesco wrote that the cause was simply "septicaemia" (Roudinesco, 1990 [1986] Vol. 2, pp. 173–174). In early 1993, Sophie Freud wrote to me that it was "one of those unsolved mysteries", but she had heard from a mutual friend that it might have been the consequence of a septic abortion.

Clearly, there was information around in the form of rumours, or folklore, and these are often precursors of documented history.

While he was at school in post-war Nice, Pierre Segond had heard stories about a granddaughter of Freud's. According to these accounts, she had also gone to school in that city and had committed suicide by throwing herself from a high window (Segond, 1993, p. 108). His curiosity was aroused and eventually he began researching her life. In the September 1993 issue of *Trames*, he published the results, a meticulously researched biographical outline, which resolved the question of her death once and for all. Afterwards, he published revised versions of it, first in *Les Temps Modernes* (1992) and subsequently on-line. In 1994, Francine Beddock and Segond broadcast a two-part programme for France-Culture based on the biography.

In this way, Eva's story entered Freud historiography. But Segond had first had to overcome his own misgivings about publishing. When invited to present a paper on his research to a group of historians of psychoanalysis, Segond subtitled it "A life crisscrossed by collective history" (Segond, 1995). He began his presentation with a brief apologia: he was not a historian; it was, in a way, his own history that had drawn him to Eva Freud. He had even been taught by some of the same teachers as her, and he had hesitated about publishing his research, imagining her life to be too personal and private to qualify as history. But Francine Beddock and Anne-Lise Stern, who read the draft,

> helped me to see it more clearly and to bring out the interest, both collective and historic, of such a study, and, in some way, to achieve the necessary distance to decipher in this individual destiny the metaphorical expression of the 'passion' of victims of the same tragedy. (Segond, 1995, p. 1)

His trajectory, progressing from the private story to its general historical significance, goes in the opposite direction to my study of this photograph. A photograph, too, has a metaphorical dimension, its relation to other images and ways of imaging. But to relate it to general history goes against its grain. Its uniqueness is the single moment cut out of time. As an object in the world of time, it is the visual world given a specific meaning. While trying to find my way into the subjective, pseudo-fictional domain of the experiences the moment evokes, I am aware that this strategy runs risks, one of which is losing oneself in a confusion of tongues, imposing premature meanings on the historical imagined subject.

By following an ascetically documentary approach, Segond has avoided most of the snares of biography. That is in contrast to a later, more florid account of Eva's short life by the biographer Eva Weissweiler, published in her family biography of the Freuds. In her research in the Library of Congress archives, she would come across photographs of Eva naked or partly dressed. She chose to interpret them as evidence of what might be termed optical sexual abuse by her photographer father.

That raises the wider question of partisan histories and the historians' transference on to their protagonist. Pierre Segond refers explicitly to the personal dimension of his biographical research, but he soberly restricts his narration to events and facts, and it is mainly his epigraph from *Les Enfants du Paradis*—'you were none the less happy because somebody loved you"—that indicates an affective involvement in Eva's fate. For Eva Weissweiler, her antipathy towards Oliver Freud as much as the pathos of Eva Freud's fate underpins her modish child abuse construction. In her version, his voyeuristic camera instigated Eva's premature sexual development. The implied consequence is that the effects of Oliver's photography culminated in her death at the hands of an abortionist.

The eye and lens of the photographer set off this inferred psycho-sexual drama. But his gaze has now, in fact, been transferred through the photograph to the viewer—or the biographer—who takes the photographer–voyeur's place. We are implicated in the image and the sense we make of it. A historian might claim to stand back in judgement on the historical scene, without being directly involved in the intentionalities of the time. But the interpreter of a photograph cannot avoid eye contact and the concomitant complications of transference.

As long as its story holds us, the photograph is haunted by the spectre of Eva's fate. That tallies with the sense of "This has been" that Barthes derived from old photographs, or the melancholy that Susan Sontag (1979) felt they exuded—the viewers' need to detach themselves from what is irrevocably lost. This melancholy translates into Freudian terms as mourning rather than melancholia (depression). Eventually, we will liberate ourselves from this image and find new objects of attachment.

And repeat that process *ad infinitum*? Alternatively, we could see the image anti-historically, as what Geoff Dyer calls the "ongoing moment". This would be to substitute Barthes' and Sontag's temporal perspective for an existential engagement. In Dyer's reading of a photograph of Charis taken by her lover, Edward Weston, that moment of mutual adoration carries a message that could be claimed for all photographs, "You are alive" (Dyer, 2005, p. 254).

In this photo, the scowling Eva is very much alive, and asking (us) questions. There is a curious counterpart to this moment. It can be found in her first school report, as copied out in the diary of her proud mother in September 1931:

> Eva is the best pupil in the class. Through her good conduct and her good application she is a good example to her classmates. She

understands how to enliven lessons with clear and well-depicted observations and nice stories. Her critical eye is constantly alert and thus gives support to the classwork. (H. Freud, 1926–1931, "Gesamtbericht", 30.9.1931)

Her teacher, the writer of the report, was Herr Lehmann. It seems as if he has benevolently co-opted the child as his representative in the class, almost a colleague, so that her critical eye can work and wake on everyone's behalf. His sympathy for her was reciprocated; according to Henny's diary, Eva had a crush on him (H. Freud, 1926–1931, mid-October 1931).

On Eva's return to school for her second year, the blue-eyed Herr Lehmann was no longer there. He had been made redundant as a result of economic cutbacks imposed on staffing levels. His absence grieved her: ". . . he was so fresh".

That summer, at the same time as Herr Lehmann lost his job and for the same economic reasons, her father was also made redundant. For a time he was able to keep going on commissions offered by his previous employer, but that was not enough. In April 1933, Goebbels' boycott of Jewish businesses made it clear which way Germany was heading; by May Oliver and his family were living in France.

The only child of refugees grows up closely attached to her parents and to their problems and anxieties. In Paris, at the beginning of the family's exile in 1933 (and, as if rehearsing what would happen ten years later and far more definitively, when they left her alone in Nice), her parents were obliged to leave the nine-year-old Eva alone one evening in the apartment. In a secret note to her mother, the girl recorded the anguish of separation after they had closed the door and left her alone:

> Then such a strange feeling came over me! Something that I can't tell you! Something like fear, I had to cry, but not for long; I put the light on and looked at the clock, hardly five minutes had passed and I thought I would not be able to stand it . . . (Weissweiler, 2006, p. 361)

Years earlier, her mother's diary had noted Eva's precocious interest in the forms and varieties of expression when she was an infant. Now her whole family existed between two languages and two cultures, with no clear prospects for the future and no firm footing in the present. The abandonment and loss that Eva experienced, and tried to express in her note, reflected the reality her uprooted parents were experiencing in the world. What is impressive about her note is its stylistic tact. It justifies Freud's comments on her quick intelligence and her mother's remarks about her sensitivity to language, for she refuses simply to define the strange feeling as "fear". She is suspicious of words and refrains from misrepresenting what for her was an unnameable sensation.

After a year of failing to find employment in Paris in his own speciality, engineering (a year of the humiliation of living off his father's charity), in 1934 Oliver and his family moved to Nice where there were more opportunities. It was here that his previous hobby became his profession: he took over an industrial photography business, which became fairly successful. He was able to acquire a second premises and hire an assistant. Henny found occasional teaching work and continued painting. Eva went to the Lycée de Jeunes Filles.

When Pierre Segond's account of Eva's life was broadcast by France-Culture in 1994, it was entitled "Nice, Land of Exile, Land of Asylum" (*Nice, Terre d'exil, Terre d'asile*). The city itself was more than just a background. It would become a living feature of her story. Her repeated refusal to leave it, first when her parents left and then after her fiancé had to go underground, would play a fatal part in what followed.

Russian and Jewish émigrés had been arriving there throughout the 1920s and 1930s and, gratefully or reluctantly, settling down along the Mediterranean. One Russian poet, Georgii Ivanov, one-time acquaintance of Mandelshtam, accepted that his half-life of nostalgia for St Petersburg was permanent. There would be no return: "The radiant sky above Nice has forever become the sky of home" (Obolensky, 1962, p. 390). During the 1930s, the Russians were joined by Germans, both Jewish and political émigrés. A week after the outbreak of war, Heinrich Mann married Emmy Kröger in the Mairie de Nice and gave an interview to *l'Éclaireur de Nice* declaring his support for the French war against Hitler. And some time later, a Russian Jewish exile from St Petersburg who had recently arrived in Nice, Woldemar (Vladimir) Mazel, would meet the sixteen-year-old Eva in her father's photo shop.

This was an apt place for a photo business, for Nice was a city of cine. In 1930, Jean Vigo had teamed up with Boris Kaufman, the Russian filmmaker Dziga Vertov's brother, to film a unique documentation of its life, *À propos de Nice*. What emerged was staccato and fractured, playful and sinister. In one vital respect at least, it matches, or responds to, *The Man with the Cine Camera*, Vertov's technically innovative record of a day in the life of a Russian city. It "bares its devices", as the Russian Formalists proposed art should do; that is, it self-consciously displays and revels in the technical means, the cuts, montage etc., which structure the cinematic illusion.

The photo of Eva, viewed as one isolated living moment, is transected by the endless falling of each of her other moments into time and history. It should be noted here that the fall which initiated Segond's research, the folklore of her suicide, did really happen, but not to her. The real protagonist was another child of refugees, Georges (Yuri) Brailowski, the son of Russian émigrés and cousin of a well-known pianist, Alexandre Brailowski. Yuri was a brilliant pupil at the Lycée, and he had just passed the second grade of his baccalauréat. Around midday on 22 June 1943, he visited Eva. After her parents had left, she had given up their apartment in the Grand Palais block and moved into a smaller place, higher up the building, on the eighth floor, just above Yuri's.

The two accounts in *l'Éclaireur de Nice*, one the following day and another the day after, differ. In the first version he came to beg a cigarette, sat on the window ledge, and fell out accidentally. The second version is more elaborate: apparently he told Eva several times about his intention of walking along the 50 cm wide ledge surrounding the balcony, to demonstrate his fearlessness to her. Eva entered her kitchen and it was at that moment he fell to his death.

Both are unsatisfactory. For a fit person to fall from a window as the result of an inept movement (*un faux mouvement*) is, of course, possible, but highly improbable. The second version bears the more feasible imprint of adolescent bravado, and even a possible literary allusion. A bright young Russian would remember the scene in *War and Peace* where Dolokhov, for a dare, drinks a bottle of rum while balancing on a high window ledge, to the envy of Pierre Bezukhov. But if the boy wanted to prove anything, why did he do it at the very time Eva was out of the room?

Obviously, the journalist was being careful to dispel any suspicion of suicide, or of possible culpability on Eva's part. The folklore Segond heard, that Eva was the actual victim, even had a certain metaphorical force. In her imagination, she could not have avoided experiencing the boy's fall. The first newspaper report on 23 June ended with the soothing formula: "Death was instantaneous", but in her mind the boy's final instants hurtling towards the stone must have been replayed over and over again.

Looking at an old photograph, we know that that particular moment, that specific person, is dead and gone. Our involvement with the image suffuses it with life, the illusion of reality. "Only as the image never to be seen again, that flashes up at the very instant of its recognizability, can the past be grasped." This is Walter Benjamin in his "Theses on the philosophy of history". The "photograph" that Benjamin conjures up is immediately obliterated—in a single breath, "nevertobeseenagain" (*auf Nimmerwiedersehen*)—as soon as recognised. In his baffling statement, the instant, a single glance (*ein Augenblick*), is "grasped" or "held fast" (*festgehalten*) at the very moment it disappears (Benjamin, 1969, p. 255, 1965, p. 81).

In Port Bou, where Benjamin committed suicide in September 1940 rather than be returned over the border into Vichy France and incarceration, the sculptor Dani Karavan erected a monument to him above the sea near the graveyard. It is a sloping tunnel through the rock, a stairwell slanted downwards to the sea below. As you look down, you become aware that it is impassable, sealed near the end by a barrier of glass.

After the boy's death, Eva suffered violent headaches, tachycardia, throat constriction, the feeling, probably well founded, that neighbours were blaming her for the accident. She heard that neighbours were also being questioned by police in search of her parents, who had fled six months previously. Her fiancé was still around and could, for the time being, offer her some moral support. But it was also in June that the Resistance organiser, Jean Moulin, had been arrested and the Resistance network in which Eva's fiancé was involved was destroyed. In consequence, Mazel was increasingly forced to leave the city and go underground. In autumn that year, he had to leave Nice for good.

In the aftermath of the fall, increasingly isolated, Eva adopted a new identity, Ève Pillon, the surname of the Grand Palais apartment manager who had been helpful to her. She had false papers manufactured by her fiancé, and moved to another address.

In accounts of the Resistance, one trope recurs; that it was often like playacting (Weitz, 1995, p. 246). Reports also speak of the solitude of this undercover existence. If it was a play, it had to be acted out in front of a silent, hostile audience. The previous year, Eva and her schoolfriends had acted Molière's *Le Misanthrope*. As Eliante, Eva had performed in the scene where Célimène rejects a life of social exclusion:

> Solitude terrifies the twenty-year-old:
> I neither feel the strength nor the grandeur of soul
> To take upon myself so daunting a role.
> (La solitude effraye une âme de vingt ans: / Je ne sens point
> la mienne assez grande, assez forte, / Pour me résoudre à
> prendre un dessein de la sorte.)
>
> (Act 5. Scene 4)

Eva was now only just eighteen years old and she was of a sociable disposition. When her cousin Sophie described her as "full of herself", she may be referring at least in part to her absorption in her social life, of which the amateur dramatics had been only one aspect. She belonged to a trio of close friends, a little clique with its own games and nicknames, and she also belonged to the Jewish Girl Scouts. (It was an international scout jamboree in Hampshire that was the occasion, or pretext, for Eva's last visit to Freud in London in 1939.) When Sophie commented that Eva might not even feel herself to be Jewish, she probably means that Eva had now adopted French as her primary identification. Yet, at the age of fifteen, she had even celebrated her Bat Mitzvah. Given her parents' indifference towards religion, this is likely to have reflected solidarity with Jewish school friends rather than pressure from her immediate family. (Although one other possibility cannot be dismissed: insinuations from Martha Freud?)

By the autumn of 1943, Eva found herself more or less alone. Her fiancé had left and, since she was now living undercover, she had to distance herself from any remaining friends in the city. All this at a time when the relatively innocuous Italian occupation was about to end and be replaced by the Germans under the notorious Alois Brunner. Having already totally extirpated the ancient Jewish culture of Salonika, in November 1943 he immediately began a systematic hunt for the remaining Jews in Nice.

This is all in the future of the photograph. The child in the picture was still at the stage of fairy tales. But she did not just have a critical eye, she also had a critical ear, and she disliked certain stories her mother read to her. In the diary, Henny recorded her antipathy to some fairy tales, such as *Hansel and Gretel*, and the *Wolf and the Seven Little Kids*. She found them unpleasant, discomforting (*unangenehm*).

A wicked stepmother casts her children out into the forest to be captured by a cannibal witch. What can be the meaning of such horror? Or a hungry wolf visits seven little kids disguised as their mother and eats them. This narrative education teaches that a mother may leave home and return as a devouring monster. Or that a child must learn to endure violence in anticipation of eventual retribution— the witch incinerated, the wolf's stomach ripped open to release the undigested infants.

Where do these fairy tales she rejected belong in that photo? The historian has to write them in.

At the school Christmas festivities in 1931, where Eva played the farmer's wife, other children in the class had acted the story of Rumpelstiltskin. According to Henny's notes, Eva had by this time overcome her earlier antipathy to fairy tales. This happened to be one that she had now learnt to enjoy (H. Freud, 1926–1931, 31 Nov. 1931).

In the story, the dwarf Rumpelstiltskin will come to take away the queen's child unless she finds out his name, which he keeps secret at the cost of his life. The story is also cited in Freud's "The occurrence in dreams of material from fairy tales" (1913d). There it serves as a screen memory for a patient's personal associations, and these include intercourse and contraception. Along this chain of associations, what the schoolchildren acted can serve as a screen memory in reverse, an anticipation of Eva's last year in Nice. Intercourse without contraception, a lost child, a secret identity.

But her secret identity was not betrayed. Or did *it* betray *her*? One counter-historical speculation drifting around her story is that her life might have been saved when she entered hospital with septicaemia, if only she had been able to use her real name and, consequently, been accorded preferential treatment.

In fact, in Rumpelstiltskin, the secret identity belongs to the dwarf, not the queen. When he betrays it to the queen's spy, she gains possession, both of him and of her child. It is assumed a little girl might identify with the queen. But to learn to take pleasure in fairy stories means learning *not* to identify too much, that is, not to identify just with one phase or one character of the story. The experienced listener has to learn a certain detachment from the suffering of the victim. An emotionally disturbing identification has to be traded for enjoyment of the games the story plays with its characters. Then the lesson can be learnt: that grotesque injustice may be remedied and murder made good—at least, in this narrative counter-world.

There was another fairy tale the child appreciated, the story of Frau Holle. An unloved daughter is forced to spin yarn until the reel is covered with her blood. Trying to wash it, she drops it in the well. The wicked mother orders her to find it. In her anguish, she throws herself after it, down into the well, and awakes in the magic realm of Frau Holle.

Because of its stillness and silence, I had begun by viewing the photo of the infant Eva as enchanted or idyllic. But any idyll is necessarily doomed and to view it in that light is also to read it as a premonition of all the ills that life can and will bring. Looking at such a photo now is looking down into a well. We see the framed figures floating on the surface of dark water, hardly distinguished from our own disturbed reflection. They are perpetually suspended, always on the verge of falling into time, falling *upwards* and into us.

The history unfolds. All the elements were there all the time, like death foreseen, only waiting to be revealed. The angel of history that Benjamin identified in Klee's *Angelus Novus*, blown backwards by the gale of time, never turns round to face a future. We live in reverse, folding up the past as we move backwards towards conclusion, the end of the story. But a photograph is not a story. All the historical indications that we find in it, and that can be stretched into narrative, are only side effects. In its entirety, it is not going forwards or backwards: it is a moment of sheer existence.

Speaking for this photograph or for this strange and familiar child, I wanted to evoke two aspects of the experience: whatever might be attributed to the child and her milieu, and how the viewer might respond. Even though Eva's role in history will always be defined by her abandonment and early death, the photo can be documented in terms of an asymptotic progression, never allowing that end (her disappearance) to be achieved. As long as the surrounding narrative continues, the image is continually regenerated as a living moment.

As so often, there happens to be another photograph of this identical scene. The characters are the same, and it was evidently taken within seconds of this one (Weissweiler, 2006, unpaginated picture between pp. 192–193). But its atmosphere is radically different. The women are laughing, and Eva has half-turned towards her grandmother, and seems to be giggling, or perhaps she is just confused. She is simply any little girl among adults. No trace of the prematurely wise child, no sense of contemplative calm, no premonitions, above all no link between the viewer of the picture and a viewer in the picture. A few seconds' difference, a different frame, a different girl and world.

Neither the sacramental angel of history nor Rublyov's angels come to rest in these images. The photograph only presents angles on history, various viewpoints as a fulcrum for our perception of the times. The documentation Pierre Segond collected and the witness statements from friends and acquaintances are like a series of snapshots from many different angles, multiple images that do not form a single coherent portrait.

During the final eighteen months (or was it two years?) of her life, it is as if Eva were moving around somewhere off-scene as far as everybody else was concerned, or as if she were just glimpsed out of the corners of their eyes. Without reference to the gaps between sightings, the documentation might create the illusion that she was the object of constant attention. But, as her friend, Anna-Lise Stern, commented, during this period she was not being looked after by anybody. She was elusive: we cannot follow all her movements. This saves her from falling prey to some exhaustive and seamlessly sequential narrative. It also saved her from the attention of the Nazi pogrom in the autumn and winter of 1943.

Under the Vichy Régime and during the Italian occupation, film had been thriving in Nice. For a short period, Eva was able to benefit. Her perfect French and her secretarial skills brought her employment, first in the unreal world of the Nice casino (a job bequeathed to her by Anne-Lise Stern, who left the city to go into hiding), and later, during the summer of 1943, in some secretarial capacity, on the production of Prévert and Carné's *Les Enfants du Paradis*. Here, too, she remained behind the scenes.

The title of the film could be translated as *The Children of Paradise*, or *The Children of the Gods*. It can be taken to refer both to the actors themselves and to their audience up in the cheapest seats, the "gods" (*paradis*). The completed film, which Eva would not live to see, is a classic of self-reflexive cinema. It glorifies what literalists consider the unreality of theatre, and celebrates the grace and humour of actors who have the courage to make that frail reality their life. It is a pity that Eva, with her acting experience, was not offered some small part, if only in one of the many crowd scenes. Or perhaps she was, and nobody has yet identified a split-second appearance? Alternatively, perhaps she was offered a part and refused it because she had to lie low.

One crossover effect of associating Rublyov's *Trinity* with this photograph is that I read into it an air of compassion, emanating from the two women behind her. This affection and concern is unfocused, passing over the head and behind the back of the worried girl between them, as if she were on another plane of reality.

To do this is, retrospectively, to read into the photo an emotional scenario that was played out over the decade following Eva's final visit to the Freuds in London. It was a correspondence/conversation between Martha and Henny about Eva that continued long after her death, both women attempting to explain to themselves what had happened to the girl and what had gone wrong.

Neither Henny nor Martha could accept fate, inevitability, or historical necessity as an "explanation". To do so would have been to abandon the past and let go of Eva for a second time. While the memory was alive, there was the necessity of conjuring her image up as she could have been, as she might have been if some mistake that they wished they could detect had not been made. If the past cannot be corrected, it must at least be understood.

But that statement is itself a misunderstanding of what it might mean to understand the past. Each version of the past is a correction. The two women in the background, by their viewing and reviewing of Eva's fate for years after her death, by their refusal to accept the inevitability of events, were contesting the idea that a death cannot be undone. If history is Benjamin's "moment of danger", it is grasped in the instant before a fact or a death can be set in stone, in the space between imagination and reality.

Martha and Henny were not the only ones concerned with writing, or rewriting, Eva's story. In February 1945, Princess Marie Bonaparte returned to France after four years of enforced exile. On 2 March 1945, René Laforgue wrote her a letter that included the following account of Eva's fate:

As far as Eva Freud is concerned, I committed her to Stern's care for a treatment that was very difficult under the circumstances, given her neurosis which prevented her from following any advice at all. She never wanted to leave Nice, despite our efforts to send her with Stern and his family to our property of Tourtour in the Haut-Var, which served as a refuge to a number of people whom we took under our protection. She died on 4th November in Marseille, where she had been operated for a cerebral abcess that was the consequence of an infection caused by an abortion procedure. She was engaged to a fine fellow who is now in Paris. He knew nothing of the drama; it was someone else, an academically qualified teacher who appears to have been responsible, whereas he was no more than the instrument of poor Eva's neurosis. . . . I will give you the details of this obscure and poignant drama when I have the opportunity of seeing you again. (René Laforgue–Marie Bonaparte, 2.3.1945, LoC)

Thanks to Pierre Segond, the details of her hospital treatment have now passed into the historiography. But it is a pity Laforgue never passed on the details he promised the Princess. In the context of the letter, the promise itself looks rather like a bait to secure her attention. Eva's story was incidental. Knowing that he was under attack as a collaborator, he urgently needed to argue his own case to her in person.

The letter is vague, too, about her treatment. Segond points out that if Laforgue did carry out a psychoanalysis, it could only have been brief, since he was very soon to consign her, as he says, to the care of his pupil, Henri Stern. According to Stern's wife, this was Laforgue's way of relieving himself of a "guardianship" that had become onerous. (He had his own troubles, a wife who was unwell and a handicapped child, a daughter named Ève with Down's syndrome.) But Stern, too, was soon forced to leave the Nice area and take refuge in the country.

During the winter of 1943–1944, there could have been no treatment and no guardians to take care of her. Mazel had totally disappeared and no communication with him was possible. She was living in solitude and constant danger. It was then she met a mathematics teacher twice her age. Under the circumstances, it is unsurprising that she should have had an affair, even though she remained emotionally attached to Mazel. The abortion, which the teacher arranged and paid for, was her initiative, an act of belated loyalty to her fiancé.

Almost the first thing that struck Freud about the infant Eva was her force of character. Perhaps that too could be read into the coal-black eyes that look out of the photograph. But in his letter, Laforgue interprets her will, as manifested in her wilful refusal to follow his advice, as a symptom. He dismisses her affair with the teacher as no more than the effect of her neurosis. In this version, Eva's will is an instrument to manipulate others, presumably in order to maintain conditions for preserving the neurosis.

In his paper "The ego and the conception of reality" (1939), Laforgue again argued for "scotomization" as an alternative to Freud's "repudiation", and in favour of a type of ego psychology. Conceptions of reality are variable, he insisted, and an ego with less libido at its disposal will form a different, more primitive, conception than might be expected from an adult in this civilisation. "It [the ego] will there-fore exhibit, from our point of view, a true 'scotoma' in its mental field of vision as regards the perception or the conception of reality in our sense of the term" (Laforgue, 1939, p. 403).

The perspectivism here is explicit—"reality in our sense of the term". The problem begins when "reality" imperceptibly slips out of its inverted commas. A defect is ascribed to the other's field of vision. But the observer's normative viewpoint is also suffering from a scotoma—the failure to put themselves into the picture.

Once again, there is a confusion of tongues, or a clash of defini-tions. Inner reality expressed in the language of symptom is at odds with the language of social reality. Laforgue's failure to situate any effective interface between the two also characterises his judgement of Eva's behaviour, as reported by Anne-Lise Stern:

> But Laforgue's testimony has to be treated with caution, for he was never very clear about this history . . . He said of us: 'You are all in revolt . . .!' . . . he is in fact the psychoanalyst in question, who '. . . assured me that my arrest should be attributed to my fundamen-tal masochism, just as the death under abject conditions of Freud's granddaughter Eva was attributable to hers'. (Telephone conversation: Anne-Lise Stern with Pierre Segond, 10.4.1991)

But who *was* clear about Eva's story? In her correspondence with Henny, Martha Freud struggled to come to terms with the girl's death. Knowing how much was attributable to Eva's interminable conflict with her mother, she wondered: could it all have been fixed if Anna had only have been brought in at the right time to mediate? In fact, the last opportunity Eva would have had to consult Anna was during her visit to London in August 1939. After that, distance and the war disposed of any realistic opportunity for any such intervention. However, the question by then was no longer one of realism.

While Eva's family situation worsened, for Anna the war brought with it the culmination of her own war with Melanie Klein, in the form of the "Controversial Discussions", the debate in the British Psycho-Analytical Society that was, in part, over her and Melanie Klein's respective theories of infant development. According to the folklore of psychoanalysis, the discussions sometimes became so heated that participants were unaware of, or chose to disregard, air raid warnings, and carried on arguing while bombs rained on London. True or not, the story survives because it neatly illustrates the clash between a war inside and a war outside. The discussions would end in a compromise, a gentlewomen's agreement to differ. But even if these controversial discussions had in fact been terminated by a German bomb, there would have been no final settlement of the question of which language must prevail, that of historical circumstances or inner reality.

Just where the voice is situated, in a continuum of inner and outer worlds, might be seen as a question of style or scientific orientation. In the last resort, it could be termed a question of faith.

What continued to trouble Martha was the knowledge that on her deathbed Eva converted to Catholicism and was baptised Eva-Maria. Not knowing that Mazel was a Russian Jew and a non-believer, Martha first thought that it might have been due to pressure from him. She might even have been projecting on to her granddaughter a distant conflict from the time of her own engagement. Under pressure from Freud to conform to his idea of her, she had, nevertheless, managed to preserve her identity. As she was non-practising, the question of her faith remains unclear. It is possible to imagine her as a sort of Marrano in his secular household, but she could well have shared his attitude towards Catholicism. Even as late as 1937, Freud told Laforgue that his true enemy was not Nazism, but the Catholic church (Molnar, 1992, p. 291). Martha had spent a lifetime with him under the shadow of the Austrian church and its potential or actual anti-Semitism. Eva's deathbed baptism was incomprehensible to her.

In 1945, she wrote, "It is obviously absurd to rack my brains about it even now, but I would dearly like to have some clarity about it" (Weissweiler, 2006, p. 416).

For years after her daughter's death, Henny was tormented by her inability to arrive at a clear image of Eva. She continued to hope that knowledge of more historical details might alleviate her mourning. In 1950, she wrote to Anna Freud, "It seems to me that it would do me good to see more clearly, if I had the opportunity of finding out something factual about Eva's illness before the final septic sickness . . ." (Weissweiler, 2006, p. 417).

What Henny was also looking for was clarity. The previous illness she refers to was Eva's neurosis. Scraps of new information about her daughter had been reaching her; about headaches her daughter had suffered which she had kept secret from her parents, or about what a teacher had considered a pathological obsession with numbers. She had also found out that the focal point of Eva's septicaemia had been a cerebral ulcer. This made her wonder whether there might not have been a previous somatic cause for Eva's headaches and psychological troubles; or an inheritance—whether the number obsession should be attributed to Oliver's mathematical precision. It is as if Henny felt these factors might all be combined into a coherent picture of her daughter that would make sense for her of the past.

She was hurt that her daughter had concealed so much from her, and that she might never have truly known or possessed her. And she, too, was concerned about the conversion to Catholicism. Martha probably saw it as disloyalty to origins and rejection of family bonds. For Henny, it was also a question of rejection. And not only was it, in her case, a far more intimate rejection, but she felt that the memory of her daughter had been monopolised or abducted by the unknown Catholic priests who were the last to see her alive. The problem she faced was how to repossess, or take possession of, a viable image. In her letter to Anna, she continued,

> I am so sorry that no trace of remembrance of such an attractive and clever person as Eva should remain, except in the memory of some catholic priests . . ., and I wondered whether the photograph that she took that time of the house with Papa and you, and which must be the last one of Papa, could be used some time in a biography, mentioning Eva's name. A tiny little place next to her immortal grandfather. (Weissweiler, 2006, p. 417)

Henny's modest hope of claiming her daughter's small place in history through her connection to Freud could be reaffirmed as a statement of a general historical imperative, of linking memory to memory, and life to life.

As for her suggestion of how her daughter's memory might be preserved, it seems to me nothing less than a flash of inspiration: that Eva, the object of so many photographs, of so much observation, of so many subsequent attempts to see her clearly, should, in the end, be remembered as a seeing eye, an invisible witness, a photographer.

NOTES

1. In Hirschmüller (2005, p. 299) this photo is captioned "ca.1929 (Berchtesgaden, Schneewinkel)". The dating, hence also the location, are clearly erroneous in the light of the photograph's internal evidence. I should add: my correction is offered in a spirit of gratitude for this excellent edition of the Freud–Minna correspondence. This chapter could not have been written without that work and I am further indebted to Professor Hirschmüller for his generous assistance during its writing.

2. It is an unfortunate irony that the photo identified as Ignaz Schönberg in E. Freud, L. Freud & Grubrich-Simitis, 1978, Pl. 64 and in Hirschmüller, 2005, p. 65 appears to be the young Eli Bernays (compare photos, Hirschmüller, 2005, p. 65 & p. 153). No photo of Schönberg has yet been identified.

3. Cited from a 10pp MS. attached to the letter from W. Ernest Freud to Richard Wells 18.12.1987 and entitled, "Detlef Berthelsen: 'Alltag bei Familie Freud: Die Erinnerungen der Paula Fichtl'" (Hoffman & Campe, 1987). "Provisional List of <u>Errors of Fact</u>" p. 5 of MS. (Comment on p. 43 of book.) Hanns Lange Papers. FML.

4. "tachtel machtel" (=Techtelmechtel)—a secret affair. "Washlappen" (=Waschlappen)—spineless person. Cited from: A. W. Freud to Henry S. Bondi, 13.7.1987. Hanns Lange Papers, FML.

5. See Roith (2008). Roith argues that the spectre of scientific racism was an important factor in impelling Freud to abandon heredity and degeneration in favour of his more universally valid sexual aetiology of neuroses. See also: Makari, 2008, p. 37.

6. It is true Freud had to shave at least part of his face for certain of the operations on his jaw, but this was hardly a matter of choice. He would remain beardless long enough for the artist Max Oppenheimer (known as Mopp) to paint his now almost unrecognisable portrait.

7. "eine tiefe verstehende harmonische Freundschaft." Cited from a note in Rosa's handwriting, appended to a letter from her brother (Freud to Rosa Freud, 3.4.1884, LoC). Rosa states that Emanuel had offered her help should she ever encounter "trouble" (in English in the original).

8. Account from the notes by Fred Hartwig (husband of Philipp Freud's daughter, Polly) attached to the Sam Freud correspondence at the John Rylands Library, Manchester. This and the preceding newspaper account are quoted from Thomas Roberts' editorial introduction to the Sigmund Freud–Sam Freud correspondence (Roberts, publication pending. Typescript FML).

9. Records of official discussions show that this, too, was a disputed term. Professor Norman Bentwich wanted to introduce the category of "friendly alien". That was rejected by Sir Herbert Emerson, the High Commissioner for Refugees. However, he did advise avoiding the term "enemy alien", except on very formal documents (see Public Record Office, HO 45/23514).

10. A copy of a seven-page extract from this diary was sent by the owner to the Freud Museum London. Subsequent attempts to contact the owner were unsuccessful.

REFERENCES

Note

Where foreign language sources are referenced, translations in the text are my own.

Archives

FML = Archive, Freud Museum London.
LoC = Freud Archives, Library of Congress, Washington.
SFC = Sigmund Freud Copyrights Archive, Albert Sloman Library, University of Essex.

Andersson, O. (1962). *Studies in the Prehistory of Psychoanalysis: The Etiology of Psychoneuroses and some Related Themes in Sigmund Freud's Scientific Writings and Letters 1886–1896*. Stockholm: Svenksa Bokförlaget.

Andreas-Salomé, L. (1999). *Russland mit Rainer: Tagebuch der Reise mit Raine Maria Rilke im Jahre 1900*. S. Michaud (Ed.). Marbach: Deutsche Schillergesellschaft.

Arendt, H. (1969). Introduction. In: Benjamin, W. *Illuminations*, H. Zorn (Trans.). New York: Schocken.

Beddock, F., & Segond, P. (1994). *Eva Freud, 1924–1944: Nice Terre d'exil, Terre d'asile*. Emission radiophonique diffusée sur France-Culture. Part 1: 3.11.1994. Part 2: 10.11.1994. (Audio cassette.)

Benedikt, M. (1894). *Hypnotismus und Suggestion; eine klinisch-psychologische Studie*. Leipzig und Wien: M. Breitenstein.

Benjamin, W. (1965). *Zur Kritik der Gewalt und andere Aufsätze*. Frankfurt: Suhrkamp.

Benjamin, W. (1969). *Illuminations*, H. Zorn (Trans.). New York: Schocken.

Berner, P., Spiel, W., Strotzka, H., & Wyklicky, H. (1983). *Zur Geschichte der Psychiatrie in Wien*. Vienna: Brandstätter.

Boehlich, W. (Ed.) (1990). *The Letters of Sigmund Freud to Eduard Silberstein 1871–1881*, A. J. Pomerans (Trans.). Cambridge, MA: Belknap Press of Harvard University Press.

Brabant, E., Falzeder, E., & Giampieri-Deutsch, P. (Eds.) (1993). *The Correspondence of Sigmund Freud and Sándor Ferenczi*, P. T. Hoffer (Trans.). Cambridge, MA: Belknap Press of Harvard University Press.

Büchner, G. (1999). Über Schädelnerven. In: H. Poschmann (Ed.), *Sämtliche Werke: Briefe und Dokumente in zwei Bänden*. Frankfurt: Deutsche Klassiker.

Charcot, J.-M. (1892–1895). *Poliklinische Vorträge*, S. Freud (Trans., preface and footnotes vol. 1); M. Kahane (Trans. vol. 2). Leipzig: Deuticke.

Coles, R. (1992). *Anna Freud. The Dream of Psychoanalysis*. Reading, MA: Addison-Wesley.

Czeike, F. (1993). *Historisches Lexikon Wien* Bd. 2. Vienna: Kremayr & Scheriau.

Davies, J. K., & Fichtner, G. (2006). *Freud's Library: A Comprehensive Catalogue*. Tübingen: edition diskord & The Freud Museum.

Dyer, G. (2005). *The Ongoing Moment*. London: Little, Brown.

Eder, J. M. (1917). *Johann Heinrich Schulze: der Erfinder des ersten photographischen Verfahrens*. Vienna: Kommissions-Verlag Lechner & Knapp.

Einladung zur 66. Versammlung Deutscher Naturforscher und Ärzte. Wien. 24 bis 30 September 1894. [Leaflet: no publication details.]

Eissler, K. R. (1953). Transcript of Interview with Oliver Freud 31.10.1953. Freud Archives, Library of Congress, Washington, DC.

Ellenberger, H. (1970). *The Discovery of the Unconscious: The History and Evolution of Dynamic Psychiatry*. New York: Basic Books.

Engelhardt, D. v. (2007). *Die Geschichte der GDNÄ*. Online at: www.gdnae.de/media/pdf/Website_Geschichte.pdf (accessed 17.12.2013).

Engelman, E. (1976). *Berggasse 19: Sigmund Freud's Home and Offices, Vienna 1938*. New York: Basic Books.

Exner, S. (1894). *Entwurf zu einer physiologischen Erklärung der psychischen Erscheinungen* Wien: Deuticke.

Falzeder, E. (Ed.) (2002). *The Complete Correspondence of Sigmund Freud and Karl Abraham 1907–1925*. London: Karnac.

Falzeder, E., & Brabant, E. (Eds.) (1996a). *Sigmund Freud & Sándor Ferenczi: Briefwechsel, Bd. II/1: 1914–1916*. Wien-Köln-Weimar: Böhlau.

Falzeder, E., & Brabant, E. (Eds.) (1996b). *The Correspondence of Sigmund Freud and Sándor Ferenczi Volume 2, 1914–1919*, P. T. Hoffer (Trans.). Cambridge, MA: Belknap Press of Harvard University Press.

Ferenczi, S. (1923). "Der Traum vom 'gelehrtem Säugling'". In: *Bausteine zur Psychoanalyse*. Bd. 3. (1939) (pp. 218–219). Bern: Huber.

Fichtner, G., Grubrich-Simitis, I., & Hirschmüller, A. (Eds.) (2011). *Sigmund Freud/Martha Bernays. Die Brautbriefe 1882–1886. Band 1.* Frankfurt: Fischer.

Fichtner, G., Grubrich-Simitis, I., & Hirschmüller, A. (Eds.) (2013). *Sigmund Freud/Martha Bernays. Die Brautbriefe 1882–1886. Band 2.* Frankfurt: Fischer.

Freud, A. (1922). Schlagephantasie und Tagtraum. In: *Die Schriften der Anna Freud* Bd.1 (pp. 141–159). Vienna: Kindler, 1980.

Freud, E. (Ed.) (1960). *Letters of Sigmund Freud*, J. & T. Stern (Trans.). New York: Basic Books.

Freud, E., Freud, L., & Grubrich-Simitis, I. (Eds.) (1978). *Sigmund Freud: His Life in Pictures and Words*, C. Trollope (Trans.). New York: Harcourt Brace Jovanovich.

Freud, H. (1926–1931). Diary 1926–1931 (Extracts). Xerox: FML.

Freud, M. (1957). *Glory Reflected: Sigmund Freud – Man and Father,* London: Angus & Robertson.

Freud, S. (1893f). Charcot. *S.E.*, 3: 11–23. London: Hogarth.

Freud, S. (1895b). On the grounds for detaching a particular syndrome from neurasthenia under the description "anxiety neurosis". *S.E.*, 3: 90–115. London: Hogarth.

Freud, S. (1896c). Aetiology of hysteria. *S.E.*, 3: 191–221. London: Hogarth.

Freud, S. (1900a). *The Interpretation of Dreams. S.E.*, 4–5. London: Hogarth.

Freud, S. (1901a). On dreams. *S.E.*, 5: 631–686. London: Hogarth.

Freud, S. (1901b). *The Psychopathology of Everyday Life. S.E.*, 6: London: Hogarth.

Freud, S. (1905c). *Jokes and their Relation to the Unconscious. S.E.*, 8. London: Hogarth.

Freud, S. (1905d). *Three Essays on the Theory of Sexuality. S.E.*, 7: 125–245. London: Hogarth.

Freud, S. (1905e). *Fragment of an Analysis of a Case of Hysteria. S.E.*, 7: 7–122. London: Hogarth.

Freud, S. (1907a). Delusions and dreams in Jensen's *Gradiva. S.E.*, 9: 3–95. London: Hogarth.

Freud, S. (1908e). Creative writers and daydreaming. *S.E.*, 9: 143–153. London: Hogarth.

Freud, S. (1910c). *Leonardo da Vinci and a Memory of his Childhood. S.E., 11*: 59–137. London: Hogarth.

Freud, S. (1911g). Greve G. Sobre psicología y psicoterapie de ciertos estados angustiosos. [Concerning psychology and psychotherapy in certain anxiety states.] 1911, I: 594–595 (*Zbl. Psychoanal.* Bd. 1 (1911) S.594f. *G.W. Nachtr.* S. 501f.)

Freud, S. (1912g). A Note on the Unconscious in Psycho-Analysis. *S.E., 12*: 257–266. London: Hogarth.

Freud, S. (1912–1913). *Totem and Taboo. S.E., 13*: 1–162. London: Hogarth.

Freud, S. (1913d). The occurrence in dreams of material from fairy tales. *S.E., 12*: 279–287. London: Hogarth.

Freud, S. (1914d). On the history of the psycho-analytic movement. *S.E., 14*: 7–66. London: Hogarth.

Freud, S. (1915b). Thoughts for the times on war and death. *S.E., 14*: 275–300. London: Hogarth.

Freud, S. (1916a). On transience. *S.E., 14*: 303–308. London: Hogarth.

Freud, S. (1917b). A childhood recollection from 'Dichtung und Wahrheit'. *S.E., 17*: 145–156. London: Hogarth.

Freud, S. (1917e). Mourning and melancholia. *S.E., 14*: 239–258. London: Hogarth.

Freud, S. (1919e). "A child is being beaten". *S.E., 17*: 175–204. London: Hogarth.

Freud, S. (1926d). *Inhibitions, Symptoms and Anxiety. S.E., 20*: 77–174. London: Hogarth.

Freud, S. (1927e). Fetishism. *S.E., 21*: 152–158. London: Hogarth.

Freud, S. (1941f). Findings, ideas, problems. *S.E., 23*: 299–300. London: Hogarth.

Freud, S. (1950a). Project for a scientific psychology. *S.E., 1*: 281–397. London: Hogarth.

Freud, Sophie (2007). *Living in the Shadow of the Freud Family*. Westport: Praeger.

Freud-Bernays, A. (2004). *Eine Wienerin in New York. Die Erinnerungen der Schwester Sigmund Freuds*, C. Tögel (Ed.). Berlin: Aufbau.

Freud-Marlé, L. (2006). *Mein Onkel Sigmund Freud. Erinnerungen an eine grosse Familie*, C. Tögel (Ed.). Berlin: Aufbau.

Gardiner, M. (Ed.) (1971). *The Wolf Man by the Wolf Man*. New York: Basic Books.

Girouard, M. (1985). *Cities and People: A Social and Architectural History*. New Haven, CT, & London: Yale University Press.

Goethe, J. W. (1989). *Schriften zur allgemeinen Naturlehre, Geologie und Mineralogie*, W. von Engelhardt & M. Wenzel (Eds.). In: *Sämtliche Werke, Briefe, Tagebücher Gespräche* (40 vols.). Frankfurt: Deutsche Klassiker.

Hamilton, G. H. (1983)[1954]. *The Art and Architecture of Russia*. Harmondsworth: Penguin.

Heller, P. (Ed.) (1992). *Anna Freud's Letters to Eva Rosenfeld*. Madison, CT: International Universities Press.

Hirschmüller, A. (1978a). *Physiologie und Psychoanalyse in Leben und Werk Josef Breuers*. Bern: Hans Huber.

Hirschmüller, A. (1978b). Eine bisher unbekannte Krankengeschichte Sigmund Freuds und Josef Breuers aus der Entstehungszeit der *Studien über Hysterie*. *Jahrbuch für Psychoanalyse*, 10: 136–168.

Hirschmüller, A. (1991). *Freuds Begegnung mit der Psychiatrie: Von der Hirnmythologie zur Neurosenlehre*. Tübingen: edition diskord.

Hirschmüller, A. (Ed.) (2005). *Sigmund Freud–Minna Bernays: Briefwechsel 1882–1938*. Tübingen: diskord.

Jones, E. (1980)[1953]. *Sigmund Freud: Life and Work*. Vol. 1. London: Hogarth.

Kerner, A., & Exner, S. (Eds.) (1894). *Tagblatt der 66. Versammlung Deutscher Naturforscher und Ärzte in Wien. 24–30 September 1894*. Wien. Kaiserlich-königliche Hof- und Staatsdruckerei.

Lafferton, E. (2006). Death by hypnosis. An 1894 Hungarian case and its European reverberations. *Endeavour*, 30(2): 65–70.

Laforgue, R. (1939). The ego and the conception of reality. *International Journal of Psycho-Analysis*, 20: 403–407.

Leggat, R. (1995). A history of photography from its beginnings till the 1920s. www.mpritchard.com/photohistory (accessed 17.12.2013).

Mach, E. (1896). *Populär-wissenschaftliche Vorlesungen*. Leipzig: Johann Ambrosius Barth.

Mach, E. (1905). *Erkenntnis und Irrtum. Skizzen zur Psychologie der Forschung*. Leipzig: Johann Ambrosius Barth.

Maciejewski, F. (2006). Freuds Geliebte. Späte Sensation im Freud-Jahr: Archivfund bestätigt Affäre zwischen Sigmund Freud und Minna Bernays. *Frankfurter Rundschau*, 28.9.2006.

Makari, G. (2008). *Revolution in Mind. The Creation of Psychoanalysis*. London: Duckworth.

Masson, J. M. (Ed. & Trans.) (1985). *The Complete Letters of Sigmund Freud to Wilhelm Fliess 1887–1904*. Cambridge, MA: Belknap Press of Harvard University Press.

Masson, J. M. (Ed.) (1986). *Briefe an Wilhelm Fließ 1887–1904*. Frankfurt: Fischer.

McGuire, W. (1974). *The Freud/Jung Letters*, R. Manheim & R. F. C. Hull (Trans.). Princeton, NJ: Princeton University Press.

Meringer, R., & Mayer, K. (1895). *Versprechen und Verlesen. Eine psychologisch-linguistische Studie*. Stuttgart: G. J. Göschen'sche.

Meyer-Palmedo, I. (Ed.) (2006). *Sigmund Freud–Anna Freud: Briefwechsel 1904–1938*. Frankfurt: Fischer.

Molnar, M. (Ed.) (1992). *The Diary of Sigmund Freud 1929–39*. London: Hogarth.

Murken, B. (1981). Tom Seidmann-Freud: Leben und Werk. *Die Schiefertafel*, *IV*(3): 163–201.

Murken, B. (2004). ". . . die Welt ist so uneben . . ." Tom Seidmann-Freud (1892–1930): Leben und Werk einer großen Bilderbuch-Künstlerin. *Luzifer-Amor*, *17*(33): 73–103.

Newhall, B. (1982). *The History of Photography from 1839 to the Present*. London: Secker & Warburg.

Obolensky, D. (Ed.) (1962). *The Penguin Book of Russian Verse*. Harmondsworth: Penguin.

Oosterhuis, H. (2001). *Stepchildren of Nature: Krafft-Ebing and the Making of Sexual Identity*. Chicago, IL: University of Chicago Press.

Ovid (1955). *Metamorphoses*, M. M. Innes (Trans.). Harmondsworth: Penguin.

Parshchikov, A. (1996). *Vybrannoe*. Moscow: ITs-Garant.

Paskauskas, R. A. (Ed.) (1993). *The Complete Correspondence of Sigmund Freud and Ernest Jones 1908–1939*. Cambridge, MA: Belknap Press of Harvard University Press.

Pearson, K. (1911). *The Grammar of Science. Part 1. – Physical*. London: Adam & Charles Black.

Pfeiffer, E., Robson-Scott, W., & Robson-Scott, E. (1963). *Sigmund Freud and Lou Andreas-Salomé. Letters*. London: International Psycho-Analytical Library.

Poe, E. A. (1950). *Tales, Poems, Essays by Edgar Allen Poe*. London: Collins.

Proust, M. (1922). *Swann's Way*, C. K. Scott Moncrieff (Trans.). New York: Henry Holt.

Reik, T. (1942). *From Thirty Years with Freud*. London: Hogarth.

Rilke, R. M. (1966)[1906]. Das Buch der Bilder. In: *Rainer Maria Rilke: Werke in drei Bänden* (Vol. 1) (pp. 123–233). Frankfurt: Insel.

Roazen, P. (1993). *Meeting the Freud Family*. Amherst, MA: University of Massachusetts Press.

Roberts, T. (Ed.) (publication pending). *The Family Letters of Sigmund Freud and the Freuds of Manchester: 1911–1938*. Typescript: FML.

Roith, E. (2008). Hysteria, heredity and anti-Semitism: Freud's quiet rebellion. *Psychoanalysis and History, 10*(2): 149–168.

Rothe, D., & Weber, I. (Eds.) (2001) *". . . als käm ich heim zu Vater und Schwester"*. *Lou Andreas-Salomé–Anna Freud Briefwechsel 1919–1937*. Göttingen: Wallstein.

Roudinesco, E. (1990)[1986]. *La bataille de cent ans, Histoire de la psychanalyse en France* (Vol. 2). Paris: Seuil.

Ruperthuz Honorato, M. (2012). The 'Return of the Repressed': the role of sexuality in the reception of psychoanalysis in Chilean medical circles (1910s–1940s). *Psychoanalysis and History, 14*(2): 285–296.

Sayers, J., & Forrester, J. (2013). The autobiography of Melanie Klein. *Psychoanalysis and History, 15*(2): 127–163.

Schönberg, I. (Trans.) (1884). *Der Hitopadescha. Altindische Märchen und Sprüche*. Wien: Carl Konegen.

Schröter, M. (1997). Der historische Kontext von Freuds "Zwangs-vorstellungen und Phobien" (1895). Einleitende Bemerkungen zum Neu-Abdruck. *Jahrbuch der Psychoanalyse, 37*: 177–195.

Schröter, M. (Ed.) (2010). *Sigmund Freud. Unterdess halten wir zusammen: Briefe an die Kinder*. Berlin: Aufbau.

Schröter, M., & Hermanns, L. M. (1994). Nachträge zu "Felix Gattel (1870–1904): Der erste Freudschüler". *Luzifer-Amor, 7*.

Segond, P. (1992). Eva Freud: one life, Berlin 1924, Nice 1934, Marseille 1944, C. Nedelea (Trans.). *Les Temps Modernes, November*(556). Translation: FML & LoC.

Segond, P. (1993). Eva Freud, une vie. *Trames*, 15 September.

Segond, P. (1995). Des Freud à Nice: Éva Freud, une vie traversée par l'histoire collective. Paper presented on 19 January 1995 at Centre de Recherche sur l'Europe. Atelier d'Histoire de la Psychanalyse en Europe et animé par Alain de Mijolla.

Segond, P. (2004). Eva Freud, une vie. Berlin 1924, Nice 1934, Marseille 1944. Online at: http://spip.systemique.eu/IMG/article_PDF/article_a356.pdf (Accessed 29.12.2013).

Seidmann-Freud, T. (1929). *Das Zauberboot*. Berlin: Herbert Stuffer.

Sontag, S. (1979)[1977]. *On Photography*. Harmondsworth: Penguin.

Spreitzer, B. (Ed.) (2014). *Anna Freud: Gedichte – Prosa – Übersetzungen*. Vienna: Böhlau.

Swales, P. J. (1988). Freud, Katharina and the first "wild analysis". In: P. Stepansky (Ed.), *Freud: Appraisals and Reappraisals* (Vol. 3) (pp. 79–164). Hillsdale, NJ: Analytic Press.

Taylor, A. J. P. (1965). *English History 1914–1945*. Oxford: Oxford University Press.

Tennyson, A. (1919). *The Works of Alfred Lord Tennyson: Poet Laureate*. London: Macmillan.

Tögel, C. (Ed.) (2002). *Sigmund Freud: Unser Herz zeigt nach dem Süden. Reisebriefe 1895–1923*. Berlin: Aufbau.

Tögel, C. (2004). Freuds Berliner Schwester Marie (Mitzi) und ihre Familie. *Luzifer-Amor, 17*(33): 33–50.

Tögel, C., & Schröter, M. (2004). Sigmund Freud "Briefe an Maria (Mitzi) Freud und ihre Familie. *Luzifer-Amor, 17*(33): 51–72.

Tolstoi, L. N. (1952). *Vospominaniya* (1903–1906). In: L. N. Tolstoi, *Polnoe Sobranie Sochinenii* Vol. 34, Moscow: G.I.Kh.L.

Wangerin, A., & Taschenberg O. (1895). *Verhandlungen der Gesellschaft deutscher Naturforscher und Ärzte. 66. Versammlung zu Wien 24.–28. September 1894. Zweiter Theil. II. Hälfte: Medicinische Abtheilung*. Leipzig: F. C. W. Vogel.

Weissweiler, E. (2006). *Die Freuds: Biographie einer Familie*. Köln: Kiepenheuer & Witsch.

Weitz, M. C. (1995). *Sisters in the Resistance: How Women Fought to Free France 1940–1945*. New York: John Wiley.

Welter, V. M. (2012). *Ernst L. Freud, Architect: The Case of the Modern Bourgeois Home*. New York: Berghahn.

Williams, R. (1980)[1976]. *Keywords: A Vocabulary of Culture and Society*. Glasgow: Fontana.

Wilsey, J. (2002). *H. Jones VC. The Life and Death of An Unusual Hero*. London: Hutchinson.

Winter, A. (1998). *Mesmerized: Powers of Mind in Victorian Britain*. Chicago, IL: University of Chicago Press.

Yates, F. A. (1979). *The Occult Philosophy in the Elizabethan Age*. London: Routledge & Kegan Paul.

Yeats, W. B. (1950). *Collected Poems of W. B. Yeats*. London: Macmillan.

Young-Bruehl, E. (1988). *Anna Freud. A Biography*. New York: Summit Books.

INDEX